Mosaic 2

READING

Brenda Wegmann

Miki Knezevic

D1666377

Lawrence J. Zwier
Contributor, Focus on Testing

Pamela Hartmann
Reading Strand Leader

Mosaic 2 Reading, Silver Edition

Published by McGraw-Hill ESL/ELT, a business unit of The McGraw-Hill Companies, Inc., 1221 Avenue of the Americas, New York, NY 10020. Copyright © 2007 by The McGraw-Hill Companies, Inc. All rights reserved. No part of this publication may be reproduced or distributed in any form or by any means, or stored in a database or retrieval system, without the prior written consent of The McGraw-Hill Companies, Inc., including, but not limited to, in any network or other electronic storage or transmission, or broadcast for distance learning.

ISBN 13: 978-0-07-325849-2 (Student Book)
ISBN 10: 0-07-325849-0
1 2 3 4 5 6 7 8 9 10 VNH 11 10 09 08 07 06

ISBN 13: 978-0-07-333739-5 (Student Book with Audio Highlights)
ISBN 10: 0-07-333739-0
1 2 3 4 5 6 7 8 9 10 VNH 11 10 09 08 07 06

Editorial director: Erik Gundersen
Series editor: Valerie Kelemen
Developmental editors: Terre Passero, Joe McVeigh
Production manager: Juanita Thompson
Production coordinator: Vanessa Nuttry
Cover designer: Robin Locke Monda
Interior designer: Nesbitt Graphics, Inc.
Artists: Burgundy Beam
Photo researcher: Photoquick Research

The credits section for this book begins on page 287 and is considered an extension of the copyright page.

Cover photo: Jeffrey Becom/Lonely Planet Images

www.esl-elt.mcgraw-hill.com

The McGraw-Hill Companies

A Special Thank You

The Interactions/Mosaic Silver Edition team wishes to thank our extended team: teachers, students, administrators, and teacher trainers, all of whom contributed invaluably to the making of this edition.

Macarena Aguilar, **North Harris College**, Houston, Texas ▪ Mohamad Al-Alam, **Imam Mohammad University**, Riyadh, Saudi Arabia ▪ Faisal M. Al Mohanna Abaalkhail, **King Saud University**, Riyadh, Saudi Arabia; Amal Al-Toaimy, **Women's College, Prince Sultan University**, Riyadh, Saudi Arabia ▪ Douglas Arroliga, **Ave Maria University**, Managua, Nicaragua ▪ Fairlie Atkinson, **Sungkyunkwan University**, Seoul, Korea ▪ Jose R. Bahamonde, **Miami-Dade Community College**, Miami, Florida ▪ John Ball, **Universidad de las Americas**, Mexico City, Mexico ▪ Steven Bell, **Universidad la Salle**, Mexico City, Mexico ▪ Damian Benstead, **Sungkyunkwan University**, Seoul, Korea ▪ Paul Cameron, **National Chengchi University**, Taipei, Taiwan R.O.C. ▪ Sun Chang, **Soongsil University**, Seoul, Korea ▪ Grace Chao, **Soochow University**, Taipei, Taiwan R.O.C. ▪ Chien Ping Chen, **Hua Fan University**, Taipei, Taiwan R.O.C. ▪ Selma Chen, **Chihlee Institute of Technology**, Taipei, Taiwan R.O.C. ▪ Sylvia Chiu, **Soochow University**, Taipei, Taiwan R.O.C. ▪ Mary Colonna, **Columbia University**, New York, New York ▪ Lee Culver, **Miami-Dade Community College,** Miami, Florida ▪ Joy Durighello, **City College of San Francisco**, San Francisco, California ▪ Isabel Del Valle, **ULATINA**, San Jose, Costa Rica ▪ Linda Emerson, **Sogang University**, Seoul, Korea ▪ Esther Entin, **Miami-Dade Community College**, Miami, Florida ▪ Glenn Farrier, **Gakushuin Women's College**, Tokyo, Japan ▪ Su Wei Feng, Taipei, Taiwan R.O.C. ▪ Judith Garcia, **Miami-Dade Community College**, Miami, Florida ▪ Maxine Gillway, **United Arab Emirates University**, Al Ain, United Arab Emirates ▪ Colin Gullberg, **Soochow University**, Taipei, Taiwan R.O.C. ▪ Natasha Haugnes, **Academy of Art University**, San Francisco, California ▪ Barbara Hockman, **City College of San Francisco**, San Francisco, California ▪ Jinyoung Hong, **Sogang University**, Seoul, Korea ▪ Sherry Hsieh, **Christ's College**, Taipei, Taiwan R.O.C. ▪ Yu-shen Hsu, **Soochow University**, Taipei, Taiwan R.O.C. ▪ Cheung Kai-Chong, **Shih-Shin University**, Taipei, Taiwan R.O.C. ▪ Leslie Kanberg, **City College of San Francisco**, San Francisco, California ▪ Gregory Keech, **City College of San Francisco**, San Francisco, California ▪ Susan Kelly, **Sogang University**, Seoul, Korea ▪ Myoungsuk Kim, **Soongsil University**, Seoul, Korea ▪ Youngsuk Kim, **Soongsil University**, Seoul, Korea ▪ Roy Langdon, **Sungkyunkwan University**, Seoul, Korea ▪ Rocio Lara, **University of Costa Rica**, San Jose, Costa Rica ▪ Insung Lee, **Soongsil University**, Seoul, Korea ▪ Andy Leung, **National Tsing Hua University**, Taipei, Taiwan R.O.C. ▪ Elisa Li Chan, **University of Costa Rica**, San Jose, Costa Rica ▪ Elizabeth Lorenzo, **Universidad Internacional de las Americas**, San Jose, Costa Rica ▪

Cheryl Magnant, **Sungkyunkwan University**, Seoul, Korea ▪ Narciso Maldonado Iuit, **Escuela Tecnica Electricista**, Mexico City, Mexico ▪ Shaun Manning, **Hankuk University of Foreign Studies**, Seoul, Korea ▪ Yoshiko Matsubayashi, **Tokyo International University**, Saitama, Japan ▪ Scott Miles, **Sogang University**, Seoul, Korea ▪ William Mooney, **Chinese Culture University**, Taipei, Taiwan R.O.C. ▪ Jeff Moore, **Sungkyunkwan University**, Seoul, Korea ▪ Mavelin de Moreno, **Lehnsen Roosevelt School**, Guatemala City, Guatemala ▪ Ahmed Motala, **University of Sharjah**, Sharjah, United Arab Emirates ▪ Carlos Navarro, **University of Costa Rica**, San Jose, Costa Rica ▪ Dan Neal, **Chih Chien University**, Taipei, Taiwan R.O.C. ▪ Margarita Novo, **University of Costa Rica**, San Jose, Costa Rica ▪ Karen O'Neill, **San Jose State University**, San Jose, California ▪ Linda O'Roke, **City College of San Francisco**, San Francisco, California ▪ Martha Padilla, **Colegio de Bachilleres de Sinaloa**, Culiacan, Mexico ▪ Allen Quesada, **University of Costa Rica**, San Jose, Costa Rica ▪ Jim Rogge, **Broward Community College**, Ft. Lauderdale, Florida ▪ Marge Ryder, **City College of San Francisco**, San Francisco, California ▪ Gerardo Salas, **University of Costa Rica**, San Jose, Costa Rica ▪ Shigeo Sato, **Tamagawa University**, Tokyo, Japan ▪ Lynn Schneider, **City College of San Francisco**, San Francisco, California ▪ Devan Scoble, **Sungkyunkwan University**, Seoul, Korea ▪ Maryjane Scott, **Soongsil University**, Seoul, Korea ▪ Ghaida Shaban, **Makassed Philanthropic School**, Beirut, Lebanon ▪ Maha Shalok, **Makassed Philanthropic School**, Beirut, Lebanon ▪ John Shannon, **University of Sharjah**, Sharjah, United Arab Emirates ▪ Elsa Sheng, **National Technology College of Taipei**, Taipei, Taiwan R.O.C. ▪ Ye-Wei Sheng, **National Taipei College of Business**, Taipei, Taiwan R.O.C. ▪ Emilia Sobaja, **University of Costa Rica**, San Jose, Costa Rica ▪ You-Souk Yoon, **Sungkyunkwan University**, Seoul, Korea ▪ Shanda Stromfield, **San Jose State University**, San Jose, California ▪ Richard Swingle, **Kansai Gaidai College**, Osaka, Japan ▪ Carol Sung, **Christ's College**, Taipei, Taiwan R.O.C. ▪ Jeng-Yih Tim Hsu, **National Kaohsiung First University of Science and Technology**, Kaohsiung, Taiwan R.O.C. ▪ Shinichiro Torikai, **Rikkyo University**, Tokyo, Japan ▪ Sungsoon Wang, **Sogang University**, Seoul, Korea ▪ Kathleen Wolf, **City College of San Francisco**, San Francisco, California ▪ Sean Wray, **Waseda University International**, Tokyo, Japan ▪ Belinda Yanda, **Academy of Art University**, San Francisco, California ▪ Su Huei Yang, **National Taipei College of Business**, Taipei, Taiwan R.O.C. ▪ Tzu Yun Yu, **Chungyu Institute of Technology**, Taipei, Taiwan R.O.C.

Authors' Acknowledgements

We are pleased to be part of the McGraw-Hill team presenting this fifth *silver* edition of *Mosaic* which we feel is distinctive, with its greater development of reading strategies, critical thinking skills and interactive tasks promoting oral and written fluency. We wish to thank Tina Carver and Erik Gundersen for their effective research which laid the foundation for this edition, and Erik in particular for his guidance and responsiveness throughout the process. We are grateful to Pam Hartmann for helpful advice and to our excellent editors: Mari Vargo who gave us a good start, Mary Sutton-Paul who assisted us in finishing up a significant part, Joe McVeigh who helped see the manuscript into print and most especially to Terre Passero who directed, encouraged and cajoled us with infinite patience and many inventive suggestions which were incorporated into the book. We are also indebted to Anne Knezevic, for her expert ESL advice and the contribution of excellent materials, Dennis McKernan and Andrew Jovanovic for their computer assistance, and to Dr. Anne Fanning for recommending the speech of Wangari Maathai, used in Mosaic 2. We would also like to thank Dr. Larry Zwier for his superb contribution to the Focus on Testing segments and to Dr. Jessica Wegmann-Sánchez for her creative ideas and technical assistance in designing activities and exercises. Finally, we wish to express our deep appreciation of ESL/EFL teachers who spend countless hours teaching their students English, a language of international communication. Better communication leads to richer understanding of others lives and cultures, and hopefully to a more peaceful co-existence.

Brenda Wegmann, Miki Prijic Knezevic

Table of Contents

Welcome to Interactions/Mosaic Silver Edition

Interactions/Mosaic **Silver Edition** is a fully-integrated, 18-book academic skills series. Language proficiencies are articulated from the beginning through advanced levels <u>within</u> each of the four language skill strands. Chapter themes articulate <u>across</u> the four skill strands to systematically recycle content, vocabulary, and grammar.

NEW to the Silver Edition:

- **World's most popular and comprehensive academic skills series**—thoroughly updated for today's global learners
- **New design** showcases compelling instructional photos to strengthen the educational experience
- **Enhanced focus on vocabulary building, test taking, and critical thinking skills** promotes academic achievement
- **New Strategies and activities for the TOEFL® iBT** build invaluable test taking skills
- **New "Best Practices" approach** promotes excellence in language teaching

NEW to Mosaic 2 Reading:

- **All new content:** Chapter 4 Beauty and Aesthetics
- **Enhanced design**—featuring larger type and 50% more instructional photos—ensures effective classroom usage.
- **Transparent chapter structure**—with consistent part headings, activity labeling, and clear guidance—strengthens the academic experience:
    - Part 1: Reading Skills and Strategies
    - Part 2: Reading Skills and Strategies
    - Part 3: Tying It All Together
- **Dynamic vocabulary acquisition program**—systematic vocabulary introduction and practice ensures students will interact meaningfully with each target word at least four times.
- **New focus on vocabulary from the Academic Word List** offers additional practice with words students are most likely to encounter in academic texts.
- **Line numbering and paragraph lettering** in reading passages allows students and teachers to easily find the information referred to in activities.
- **Expanded audio program** includes all reading selections, vocabulary words, and selected listening activities to accelerate reading fluency.
- **New *Vocabulary index*** equips student and instructors with chapter-by-chapter lists of target words.

---

* TOEFL is a registered trademark of Educational Testing Service (ETS). This publication is not endorsed or approved by ETS.

Interactions/Mosaic
Best Practices

Our Interactions/Mosaic Silver Edition team has produced an edition that focuses on Best Practices, principles that contribute to excellent language teaching and learning. Our team of writers, editors, and teacher consultants has identified the following six interconnected Best Practices:

Making Use of Academic Content

Materials and tasks based on academic content and experiences give learning real purpose. Students explore real world issues, discuss academic topics, and study content-based and thematic materials.

Organizing Information

Students learn to organize thoughts and notes through a variety of graphic organizers that accommodate diverse learning and thinking styles.

Scaffolding Instruction

A scaffold is a physical structure that facilitates construction of a building. Similarly, scaffolding instruction is a tool used to facilitate language learning in the form of predictable and flexible tasks. Some examples include oral or written modeling by the teacher or students, placing information in a larger framework, and reinterpretation.

Activating Prior Knowledge

Students can better understand new spoken or written material when they connect to the content. Activating prior knowledge allows students to tap into what they already know, building on this knowledge, and stirring a curiosity for more knowledge.

Interacting with Others

Activities that promote human interaction in pair work, small group work, and whole class activities present opportunities for real world contact and real world use of language.

Cultivating Critical Thinking

Strategies for critical thinking are taught explicitly. Students learn tools that promote critical thinking skills crucial to success in the academic world.

Highlights of Mosaic 2 Reading Silver Edition

New design showcases compelling instructional photos to strengthen the educational experience.

Interacting with Others
Questions and topical quotes stimulate interest, activate prior knowledge, and launch the topic of the unit.

Chapter

4

Beauty and Aesthetics

In This Chapter

Aesthetics is the philosophy of beauty. So, we begin this chapter with a look at what many consider the most beautiful building in the world: the great Taj Mahal of India with its Muslim influences, mixing the traditions of Persia, India, and central Asia. Then we turn to look at current ideas about human beauty, with an article on the popularity of plastic surgery in Korea and some other Asian countries.

❝ Beauty is in the eye of the beholder. ❞

—English proverb

Connecting to the Topic

1 Look at the photo of Da Vinci's famous painting, *The Mona Lisa*. Can you see why many people consider it an example of ideal beauty?

2 What does it mean to say that beauty is in the eye of the one who beholds (sees) it? Do you agree with this English saying? Why or why not?

3 What is the most beautiful place or thing that you have ever seen?

2 Skimming for Main Ideas Take two minutes and skim the reading below. Then look at the list of themes below. Put a check in front of the themes related to ideas that are discussed in the reading.

- ❏ How English is taught in different countries
- ❏ Where English is taught
- ❏ The use of English among young people
- ❏ The use of English in literature and poetry
- ❏ The use of English in business, science, and diplomacy
- ❏ Comparisons of the use of English and the use of some other languages

Read

Introduction
Is English truly a universal language, or will it be at some time in the near future? The following selection from the book *Megatrends 2000* presents one opinion on this subject and supports the opinion with numerous details and statistics. Answer the questions below. Then read to see if you agree with the authors' opinion.

- ■ Are you learning English because you think it is a universal language, or is there some other reason for you to learn it?
- ■ What uses does learning English have for people from your culture?

English as a Universal Language

A English is becoming the world's first truly universal language. It is the native language of some 400 million people in 12 countries. That is a lot fewer than the 885 million people or so who speak Mandarin Chinese. But another 400 million speak English as a second language. And several hundred million more have some knowledge of English, which has official or semiofficial status in some 60 countries. Although there *may* be as many people speaking the various dialects of Chinese as there are English speakers, English is certainly more widespread geographically, more genuinely universal than Chinese. And its usage is growing at an extraordinary pace. 10

B Today there are about 1 billion English speakers in the world, and the number is growing. The world's most taught language, English is not replacing other languages; it is supplementing them:
- ■ More than two hundred and fifty million Chinese study English.
- ■ In eighty-nine countries, English is either a common second language or 15 widely studied.
- ■ In Hong Kong, nine of every ten secondary school students study English.
- ■ In France, state-run secondary schools require students to study four years of English or German; most—at least 85 percent—choose English.
- ■ In Japan, secondary students are required to take six years of English 20 before graduation.

▲ University students in Shanghai, China

Media and Transportation
C English prevails in transportation and the media. The travel and communication language of 25 the international airwaves is English. Pilots and air traffic controllers speak English at all international airports. Maritime traffic uses flag 30 and light signals, but "if vessels needed to communicate verbally, they would find a common language, which would 35 probably be English," says the U.S. Coast Guard's Werner Siems.

D Five of the largest broadcasters—CBS, NBC, ABC, the BBC, and the CBC*—reach a potential audience of about 300 million people through 40 English broadcast. It is also the most popular language of satellite TV.

The Information Age
E The language of the information age is English.
F More than 80 percent of all the information stored in the more than 100 million computers around the world is in English.
G Eighty-five percent of international telephone conversations are 45 conducted in English, as are three-fourths of the world's mail, telexes, and

---
* In addition to the five broadcasters mentioned, CNN news reaches 186 million households and hotel rooms around the world.

6 **Guided Academic Conversation** Use the guide words *who, when, where, what, why* to discuss the following topics with a small group of classmates. Then look at the questions in parentheses for more ideas. Be prepared to describe to the class what your group talked about after you finish.

1. Mountain climbing the world over. (Is it done by men, by women, by all nationalities, or only by some? What is the most exciting, the most difficult, the most pleasant, the most famous mountain? What do you think of the climbers who pay $65,000 to be brought to the top of Everest?)

2. Taking risks: physical, intellectual, social, financial. (Is danger a stimulant? Can it be an addiction? Does risky behavior bring about the ruin of some people? How?)

3. Extreme sports. (Which ones are the most dangerous: hang gliding, scuba diving, auto racing, rock climbing? Is boxing an extreme sport?)

▲ Which sports do you think are dangerous?

Part 2 Reading Skills and Strategies

The World We Lost

Before You Read

1 **Previewing the Reading** Work with a partner to preview the next reading. To preview, answer the questions below.

1. Look at the photo and its caption on page 40. What do they tell you about the subject of the selection? What do you already know about these animals?

2. Look at the title. Its meaning is not obvious. Can you make a guess about how it connects with the photo? What "world" could the author be referring to?

3. Skim the first paragraph of the reading. To *skim* means to read quickly for general meaning without stopping to look up words you don't understand. What do you find out about the author and his work? Describe the way he feels at the beginning of the story.

2 **Getting Meaning from Context** Look at the following excerpts from the reading selection and choose the best definition for each italicized word. Use the context in the sentences and the hints in parentheses to help you.

1. In order to round out my study of wolf family life, I needed to know what the *den* was like inside—how deep it was, the diameter of the passage, the presence (if any) of a nest at the end of the *burrow*, and such related information. (**Hint:** Since the author wants to study the "family life" of wolves and states a need to know the "inside," you can infer the meaning of the first word.)

The *den* is the place where the wolves go to _____.
- Ⓐ hunt
- Ⓑ sleep
- Ⓒ die

A *burrow* is _____. (**Hint:** The reference in the reading to a nest at the *end* of this gives a clue to the correct meaning.)
- Ⓐ a pile of sticks and mud
- Ⓑ a young wolf or dog
- Ⓒ a hole dug by an animal

2. The *Norseman* came over at about 50 feet. As it roared past, the plane waggled its wings gaily in salute, then lifted to skim the crest of the wolf *esker*, sending a blast of sand down the slope with its propeller wash. (**Hint:** The word *esker* is not well known even to English speakers, but the reader can use clues from the context: the word *crest*, your knowledge of where the man is going, what happens when the propeller gets near the esker.)

The *Norseman* is a type of _____.
- Ⓐ animal
- Ⓑ wind
- Ⓒ plane

An *esker* is _____.
- Ⓐ a ridge of sand
- Ⓑ a small river
- Ⓒ a kind of fruit tree

Cultivating Critical Thinking
Enhanced focus on critical thinking skills promotes academic achievement.

After You Read

Strategy

Using a Graphic Organizer to Determine the Order of Events
The order in which events are described in a reading selection is not always the order in which they actually occurred.

You can use a graphic organizer like the one in the next exercise to show the order of events. Using a graphic organizer of this type helps to organize and retain information.

3 **Determining the Order of Events** The following events are from the case study described in the article. Put them in the order in which they occurred in real life. Write one letter in each box.

1. Tara and Abe fell in love.
2. Tara began to cling to Abe.
3. Tara would become concerned and insist on talking about what was wrong.
4. Tara and Abe met at a party.
5. Abe would come home tired and annoyed.
6. Tara wanted more closeness with her father, and Abe more respect for his privacy from his mother.
7. Abe began to withdraw from Tara.
8. Tara and Abe got married.

Chain-of-Events Diagram

Beginning: First Event → □ → □ → □

→ □ → □ → End: Last Event

4 **Identifying Causes** The article points out common patterns in the behavior of people involved in intimate relationships. Complete each statement to show the cause for the behavior described.

1. According to Dr. Ayala Malach Pine, we often fall in love with someone because he or she reminds us of *a significant person from our childhood, such as one of our parents*

4 **Guided Academic Conversation** Work with another student. Take turns asking and answering the following questions. After you finish, compare your answers with those of another pair of students.

1. Why do the authors feel that English is more universal than Chinese?
2. Where is English used as a common second language?
3. In your opinion, why do people in many parts of the world study English? Why are you studying English?
4. In what situations can you imagine that a knowledge of English could mean the difference between life and death?
5. How has technology helped to make English popular?
6. Can you explain the meaning of *lingua franca* in the selection? Is English a lingua franca or not? Why?
7. What English terms or phrases are common in your culture?

TOEFL® iBT   **Focus on Testing**

Analyzing Summary Statements
On reading comprehension tests, you may be given several statements and asked to select the one that best summarizes a selection. In order to do this, first read the statements and see if any of them does not match the information in the reading. If so, eliminate it. Next, look at the other statements and decide which one best expresses the main idea of the reading selection. This statement must be *short* (one sentence) but *complete*. It should not just state a secondary idea or summarize small details of the selection. If there are subheads in the selection, they can help to remind you of the important ideas that should be included in a summary statement.

Practice Choose the statement below that best summarizes the article *English as a Universal Language*. Then explain your answer.

Ⓐ English is replacing the dominant European languages of the past, and serves as a common means of communication in India and Africa and for scientists all over the world.

Ⓑ English is the most important language in the world for transportation, information, business, diplomacy, trade, and communication among the young.

Ⓒ English is the predominant language in the world because it is spoken by many more people than any other language and is used in most multinational companies.

Testing Notes
The TOEFL® iBT Test Over 2,300 colleges and universities in the United States and Canada require students who do not speak English as their first language to take the TOEFL® (TEST OF ENGLISH AS A FOREIGN

Organizing Information
Graphic organizers provide tools for organizing information and ideas.

New strategies and activities for the TOEFL® iBT build invaluable test taking skills.

Scope and Sequence

 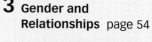

Critical Thinking Skills	Vocabulary Building	Focus on Testing
Comparing ideas about a reading Reacting to an opinion Interviewing and answering interview questions Synthesizing Internet content: Taking notes and presenting results Writing Tip: Writing a summary statement	Getting meaning from word structure and context Understanding acronyms and abbreviations Guessing the meaning of strong verbs from context Focusing on words from the Academic Word List	Analyzing summary statements on standardized tests TOEFL® IBT
Recapitulating the action of a narrative with a graphic organizer (storyboard) Analyzing discussion questions Using a graphic organizer (chain diagram) to sequence events and emotions Summarizing group opinions Synthesizing Internet content: Taking notes and presenting results Writing Tip: Structuring a letter	Identifying more exact or colorful synonyms Getting the meaning of everyday phrases from context Recalling vocabulary of fear and anger Focusing on words from the Academic Word List Inventing sentences on the spot for vocabulary words	Answering schematic-table questions TOEFL® IBT
Using a graphic organizer to determine the order of events Identifying causes Comparing opinions and interpretations Drawing conclusions from a chart Clarifying ideas and speculating on outcomes Taking a side in a debate Writing Tip: Using a cluster diagram to organize ideas Synthesizing Internet content: Taking notes and presenting results	Identifying more exact or colorful synonyms Getting meaning from word structure and context Focusing on words from the Academic Word List	Answering prose-summary questions TOEFL® IBT

Critical Thinking Skills	Vocabulary Building	Focus on Testing
Comparing opinions Illustrating ideas Using a graphic organizer (Venn diagram) to draw a comparison Analyzing facts Evaluating opinions Structuring an argument: Weakest to strongest point Synthesizing Internet content: Taking notes and presenting results Writing Tip: Supporting an argument	Getting meaning from context for specialized terms related to architecture Getting meaning from structure and context: Identifying synonyms for adjectives Understanding specialized terms relating to personal beauty Getting meaning from context by choosing synonyms or antonyms Focusing on words from the Academic Word List	Answering vocabulary questions **TOEFL® IBT**
Paraphrasing Comparing answers Interviewing and answering interview questions Summarizing a story Role playing Synthesizing Internet content: Taking notes and presenting results Writing Tip: Using a flashback	Identifying differences between standard English and global English Getting meaning from word structure and context Recognizing regional vocabulary differences Selecting adjectives to fit the context Identifying regional spelling differences Focusing on words from the Academic Word List	Avoiding traps in standardized vocabulary tests
Improving study skills: Underlining and marginal glossing Understanding mnemonic systems Supporting or challenging a hypothesis Summarizing from a different point of view Writing Tip: Illustrating with strong examples	Identifying synonyms Getting the meaning of words from context Focusing on words from the Academic Word List	Reading for speed and fluency on standardized tests: Skimming and scanning

Critical Thinking Skills	Vocabulary Building	Focus on Testing
Interviewing and answering interview questions	Forming adjectives from nouns	Understanding grammar-oriented reading questions
Applying inferences to a situation	Understanding idiomatic phrases from the context	**TOEFL® IBT**
Making comparisons with a chart	Focusing on words from the Academic Word List	
Synthesizing Internet content: Taking notes and presenting results		
Writing Tip: Summarizing by writing a sentence to cover each of the main points		
Analyzing the author's point of view	Building new words with prefixes and suffixes	Speaking in front of people during an oral exam, interview, or meeting
Separating fact from opinion	Building new words from the same root	
Synthesizing Internet content: Taking notes and presenting results	Identifying compound words	
Expressing opinions and justifying answers	Understanding idiomatic phrases in context	
Writing Tip: Clearly separating a summary from an opinion	Focusing on words from the Academic Word List	
Paraphrasing ideas	Getting meaning through word structure and context: Verbs	Understanding inference questions
Comparing answers to discussion questions	Matching words to their meanings	**TOEFL® IBT**
Using a Venn diagram to make a comparison	Focusing on words from the Academic Word List	
Summarizing information		
Comparing opinions		
Interpreting meaning in poetry		
Synthesizing Internet content: Taking notes and presenting results		
Writing Tip: Using a Venn diagram to compare and contrast		
Analyzing causes and effects	Getting meaning from word structure and context	Understanding negative questions and sentence-insertion questions
Synthesizing information and applying to real-life situations: Using a chart for comparison	Inferring the meaning of idioms and expressions	**TOEFL® IBT**
Comparing opinions	Focusing on words from the Academic Word List	
Interpreting an anecdote	Identifying synonyms	
Synthesizing Internet content: Taking notes and presenting results		
Writing Tip: Writing a strong first sentence		

Language and Learning

In This Chapter

Why learn English? The first selection in this chapter argues that English is a universal language that people around the world use to communicate in a variety of different areas. The second selection looks at the case of one particular nation, Mongolia, where the government is implementing an extensive national education program to make its residents bilingual in English, a move that has become popular in a number of countries.

" Whoever comes to learn, will always find a teacher. **"**

—German, anonymous

Connecting to the Topic

1 What is happening in the photo below? Why is good communication important for people with this job?

2 What challenges are faced by people when they speak different languages? How can they communicate?

3 What has been your own experience of learning English? How do you think that people best learn languages?

English as a Universal Language

Strategy

Getting Meaning from Word Structure and Context
Try to guess the meaning of new or unfamiliar words as you read. To do this, break them into smaller words, into prefixes and suffixes, or use clues from the context—the words that come before and after the new word.

1 **Getting Meaning from Word Structure and Context** Choose the best meaning for the italicized words in the following excerpts (parts) taken from the reading selection. Use the hints about word structure and context to help you.

1. English as a *Universal* Language (**Hint:** This is the title, which often, but not always, relates to the main idea. Break the word into its two parts: *universe* and the suffix *–al*, which simply makes an adjective of a noun, and think about their meanings.)
   - (A) beautiful
   - (B) difficult
   - (C) global
   - (D) political

2. And several hundred million more [people] have some knowledge of English, which has official or semiofficial *status* in some 60 countries. (**Hint:** Look at the words that come before and after and decide which option makes the most sense, considering the idea expressed in the title.)
   - (A) existence (condition, usage, rank)
   - (B) enjoyment
   - (C) problems
   - (D) rejection (hatred, dislike)

3. Although there may be as many people speaking the various *dialects* of Chinese as there are English speakers, English is certainly more widespread geographically . . . (**Hint:** A comparison is being made between those who speak English and those who speak different *dialects* of Chinese.)
   - (A) words
   - (B) dialogs
   - (C) lists of rules
   - (D) ways of speaking

4. English is certainly more *widespread* geographically. (**Hint:** Break this word into its two parts and think of what each one means.)
   - (A) restricted
   - (B) extended
   - (C) regional
   - (D) popular

5. English is not replacing other languages; it is *supplementing* them. (**Hint:** Think of the word *supply*, which starts out the way this word does. Also, take note of the general idea of the article expressed in its title.)
   - (A) proving its superiority over
   - (B) taking the place of
   - (C) being used in addition to
   - (D) being used exclusively by

6. English *prevails* in transportation and the media. (**Hint:** Once again, consider the general idea of the article.)
   - (A) exists
   - (B) preserves
   - (C) continues
   - (D) predominates

7. *Maritime* traffic uses flag and light signals, but "if vessels needed to communicate verbally, they would find a common language, which would probably be English. . ." (**Hint:** Notice the word *vessels*, which means *ships.*)
   - (A) sea
   - (B) air
   - (C) ground
   - (D) rail

8. It is a foreign *tongue* for all six member nations. (**Hint:** Consider that this word also refers to a part of the body.)
   - (A) challenge
   - (B) figure
   - (C) trade
   - (D) language

Strategy

Skimming for Main Ideas
Skimming is a useful way to get an overview of a reading selection. To skim, move your eyes quickly through the whole reading, making sure to look at titles, headings, and illustrations. Do not stop for details or worry about words you don't understand. Keep going like a fast-moving train from beginning to end. Afterward, you will have a general idea of the contents. Then you can read the selection again with better comprehension.

    ❏ How English is taught in different countries

    ❏ Where English is taught

    ❏ The use of English among young people

    ❏ The use of English in literature and poetry

    ❏ The use of English in business, science, and diplomacy

    ❏ Comparisons of the use of English and the use of some other languages

Read

Introduction

Is English truly a universal language, or will it be at some time in the near future? The following selection from the book *Megatrends 2000* presents one opinion on this subject and supports the opinion with numerous details and statistics. Answer the questions below. Then read to see if you agree with the authors' opinion.

■ Are you learning English because you think it is a universal language, or is there some other reason for you to learn it?

■ What uses does learning English have for people from your culture?

English as a Universal Language

A   English is becoming the world's first truly universal language. It is the native language of some 400 million people in 12 countries. That is a lot fewer than the 885 million people or so who speak Mandarin Chinese. But another 400 million speak English as a second language. And several hundred million more have some knowledge of English, which has official 5 or semiofficial status in some 60 countries. Although there *may* be as many people speaking the various dialects of Chinese as there are English speakers, English is certainly more widespread geographically, more genuinely universal than Chinese. And its usage is growing at an extraordinary pace. 10

B   Today there are about 1 billion English speakers in the world, and the number is growing. The world's most taught language, English is not replacing other languages; it is supplementing them:

- More than two hundred and fifty million Chinese study English.
- In eighty-nine countries, English is either a common second language or widely studied.
- In Hong Kong, nine of every ten secondary school students study English.
- In France, state-run secondary schools require students to study four years of English or German; most—at least 85 percent—choose English.
- In Japan, secondary students are required to take six years of English before graduation.

Media and Transportation

C   English prevails in transportation and the media. The travel and communication language of the international airwaves is English. Pilots and air traffic controllers speak English at all international airports. Maritime traffic uses flag and light signals, but "if vessels needed to communicate verbally, they would find a common language, which would probably be English," says the U.S. Coast Guard's Werner Siems.

▲ University students in Shanghai, China

D   Five of the largest broadcasters—CBS, NBC, ABC, the BBC, and the CBC*—reach a potential audience of about 300 million people through English broadcast. It is also the most popular language of satellite TV.

The Information Age

E   The language of the information age is English.

F   More than 80 percent of all the information stored in the more than 100 million computers around the world is in English.

G   Eighty-five percent of international telephone conversations are conducted in English, as are three-fourths of the world's mail, telexes, and

___
* In addition to the five broadcasters mentioned, CNN news reaches 186 million households and hotel rooms around the world.

cables. Computer program instructions and the software itself are often supplied only in English.

H   German was once the language of science. Today more than 80 percent of all scientific papers are published first in English. Over half the world's technical and scientific periodicals are in English, which is also the language of medicine, electronics, and space technology. 50

International Business

I   English is the language of international business.

J   When a Japanese businessman strikes a deal anywhere in Europe, the chances are overwhelming that the negotiations were conducted in English. 55

▲ English is the international language of business.

K   Manufactured goods indicate their country of origin in English: "Made in Germany," not *Fabriziert in Deutschland*. It is the language of choice in multinational corporations. Datsun and Nissan write international memorandums in English. As early as 1985, 80 percent of the Japanese Mitsui and Company's employees could speak, read, and write English. Toyota provides in-service English courses. English classes are held in Saudi Arabia for the ARAMCO workers and on three continents for Chase Manhattan Bank staff. 60 65

Diplomacy

L   English is replacing the dominant European languages of centuries past. English has replaced French as the language of diplomacy; it is one of the official languages of international aid organizations such as Oxfam and Save the Children as well as of UNESCO, NATO, and the UN. 70

Lingua Franca

M   English serves as a common tongue in countries where people speak many different languages. In India, nearly 200 different languages are spoken; only 30 percent speak the official language, Hindi. When Rajiv Gandhi addressed the nation after his mother's assassination, he spoke in English. The European Free Trade Association works only in English even though it is a foreign tongue for all six member countries. 75

Official Language

N   English is the official or semiofficial language of 20 African countries, including Sierra Leone, Ghana, Nigeria, Liberia, and South Africa. Students are instructed in English at Makerere University in Uganda, the University of Nairobi in Kenya, and the University of Dar es Salaam in Tanzania. 80

o   English is the ecumenical language of the World Council of Churches, and one of the official languages of the Olympics and the Miss Universe competition.

Youth Culture

P   English is the language of international youth culture. Young people worldwide listen to and sing popular songs in English often without fully understanding the lyrics. "Break dance," "rap music," "bodybuilding," "windsurfing," and "computer hacking" are invading the slang of German youth.

Source: "English as a Universal Language" *Megatrends 2000* (Patricia Aburdene & John Naisbitt)

▲ Often people learn English to understand the lyrics of popular music.

After You Read

Strategy

Scanning for Specific Information

Scanning is different from skimming. You skim for general ideas. You scan for specific facts or details. To scan, move your eyes quickly over the reading until you come to the specific piece of information that you want. If you know that it is in the middle or toward the end of the reading, start there. Do not be distracted by other items. Concentrate. When you find what you want, use it. Then go to the next point.

3 **Scanning for Specific Information: Statistics** The selection supports its ideas with many and varied statistics from the time the article was written. Scan for the following information and write it in the blanks.

1. the number of English speakers in the world: _____

2. the number of Chinese studying English: _____

3. the approximate number of computers in the world: _____

4. the percentage of scientific papers published first in English: _____

5. the number of different languages spoken in India: _____

6. the number of African countries in which English has official or semiofficial status: _____

4 Guided Academic Conversation Work with another student. Take turns asking and answering the following questions. After you finish, compare your answers with those of another pair of students.

1. Why do the authors feel that English is more universal than Chinese?

2. Where is English used as a common second language?

3. In your opinion, why do people in many parts of the world study English? Why are you studying English?

4. In what situations can you imagine that a knowledge of English could mean the difference between life and death?

5. How has technology helped to make English popular?

6. Can you explain the meaning of *lingua franca* in the selection? Is English a lingua franca or not? Why?

7. What English terms or phrases are common in your culture?

TOEFL® IBT

Focus on Testing

Analyzing Summary Statements

On reading comprehension tests, you may be given several statements and asked to select the one that best summarizes a selection. In order to do this, first read the statements and see if any of them does not match the information in the reading. If so, eliminate it. Next, look at the other statements and decide which one best expresses the main idea of the reading selection. This statement must be *short* (one sentence) but *complete*. It should not just state a secondary idea or summarize small details of the selection. If there are subheads in the selection, they can help to remind you of the important ideas that should be included in a summary statement.

Practice Choose the statement below that best summarizes the article *English as a Universal Language*. Then explain your answer.

(A) English is replacing the dominant European languages of the past, and serves as a common means of communication in India and Africa and for scientists all over the world.

(B) English is the most important language in the world for transportation, information, business, diplomacy, trade, and communication among the young.

(C) English is the predominant language in the world because it is spoken by many more people than any other language and is used in most multinational companies.

Testing Notes

The TOEFL® iBT Test Over 2,300 colleges and universities in the United States and Canada require students who do not speak English as their first language to take the TOEFL® (TEST OF ENGLISH AS A FOREIGN

LANGUAGE). But many more organizations around the world accept TOEFL® scores. Many practice tests are commercially available to help you prepare for the TOEFL® test. These are available in bookstores and from the Internet. In addition, there is a lot of information on the Internet about the TOEFL® test, including the official website at www.toefl.org.

TOEIC® Test The TOEIC® (TEST OF ENGLISH FOR INTERNATIONAL COMMUNICATION) is used by companies, government agencies, colleges, and universities to measure English-language proficiency. More than 4.5 million non-native English speakers around the world take the TOEIC® test every year. More information about the TOEIC® test can be found at www.toeic.org.

TOEFL and TOEIC are registered trademarks of Educational Testing Service (ETS). This publication is not endorsed or approved by ETS.

Strategy

Understanding Acronyms and Abbreviations
Acronyms are words formed from the first letters of a phrase, such as LASER, which stands for **l**ightwave **a**mplification by **s**timulated **e**mission of **r**adiation or SCUBA—**s**elf-**c**ontained **u**nderwater **b**reathing **a**pparatus. Abbreviations are letters that stand for names and phrases, such as UN—**U**nited **N**ations—or they are the first letters of a word such as Inc. for Incorporated.

5 **Understanding Acronyms and Abbreviations** Can you identify what the following acronyms and abbreviations stand for? If you don't know, ask a classmate, look in a dictionary, or on the Internet. Write the information in the blanks. The first five items were used in the reading selection on pages 6–9.

1. ABC _____
2. BBC _____
3. CBC _____
4. UNESCO _____
5. NATO _____
6. NAFTA _____
7. etc. _____
8. RADAR _____
9. INTERPOL _____
10. ASAP _____
11. CD _____

12. DVD   _____

13. ESL   _____

14. TOEFL   _____

 6 **Reacting to an Opinion** In a small group, tell what you think about the following opinion. Do you agree with it, or do you agree with the article? Explain. What reasons do you have for your point of view? Compare the opinions of your group with those of other groups.

> "This article expresses a one-sided and nationalistic view in favor of the English language. The authors admit that French used to be the language of diplomacy and German used to be the language of science. Now it is the turn of English to predominate in these two areas, but it will soon change. There is no doubt about that! Technology is actually helping other languages to expand, not just English. No one can predict the future. There are many important languages in the world today. No one language can claim to be universal."

7 **Reading a Map** Look at the map of the world on page 13, read its legend (the explanation of the shading and the explanation under the map), and answer the following questions.

1. What do the shaded parts of the map indicate?

2. What is the difference between the two types of shading?

3. On what continents is English spoken as the mother tongue in some countries?

4. On what continents is English spoken as a second language?

5. Which of these two groups is larger? Which is more important for the status of English as a _global_ language?

 8 **What Do You Think?** Read the paragraph below and discuss the questions that follow on page 14.

Attack on English

In 1994, the French Cultural Minister promoted a law, which has continued into 2006, requiring that 3,000 English words widely used in France be replaced by newly created French equivalents. He felt the French were losing an important part of their culture by using English words. This would mean changing "prime time" to _heure de grande écoute_, or calling a "corner kick" in soccer a _jet de coin_. Although government officials will have to follow the new law, the French Constitutional Congress ruled that the law violates the "freedom of expression" of the general public.

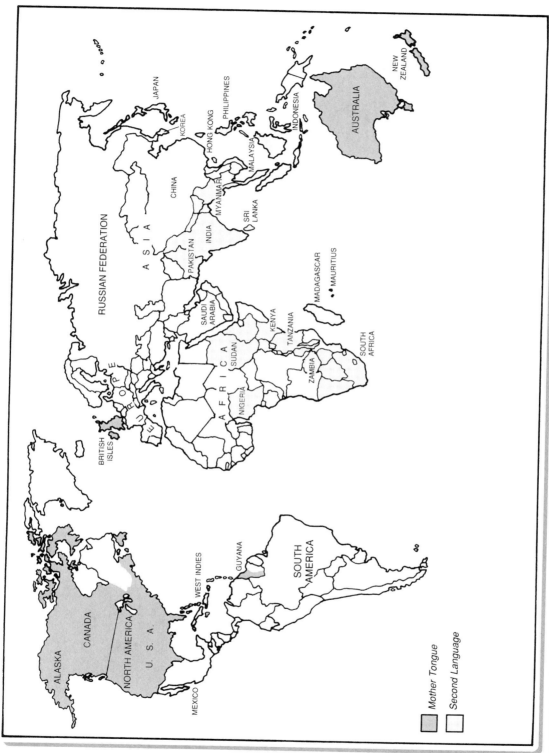

▲ English today is spoken as a mother tongue by about 400 million people, and at least 400 million more use it as a second language in societies—Africa, for instance—with dozens of competing languages. In total, there are probably more than a billion speakers of English.

1. Do you think the minister was right in trying to keep foreign words out of the French language?

2. Does your language include words of English origin? What are some examples?

3. What words do you know in English that come from other languages?

Mongolians Learn to Say "Progress" in English

Before You Read

1 Getting Meaning from Word Structure and Context Guess the meaning of the word or expression in italics by breaking it apart into smaller words, into prefixes and suffixes, or by using clues from the context. Use these skills, the hints given in parentheses, and your own logic to help you finish each statement with the correct option.

1. She searched for the English words to name the *razortooth* fish swimming around her stomach on her faded blue-and-white T-shirt. (**Hint:** A *razor* is an instrument that men and women use to shave their facial or leg hair.) Therefore, a *razortooth* fish is a fish _____.
   - (A) with whiskers or hair
   - (B) with very sharp teeth
   - (C) that swims quickly

2. Camel herders (people who take care of camels) may not yet refer to each other as "*dude*," but Mongolia, thousands of kilometers from the nearest English-speaking nation, is a reflection of the steady march of English as a world language. (**Hint:** *Dude* is an English slang word used to talk to a male friend.) Therefore, the first part of the sentence means that the common people in rural Mongolia do not _____.
   - (A) have much skill for herding animals
   - (B) speak the way young men like to speak
   - (C) know English perfectly at this time

3. The rush toward English in Mongolia *has not been without its bumps.* (**Hint:** Think about what bumps are like on a road.) So, this sentence means that the process of learning English in Mongolia has been _____.
   - (A) somewhat difficult
   - (B) really simple
   - (C) often boring

4. The first private English school when it started in 1999, this Mongolian-American *joint venture* now faces competition on all sides. (**Hint:** *Joint* means something done together by more than one person or group and *venture* is a business enterprise.) Therefore, a Mongolian-American joint venture is a business in which _____.

- (A) Mongolians learn from Americans.
- (B) Americans compete against Mongolians.
- (C) People from both countries participate.

5. Foreign arrivals are up *across the board*, with the exception of Russians, who experienced a 9.5 percent drop. (**Hint:** A board is often used to list numbers, such as the scores in a football game or prices at a market.) This means that, in general, the arrival of foreigners to Mongolia has _____.

- (A) moved across the border to Russia
- (B) decreased
- (C) increased

6. So far, Beijing has adopted a *laissez-faire stance* to Mongolia's flirtation with English. (**Hint:** *Laissez-faire* is an expression coming from the French language that means "to leave alone." *Flirtation* describes a playful interaction, often in a romantic sense between two people.) Therefore, Beijing's opinion of the Mongolian interest in English is that this is _____.

- (A) a great idea
- (B) a bad idea
- (C) no problem for Beijing

7. Chinese language studies are undergoing a *boom* here. (**Hint:** An example of a *boom* is when you talk about an "oil boom" in a region where a lot of oil has been discovered.) This phrase means that Chinese language studies are _____.

- (A) doing very well
- (B) doing poorly
- (C) an intellectual challenge

8. If there is a *shortcut* to development, it is English. (**Hint:** Look at the two smaller words inside this word.) This means that English provides _____.

- (A) a faster way for a country to develop
- (B) a danger for a country that is developing
- (C) a longer path to development

9. If we combine our academic knowledge with the English language, we can do *outsourcing* here, just like in Bangalore. (**Hint:** Once again, break the word apart and think about the meaning of its two parts.) *Outsourcing* here means _____.

- (A) finding the sources of foreign words in the English language
- (B) using people in one country as a source of workers for companies in other countries
- (C) paying out sums of money to Mongolians from government sources in other countries

Introduction

If English is becoming a universal language, how are countries assisting their residents to acquire proficiency in this language? The article below shows how Mongolia is implementing a deliberate program to become bilingual in the next generation, and it explains the reasons behind this radical move.

- What is your native country doing to assist non-English speakers to learn English as a second language?
- What kind of national policies or programs can you imagine that could help more people in a country to learn English more quickly?

Mongolians Learn to Say "Progress" in English

A **Ulan Bator, Mongolia** As she searched for the English words to name the razortooth fish swimming around her stomach on her faded blue-and-white T-shirt, ten-year-old Urantsetseg hardly seemed to embody an urgent new national policy.

B "Father shark, mother shark, sister shark," she recited carefully. Stumped by a smaller, worried-looking fish, she paused and frowned. Then she cried out: "Lunch!"

▲ Mongolian children learning English

C Even in the settlement of dirt tracks, plank shanties, and the circular felt yurts of herdsmen, the sounds of English can be heard from the youngest of students, part of a nationwide drive to make it the primary foreign language learned in Mongolia.

D "We are looking at Singapore as a model," Tsakhia Elbegdorj, Mongolia's prime minister, said in an interview, his own American English honed at graduate school at Harvard University. "We see English not only as a way of communicating, but as a way of opening windows on the wider world."

E   Camel herders may not yet refer to each other as "dude," but Mongolia, thousands of kilometers from the nearest English-speaking nation, is a reflection of the steady march of English as a world language. 25

F   Fueled by the Internet, the growing dominance of U.S. culture, and the financial realities of globalization, English is now taking hold in Asia, and elsewhere, just as it has done in many European countries.

G   In Korea, six "English villages" are being established where paying 30 students can have their passports stamped for intensive weeks of English-language immersion, taught by native speakers imported from all over the English-speaking world.

H   The most ambitious, an $85 million English town near Seoul, will have Western architecture, signs, and a resident population of English-speaking 35 foreigners.

I   In Iraq, where Arabic and Kurdish are to be the official languages, there is a growing movement to add English, a neutral link for a nation split along ethnic lines.

J   In Iraqi Kurdistan, there is an explosion in English-language studies, 40 fueled partly by an affinity for Britain and the United States, and partly by the knowledge that neighboring Turkey may soon join the European Union, where English is emerging as the dominant language.

K   In Chile, the government has embarked on a national program of teaching English in all elementary and high schools. The goal is to make 45 that nation of 15 million people bilingual in English within a generation. The models are the Netherlands and the Nordic nations, which have achieved virtual bilingualism in English since World War II.

L   The rush toward English in Mongolia has not been without its bumps. After taking office after the elections here in June, Elbegdorj shocked 50 Mongolians by announcing that it would become a bilingual nation, with English as the second language.

M   For Mongolians still debating whether to jettison the Cyrillic alphabet imposed by Stalin in 1941, this was too much, too fast.

N   Later, on his bilingual English-Mongolian website, the prime minister 55 fine-tuned his program, drawing up a national curriculum designed to make English replace Russian next September as the primary foreign language taught here.

O   Still, as fast as Elbegdorj wants the Mongolian government to proceed, the state is merely catching up with the private sector. "This 60 building is three times the size of our old building," Doloonjin Orgilmaa, director general of Santis Educational Services, said, showing a visitor around her three-story English school, which opened in November near Mongolia's Sports Palace. The first private English school when it started in 1999, this Mongolian-American joint venture now faces competition 65 on all sides.

P   With schools easing the way, English is penetrating Ulan Bator through the electronic media and at Mongolian International University, all classes are in English . . . "If there is a shortcut to development it is English," Munh-Orgil Tsend, Mongolia's foreign minister, said in an interview, 70 speaking American English, also honed at Harvard. "Parents understand that, kids understand that . . ."

Q   Increased international tourism and a growing number of resident foreigners explain some moves, like the two English-language newspapers here and the growing numbers of bilingual store signs and restaurant 75 menus. . . . Foreign arrivals are up across the board, with the exception of Russians, who experienced a 9.5 percent drop. Their decrease reflects a wider decline here of Russian influence and the Russian language. Until the collapse of the Soviet Union, Russian was universally taught here and was required for admission to university in Mongolia . . . 80

R   So far, Beijing has adopted a laissez-faire stance to Mongolia's flirtation with English, even though China is now the leading source of foreign investment, trade, and tourism. Such a stance is easy to maintain, because Chinese language studies are also undergoing a boom here.

S   A trading people famed for straddling the east-west Silk Road, 85 Mongolians have long been linguists, often learning multiple languages.

T   After attempting during the 1990s to retrain about half of Mongolia's 1,400 Russian language teachers to teach English, Mongolia now is embarking on a program to attract hundreds of qualified teachers from around the world to teach here. "I need 2,000 English teachers," said 90 Puntsag Tsagaan, Mongolia's minister of education, culture, and science. A graduate of a Soviet university, he laboriously explained in English that Mongolia hoped to attract English teachers, not only from Britain and North America, but also from India, Singapore, and Malaysia.

U   Tsagaan spins an optimistic vision of Mongolia's bilingual future. "If we 95 combine our academic knowledge with the English language, we can do outsourcing here, just like in Bangalore," he said.

Source: "Mongolians Learn to Say 'Progress' in English" *New York Times* (James Brooke)

After You Read

Strategy

Completing a Summary

A summary is a longer version of a summary statement. It reviews the main points of a selection in a shorter format. Filling in blanks in a summary can help you to understand key vocabulary terms, to review the meaning of the selection as a whole, and to remind you of the purpose of a summary.

2 Completing a Summary Fill in the blanks with the words from the list below to complete the summary of *Mongolians Learn to Say "Progress" in English*.

bilingual	immersion	model	replace
established	intensive	policy	resident
ethnic	link	primary	shocked

Mongolia has an urgent new national _____ 1 to make English the _____ 2 foreign language learned in Mongolia. The Prime Minister is looking at Singapore as a _____ 3. Other countries also have growing English programs. In Korea, "English villages" are being _____ 4 where paying students 5 can have their passports stamped for _____ 5 weeks of English-language _____ 6. In Iraq, the English language may serve as a neutral _____ 7 for a nation split along _____ 8 lines (divided into different cultural groups). Iraqi Kurdistan and Chile provide other examples of a new interest in 10 learning English. Right after being elected, the Prime Minister _____ 9 Mongolians by announcing that their country would become a _____ 10 nation. On his English-Mongolian website, he explained his plans for how English would _____ 11 Russian as the main foreign language taught. 15 Increased international tourism and a growing number of _____ 12 foreigners explain this move.

Guessing the Meaning of Strong Verbs

Strong verbs are verbs that express the action in a more complete, exact, or picturesque way than common verbs. Using strong verbs improves one's writing. The selection you just read uses many strong verbs. For instance, instead of saying that "ten-year-old Urantsetseg hardly seemed to be a representative for an urgent new national policy," it says that she "hardly seemed to *embody* an urgent new national policy."

3 **Guessing the Meaning of Strong Verbs** Match the strong verbs on the left with their meaning in the column on the right. Check your answers by looking up the verb and its context in the selection if necessary.

1. __d__ (she) hardly seemed to *embody* an urgent new national policy (line 3)

2. _____ she *recited* carefully (line 7)

3. _____ *Stumped* by a smaller, worried-looking fish (line 7)

4. _____ American English *honed* at graduate school (line 21)

5. _____ *fueled* partly by an affinity for Britain and the United States (line 41)

6. _____ the government has *embarked on* a national program (line 44)

7. _____ debating whether to *jettison* the Cyrillic alphabet (line 53)

8. _____ the prime minister *fine-tuned* his program (line 56)

9. _____ the state is merely *catching up* with the private sector (line 60)

10. _____ With schools *easing the way* (line 67)

11. _____ English is *penetrating* Ulan Bator (line 67)

12. _____ Tsagaan *spins* an optimistic vision of (line 95)

a. learned well, made perfect

b. throw away, discard

c. making things easier to do

d. represent, stand for

e. entering, making its way into

f. made small improvements to

g. confused, puzzled

h. tells of, narrates

i. pushed forward, promoted

j. becoming equal, coming closer

k. said, spoke out loud

l. started, begun

THE ACADEMIC WORD LIST

There is a list of words that college students should know because these words occur frequently in academic English. This list is called the "Academic Word List." You will find an activity in each chapter of this book that will help you focus on these words. Also, in the Self-Assessment Log at the end of each chapter these words have an asterisk (*) next to them. For more information on Averil Coxhead's Academic Word List, see www.vuw.ac.nz/lals/research/awl.

4 Focusing on Words from the Academic Word List Read the following excerpt taken from the reading in Part 2. Fill in the blanks with a word from the box. Do not look back at the reading right away; instead, see if you can remember the vocabulary.

debating	dominant	generation	imposed	site
designed	emerging	goal	primary	virtual

A In Iraqi Kurdistan, there is an explosion in English-language studies, fueled partly by an affinity for Britain and the United States, and partly by the knowledge that neighboring Turkey may soon join the European Union, where English is _____ as the _____ language.
                                   1   2

5

B In Chile, the government has embarked on a national program of teaching English in all elementary and high schools. The _____ is
                                                                    3
to make that nation of 15 million people bilingual in English within a _____. The models are the Netherlands and the Nordic
                4
nations, which have achieved _____ bilingualism in
                              5
English since World War II.

10

C The rush toward English in Mongolia has not been without its bumps. After taking office after the elections here in June, Elbegdorj shocked Mongolians by announcing that it would become a bilingual nation, with English as the second language.

15

D For Mongolians still _____ whether to jettison the
                        6
Cyrillic alphabet _____ by Stalin in 1941, this was too
                   7
much, too fast.

E Later, on his bilingual English-Mongolian web _____,
                                                   8
the prime minister fine-tuned his program, drawing up a national curriculum

20

_____ to make English replace Russian next September
         9
as the _____ foreign language taught here.
       10

5 Guided Academic Discussion Get into groups and answer the following questions. After you finish, get together with another group and compare your answers to one of the questions which your teacher will assign to you. Are your answers similar or different? Explain.

1. According to the article, what is happening with the teaching of English in the following places: Korea, Iraq, Iraqi Kurdistan, and Chile? What do you think of these programs?

2. Why are Mongolians used to learning more than one language? What second language will English replace as a primary second language there? How many languages do you know? In your opinion, how many languages should a person learn? Why?

3. Why do many Mongolians want to learn English? How is the transition to bilingualism in English to be accomplished?

4. Should countries have programs to promote bilingualism in English, or should countries be more focused on programs to develop their original native languages? Why?

Part 3 Tying It All Together

 1 Your Views on Education—an Interview Find a partner and take turns interviewing each other using the questions below, relating to education. Afterwards, be prepared to tell the class something you have learned about your partner.

1. What are the most important qualities of a good teacher? What are the worst qualities that a teacher could have? Why?

2. How do you like your classes to be structured? Which of the following elements would you like to have included in a course: lectures, discussions, debates, movies or videos, music, presentations, group work, writing, homework, dramatic plays, or other elements? Explain.

3. Describe the best class you have ever taken. Why did you like it?

 2 Making Connections Do some research on the Internet and take notes on one of the following topics. Share your results with the class or in a small group.

Preserving Languages Search for groups or movements that are attempting to preserve their original languages. Which languages are people united in trying to preserve? Take notes on one or two of these groups and the languages they want to preserve.

English Use in Non-English-Speaking Countries Choose a country whose primary language is not English and look up some facts about how much the English language is used in that country. Are people there interested in learning English? What kind of programs or national policies are there in that country for learning English?

The Future of Languages Find out how many languages exist in the world today. How many do the experts think will still exist 50 years from now? What determines whether the use of a language increases or decreases? Just as in nature, certain species of animals have survived and others have gone extinct (completely died off), languages also either grow or die. Which languages will probably survive in the future and which ones will go extinct? Why?

Responding in Writing

WRITING TIP: WRITING A SUMMARY STATEMENT

Learning how to write a summary statement—a single sentence giving the essence of a piece of writing—is a useful skill. There will be occasions when you have limited time and want to explain something briefly. As is mentioned in the Focus-on-Testing section in this chapter, a good summary statement is *short* (one sentence) and *inclusive* (relatively complete, referring to different parts, not just to one).

To write a summary statement of a short piece of writing, put down the main idea and the most important details in one sentence. Try to express this in *your own words,* not in the same words that were written. Use the most important details from the whole piece, not just from the beginning.

3 **Writing a Summary Statement** Follow the steps below to write a summary statement of a paragraph. In a later chapter, you will be asked to summarize a longer piece of writing.

Step 1 Look at the first paragraph of the reading from Part 1, copied below.

1. How many sentences does it have?

2. A summary statement must *distill* (reduce, bring down, compress) this into one good sentence. Read this paragraph and the three statements that follow it. Which statement is the best summary statement? Remember it should be *short* and *inclusive.*

3. Why are the others not as good?

English is becoming the world's first truly universal language. It is the native language of some 400 million people in 12 countries. That is a lot fewer than the 885 million people or so who speak Mandarin Chinese. But another 400 million speak English as a second language. And several hundred million more have some knowledge of English, which has official or semiofficial status in some 60 countries. Although there *may* be as many people speaking the various dialects of Chinese as there are English speakers, English is certainly more widespread geographically, more genuinely universal than Chinese. And its usage is growing at an extraordinary pace.

a. English is turning into the most popular language on the planet because it is the native language of 400 million people in 12 countries and the second language of 400 million, almost as many as the 885 million who speak Mandarin Chinese, and also several million people have some knowledge of English.

b. English is developing into the most common international language since hundreds of millions of people speak it as a first or second language, it is the official or semiofficial language of some 60 countries and, unlike its closest rival, Chinese, it is used more and more all over the globe.

c. English is evolving into the most truly global language, being the native language of many people in 12 different countries and well known to hundreds of millions of others, and although there may be as many speakers of the various dialects of Chinese as there are English speakers, English is growing at a very fast pace.

Step 2 Now, farther on in the same reading, there is a section subtitled *Media and Transportation* (copied below). How many sentences does it have? Read it carefully and consider the main idea.

English prevails in transportation and the media. The travel and communication language of the international airwaves is English. Pilots and air traffic controllers speak English at all international airports. Maritime traffic uses flag and light signals, but "if vessels needed to communicate verbally, they would find a common language, which would probably be English," says the U.S. Coast Guard's Werner Siems.

Five of the largest broadcasters—CBS, NBC, ABC, the BBC, and the CBC—reach a potential audience of about 300 million people through English broadcast. It is also the most commonly used language of satellite TV.

Step 3 Write a one-sentence summary statement of the section in Step 2. Include the main idea in different words from those used in the text and some details that support the main idea. Make sure to express what is said, *not your opinions*. That is another type of writing that will be studied in a later chapter.

_____

_____

_____

Step 4 Check over your summary statement. Is it one sentence long? Is it inclusive? Do you have the correct spelling of the words and good punctuation? Make sure that your statement expresses the main ideas of the author, not your own personal opinion. But also make sure that your statement is in your own words, not just a copy of a sentence taken from the reading selection.

Step 5 Work with two or three others to revise your writing. Everyone reads his or her statement aloud. Then all of you discuss the statements and vote on which one is the best: short but inclusive, correctly written in words that are not copied directly from the text, clear and interesting. Congratulations to the winner. He or she should take a bow!

Self-Assessment Log

Read the lists below. Check (✓) the strategies and vocabulary that you learned in this chapter. Look through the chapter or ask your instructor about the strategies and words that you do not understand.

Reading and Vocabulary-Building Strategies
- ❏ Getting meaning from word structure and context
- ❏ Skimming for main ideas
- ❏ Scanning for specific information
- ❏ Analyzing summary statements
- ❏ Understanding acronyms and abbreviations
- ❏ Reacting to an opinion
- ❏ Reading a map
- ❏ Completing a summary
- ❏ Guessing the meaning of strong verbs
- ❏ Writing a summary statement

Target Vocabulary

Nouns
- ❏ boom
- ❏ dialects
- ❏ dude
- ❏ generation*
- ❏ goal*
- ❏ immersion
- ❏ joint venture
- ❏ laissez-faire stance
- ❏ link*
- ❏ model
- ❏ outsourcing
- ❏ policy*
- ❏ shortcut
- ❏ site*
- ❏ status*
- ❏ tongue

Verbs
- ❏ catching up
- ❏ debating*
- ❏ designed*
- ❏ embarking
- ❏ embody
- ❏ emerging*
- ❏ established*
- ❏ fine-tuned
- ❏ jettison
- ❏ penetrating
- ❏ prevails
- ❏ recited
- ❏ replace
- ❏ shocked
- ❏ spins
- ❏ supplementing*

Adjectives
- ❏ bilingual
- ❏ dominant*
- ❏ ethnic*
- ❏ fueled
- ❏ honed
- ❏ imposed*
- ❏ intensive*
- ❏ maritime
- ❏ primary*
- ❏ razortooth
- ❏ resident*
- ❏ stumped
- ❏ virtual*
- ❏ widespread*

Idioms and Expressions
- ❏ across the board
- ❏ easing the way
- ❏ has not been without its bumps

* These words are from the Academic Word List. For more information on this list, see www.vuw.ac.nz/lals/research/awl.

2

Danger and Daring

In This Chapter

Why take risks? Why face danger and death when you could stay home in safety and comfort? Throughout history, there have been many who dared: explorers, mountain climbers, travelers, soldiers, and religious leaders, to name a few. The first selection is an excerpt from a book about the tragic and terrifying events that occurred a few years ago on the slopes of the highest mountain in the world. The second selection is the true account of a Canadian naturalist and writer who lived among wild animals and made an important discovery—about himself.

❝ I'll try anything once. ❞

—Alice Roosevelt Longworth (1884–1980), daughter of Theodore Roosevelt, 26th president of the United States as she was about to give birth at age 41, to her first child

Connecting to the Topic

1. Look at the picture below and imagine that you are the skier. Does it look like something you would like to do? How would you feel? Excited? Terrified?

2. Alice Roosevelt Longworth said that she would try anything once. Are you willing to try new things or do you prefer to do things you have done before?

3. Have you ever done anything dangerous? What did you do? What was the result?

Into Thin Air

Before You Read

> **Strategy**
>
> **Previewing a Reading**
> The prefix *pre-* means "before," so *previewing* means "viewing (looking) before." It aids comprehension to look through a selection before reading it and predict its contents. Find clues to what the selection is about. Just as it is easier to drive through a neighborhood you know rather than through a strange one, it is easier to read something if you get acquainted with it first.
>
> To preview a reading, look at the title and any photos, charts, or illustrations, the first and last paragraphs, and the first line of each of the other paragraphs. Think about what associations or connections there are between your life and the topic. Ask yourself: What is the topic and what do I already know about it?

 1 Previewing a Reading Work with a partner and answer these questions about the reading on pages 31–33.

1. Look at the photos. What do they tell you about the subject of the selection?

2. In English, people often talk about disappearing "into thin air," even when it has nothing to do with falling off a mountain. Look at the title. What does it suggest to you? What feelings does it give you?

3. Skim lines 1–37 very quickly. Is the reading about a difficult or an easy experience? Dangerous or safe? Comfortable or demanding? Give some details to support each of your answers.

Identifying More Exact or Colorful Synonyms

Good writers choose their words carefully. To appreciate their style, learn how to identify the exact and colorful (interesting, exciting) words they choose instead of plain or boring ones. Identifying words like these can help you to choose exact and colorful words in your own writing, too.

Example

Standing on the top of the world, one foot in China and the other in Nepal, I cleared the ice from my oxygen mask, *leaned* a shoulder against the wind, and *looked* absently down the vastness of Tibet.

Now, look at the first sentence in the reading on page 31. What three synonyms are used instead of the words in italics above?

standing on = _____

leaned = _____

looked = _____

Notice that the synonym for *standing on* is more concise and the synonyms for *leaned* and *looked* are more exact and colorful.

2 **Identifying More Exact or Colorful Synonyms** Read the phrases below from the reading. Scan the reading for the more exact, concise, or colorful synonyms of the words in parentheses. The phrases are listed in the order of their appearance in the reading.

1. I understood on some dim, detached level that the sweep of earth beneath my feet was a (wonderful) ____*spectacular*____ sight.

2. I'd (thought) _____ about this moment, and the release of emotion that would accompany it for many months.

3. But now that I was finally here, actually standing on the (peak) _____ of Mount Everest.

4. Weeks of violent coughing had left me with two separated ribs that made ordinary breathing (a painful) an _____ trial.

5. I (took) _____ four quick photos . . .

6. . . . after surgeons had (cut off) _____ the gangrenous right hand of my teammate . . .

7. . . . why, if the weather had begun to (get worse) _____ , had climbers on the upper mountain not (paid attention to) _____ the signs?

8. Why did veteran Himalayan guides keep moving upward, ushering a (group) _____ of . . . amateurs . . .? (**Hint:** This is a picturesque word because it usually refers to a group of geese and so implies disdain or disrespect for people without skill.)

9. Moving at the snail's pace that is the norm above 26,000 feet, the (crowd) _____ labored up the Hillary Step.

10. As I exchanged (commonplace) _____ congratulations with the climbers filing past . . .

11. . . . it began to snow lightly and (the ability to see) _____ went to hell.

12. . . . my (close friends) _____ (took their time) _____ unfurling flags and snapping photos. (**Hint:** The first word is a Spanish word well-known to many English speakers.)

Read

Introduction

The peak of Mt. Everest, which lies between China and Tibet, is the highest place on Earth, 29,028 feet above sea level, and many have tried to reach it. Some have achieved this goal, especially in recent decades when it has become possible to carry oxygen tanks. Some have died in the attempt. Others have returned with permanent physical injuries or psychological damage.

Almost all of the climbers, no matter what country they come from, use natives called Sherpas to carry their equipment and aid them in the dangerous journey to the summit. The Sherpas know this mountain well and consider it sacred. They earn their living carrying heavy loads and serving as guides.

- Why do you think so many people try to climb Mt. Everest?
- If you had the money and opportunity, would you do it? Why or why not?

The following selections are excerpts from the true narrative book *Into Thin Air* by John Krakauer. This book has been called "the definitive account of the deadliest season in the history of Everest." The selection begins at the moment that Krakauer arrives at the peak of the mountain in the early afternoon of May 10, 1996.

▲ Climbers experience a personal high when they reach "the roof of the world."

Into Thin Air

A   Straddling the top of the world, one foot in China and the other in Nepal, I cleared the ice from my oxygen mask, hunched a shoulder against the wind, and stared absently down the vastness of Tibet. I understood on some dim, detached level that the sweep of earth beneath my feet was a spectacular sight. I'd fantasized about this moment, and the release of emotion that would accompany it for many months. But now that I was finally here, actually standing on the summit of Mount Everest, I just couldn't summon the energy to care. It was early in the afternoon of May 10, 1996. I hadn't slept in 57 hours. The only food I'd been able to force down over the preceding three days was a bowl of ramen soup and a handful of peanut M&Ms. Weeks of violent coughing had left me with two separated ribs that made ordinary breathing an excruciating trial. At 29,028 feet up . . . so little oxygen was reaching my brain that my mental capacity was that of a slow child . . . I was incapable of feeling much of anything except cold and tired.

B   I'd arrived on the summit a few minutes after Anatoli Boukreev, a Russian climbing guide . . . and just ahead of Andy Harris, a guide on the New Zealand-based team to which I belonged . . . I snapped four quick photos of Harris and Boukreev striking summit poses, then turned and headed down. My watch read 1:17 P.M. All told, I'd spent less than five minutes on the roof of the world.

C   A moment later, I paused to take another photo. . . . Training my lens on a pair of climbers approaching the summit, I noticed something that until that moment had escaped my attention. To the south, where the sky had been perfectly clear just an hour earlier, a blanket of clouds now hid Pumori, Ama Dablam, and the other lesser peaks surrounding Everest.   25

D   Later—after six bodies had been located, after a search for two others had been abandoned, after surgeons had amputated the gangrenous right hand of my teammate Beck Weathers—people would ask why, if the weather had begun to deteriorate, had climbers . . . not heeded the signs? Why did veteran Himalayan guides keep moving upward, ushering a gaggle   30 of amateurs—each of whom had paid as much as $65,000—into an apparent death trap?

E   Nobody can speak for the leaders of the two guided groups involved, because both men are dead. But I can attest that nothing I saw early on the afternoon of May 10 suggested that a murderous storm was bearing down.   35 To my oxygen-depleted mind, the clouds drifting up the grand valley . . . looked innocuous, wispy, insubstantial.

As Krakauer began his descent from the summit of Mt. Everest, he became extremely concerned because his oxygen tanks were running low. He knew he had to climb down to the South Summit camp to get oxygen. On his way down, however, he ran into a "traffic jam" of more than a dozen climbers trying to reach the summit. He stepped aside to let them pass.

F   The traffic jam was comprised of climbers from three expeditions . . . Moving at the snail's pace that is the norm above 26,000 feet, the throng labored up the Hillary Step one by one,   40 while I nervously bided my time.

▲ Korean mountaineer Ko Sang-don reached the top of Mt. Everest in 1977.

G   Harris, who'd left the summit shortly after I did, soon pulled up behind me. Wanting to conserve whatever oxygen remained in my tank, I asked him to reach   45 inside my backpack and turn off the valve of my regulator, which he did. For the next ten minutes I felt surprisingly good. My head cleared. I actually seemed less tired than I had with the gas turned on. Then abruptly, I   50 sensed that I was suffocating. My vision dimmed and my head began to spin. I was on the brink of losing consciousness.

H   Instead of turning my oxygen off, Harris, had mistakenly cranked the valve open to full flow, draining the tank. I'd just squandered the last of my   55 gas going nowhere. There was another tank waiting for me at the South

Summit, 250 feet below, but to get there I would have to descend the most exposed terrain on the entire route without the benefit of supplemental oxygen.

I   And first I had to wait for the mob to disperse. I removed my now useless mask . . . and hunkered on the ridge. As I exchanged banal congratulations with the climbers filing past, inwardly I was frantic: "Hurry it up, hurry it up!" I silently pleaded . . .

60

The climbers, many of them exhausted, passed Krakauer on their way to the summit. They were behind schedule. After they passed, Krakauer continued his descent to the South Summit.

J   It was after three o'clock when I made it down to the South Summit. By now tendrils of mist were . . . lapping at Everest's summit pyramid. No longer did the weather look so benign. I grabbed a fresh oxygen cylinder, jammed it onto my regulator, and hurried down into the gathering cloud. Moments after I dropped below the South Summit, it began to snow lightly and visibility went to hell.

65

K   Four hundred vertical feet above, where the summit was still washed in bright sunlight . . . my compadres dallied . . . unfurling flags and snapping photos, using up precious ticks of the clock. None of them imagined that a horrible ordeal was drawing nigh. Nobody suspected that by the end of that long day, every minute would count.

70

Source: *Into Thin Air* (John Krakauer)

Nine climbers from four expeditions, many of those whom Krakauer passed on his way down from the summit, perished in that unexpected storm on Mt. Everest on May 10, 1996. Impaired judgment seems to have been a significant factor in their deaths.

After You Read

Strategy

Making Inferences

Inferences are ideas or opinions that are not stated but that can be *inferred* (concluded) from the information given. For example, if your friend says, "Shoot! I have to wear my heavy coat today," you can infer that he thinks it is cold outside and that he is not happy about this. Learning how to make inferences makes you a better reader and a clearer thinker.

3 **Making Inferences** Practice recognizing inferences by matching each of the following inferences on the left to the statements from the article on the right that give the basis for the inference.

_d_ **1.** Weather can change very quickly in the mountains.

_____ **2.** Climbing at high altitude causes problems with the respiratory (breathing) system.

_____ **3.** Climbing at high altitude makes normal eating and sleeping difficult.

_____ **4.** Mountain climbers are proud people who do not like to show their fear.

_____ **5.** Lack of oxygen can result in a person making poor decisions.

a. I hadn't slept in 57 hours. The only food I'd been able to force down over the preceding three days was a bowl of ramen soup and a handful of peanut M&Ms.

b. Weeks of violent coughing had left me with two separated ribs that made ordinary breathing an excruciating trial.

c. . . . so little oxygen was reaching my brain that my mental capacity was that of a slow child.

d. To the south, where the sky had been perfectly clear just an hour earlier, a blanket of clouds now hid Pumori, Ama Dablam, and the other lesser peaks surrounding Everest.

e. As I exchanged banal congratulations with the climbers filing past, inwardly I was frantic: "Hurry it up, hurry it up!"

Strategy

Getting Meaning from Context: Everyday Phrases
Sometimes you know the meaning of each word in a phrase but don't understand the whole phrase. You have to infer the meaning of a phrase from its context (the words before and after it.)

---

4 **Getting Meaning from Context: Everyday Phrases** Use context to explain the italicized phrases below.

1. I'd fantasized about this moment and *the release of emotion* that would accompany it . . . (line 5)

The author is on the summit and expects to feel strong emotions

that he had to keep inside himself before.

2. I snapped four quick photos of Harris and Boukreev *striking summit poses* . . . (line 18)

_____

3. All told, I'd spent less than five minutes *on the roof of the world.* (line 19)

_____

4. A *blanket of clouds* now hid Pumori, Ama Dablam, and the other lesser peaks . . . (line 24)

_____

5. Why did veteran Himalayan guides keep moving upward . . . *into an apparent death trap?* (line 30)

_____

6. *Moving at the snail's pace* that is the norm above 26,000 feet . . . (line 39)

_____

7. . . . my compadres dallied . . . unfurling flags and snapping photos, *using up precious ticks of the clock.* (line 71)

_____

CREATING A STORYBOARD

A storyboard is a visual representation of a story from beginning to end. It illustrates each part of a story's plot—like a sort of cartoon. It is used by directors who are making TV shows or movies, and it is shown to the actors to guide them. Storyboards may also include written descriptions along with the pictures that illustrate them.

5 **Creating a Storyboard** Imagine that you have to make a storyboard for a TV docudrama called *Tragedy on Top of the World,* based on the selection from John Krakauer's book. Work in small groups and think of four to six scenes that you think best show the story. Briefly describe the scene in the column on the left and then an "artist" (or artists) from your group should draw a picture of each scene, using stick figures if necessary. (You can copy the storyboard below on a separate sheet of paper, leaving enough room for the words and the illustrations.) Show your storyboard to the class or to another group, and tell the story, explaining what emotions the actors must convey in each scene.

A Storyboard for *Tragedy on Top of the World*	
Descriptions	**Illustrations**
1.	
2.	
3.	
4.	

6 Guided Academic Conversation Use the guide words *who, when, where, what, why* to discuss the following topics with a small group of classmates. Then look at the questions in parentheses for more ideas. Be prepared to describe to the class what your group talked about after you finish.

1. Mountain climbing the world over. (Is it done by men, by women, by all nationalities, or only by some? What is the most exciting, the most difficult, the most pleasant, the most famous mountain? What do you think of the climbers who pay $65,000 to be brought to the top of Everest?)

2. Taking risks: physical, intellectual, social, financial. (Is danger a stimulant? Can it be an addiction? Does risky behavior bring about the ruin of some people? How?)

3. Extreme sports. (Which ones are the most dangerous: hang gliding, scuba diving, auto racing, rock climbing? Is boxing an extreme sport?)

▲ Which sports do you think are dangerous?

Part 2 Reading Skills and Strategies

The World We Lost

Before You Read

 1 Previewing the Reading Work with a partner to preview the next reading. To preview, answer the questions below.

1. Look at the photo and its caption on page 40. What do they tell you about the subject of the selection? What do you already know about these animals?

2. Look at the title. Its meaning is not obvious. Can you make a guess about how it connects with the photo? What "world" could the author be referring to?

3. Skim the first paragraph of the reading. To *skim* means to read quickly for general meaning without stopping to look up words you don't understand. What do you find out about the author and his work? Describe the way he feels at the beginning of the story.

2 **Getting Meaning from Context** Look at the following excerpts from the reading selection and choose the best definition for each italicized word. Use the context in the sentences and the hints in parentheses to help you.

1. In order to round out my study of wolf family life, I needed to know what the *den* was like inside—how deep it was, the diameter of the passage, the presence (if any) of a nest at the end of the *burrow*, and such related information. (**Hint:** Since the author wants to study the "family life" of wolves and states a need to know the "inside," you can infer the meaning of the first word.)

   The *den* is the place where the wolves go to _____.
   - (A) hunt
   - (B) sleep
   - (C) die

   A *burrow* is _____. (**Hint:** The reference in the reading to a nest at the *end* of this gives a clue to the correct meaning.)
   - (A) a pile of sticks and mud
   - (B) a young wolf or dog
   - (C) a hole dug by an animal

2. The *Norseman* came over at about 50 feet. As it roared past, the plane waggled its wings gaily in salute, then lifted to skim the crest of the wolf *esker*, sending a blast of sand down the slope with its propeller wash. (**Hint:** The word *esker* is not well known even to English speakers, but the reader can use clues from the context: the word *crest*, your knowledge of where the man is going, what happens when the propeller gets near the esker.)

   The *Norseman* is a type of _____.
   - (A) animal
   - (B) wind
   - (C) plane

   An *esker* is _____.
   - (A) a ridge of sand
   - (B) a small river
   - (C) a kind of fruit tree

3. My mouth and eyes were soon full of sand, and I was beginning to suffer from *claustrophobia*, for the tunnel was just big enough to admit me. (**Hint:** *Phobia* is a term used in psychology to refer to a deep, irrational fear. If you remember that the word *for* means "because" when it starts a secondary clause, you will understand what kind of fear is referred to by this word.)

Claustrophobia is the unreasonable fear of _____ .

(A) high, open places
(B) small, enclosed places
(C) wild animals

4. Despite my close *familiarity* with the wolf family, this was the kind of situation where irrational but deeply ingrained *prejudices* completely overmaster reason and experience. (**Hint:** If you break up the word *prejudice*, you get the prefix *pre-* meaning "before," and the root *jud*, which also appears in words such as *judge* and *judgment*.)

In this context, *familiarity* means _____ .

(A) similarity
(B) hatred
(C) acquaintance

Prejudices are _____ .

(A) strong and warm emotions
(B) opinions formed with no basis in fact
(C) conclusions drawn from observation and action

5. It seemed *inevitable* that the wolves *would* attack me, for even a *gopher* will make a fierce defense when he is cornered in his den. (**Hint:** The word *even* is your best clue to the meaning of the first and third italicized words.)

Inevitable means _____ .

(A) certain
(B) highly unlikely
(C) possible

A *gopher* is an animal that is _____ .

(A) large and dangerous
(B) small and defenseless
(C) similar to a wolf

6. I was *appalled* at the realization of how easily I had forgotten, and how readily I had denied, all that the summer *sojourn* with the wolves had taught me about them . . . and about myself.

Appalled means _____ .

(A) pleased
(B) shocked
(C) relieved

Sojourn means _____ .

(A) reading
(B) weather
(C) stay

Introduction

Do you ever have nightmares? What is your secret fear? Poisonous snakes? Earthquakes? Water? Fire? Everyone is afraid of something, and wild animals appear high on the list for many people. Farley Mowat, the world-famous Canadian writer and naturalist, shared this fear but still accepted a job that meant living alone in the far north in direct contact with wolves. The Wildlife Service of the Canadian government hired him to investigate claims that wolves were killing the arctic caribou (large animals of the deer family). Much to his surprise, Mowat discovered that the wolves were not savage killers, but cautious and predictable animals. He gave names to the ones he studied and became fond of them.

Later he wrote a book called *Never Cry Wolf* about his experiences. It became a best-seller and was made into a popular movie that has changed many people's ideas about wolves. The following selection is the last chapter of his book. It tells of an incident that led the author to an important discovery, not about the wolves but about himself.

- Have you had experiences dealing with wild animals before? What do you imagine will happen to the author when he deals closely with the wolves?
- What do you anticipate he might mean by the title *The World We Lost*?

▲ Wolves can be fierce when hunting prey.

The World We Lost

A   In order to round out my study of wolf family life, I needed to know what the den was like inside—how deep it was, the diameter of the passage, the presence (if any) of a nest at the end of the burrow, and such related information. For obvious reasons, I had not been able to make the investigation while the den was occupied, and since that time I had been   5 too busy with other work to get around to it. Now, with time running out, I was in a hurry.

B   I trotted across country toward the den, and I was within half a mile of it when there was a thunderous roar behind me. It was so loud and unexpected that I involuntarily flung myself down. The *Norseman* came   10 over at about 50 feet. As it roared past, the plane waggled its wings, then lifted to skim the crest of the wolf esker, sending a blast of sand down the slope. I picked myself up and quieted my thumping heart, thinking black thoughts about the humorist in the now rapidly vanishing aircraft.

C   The den ridge was, as I had expected . . . wolfless. Reaching the entrance   15 to the burrow, I shed my heavy trousers, tunic, and sweater, and taking a flashlight (whose batteries were very nearly dead) and measuring tape from my pack, I began the difficult task of wiggling down the entrance tunnel.

D   The flashlight was so dim it cast only an orange glow—barely sufficient to enable me to read the marks on the measuring tape. I squirmed onward,   20 descending at a 45-degree angle, for about eight feet. My mouth and eyes were soon full of sand, and I was beginning to suffer from claustrophobia, for the tunnel was just big enough to admit me.

E   At the eight-foot mark the tunnel took a sharp upward bend and swung to the left. I pointed the torch in the new direction and pressed the switch.   25
    Four green lights in the murk ahead reflected back the dim torch beam.

F   I froze where I was, while my startled brain tried to digest the information that at least two wolves were with me in the den.

G   Despite my close familiarity with the   30 wolf family, this was the kind of situation where irrational but deeply ingrained prejudices completely overmaster reason and experience. To be honest, I was so frightened that paralysis gripped me. I had no weapon of   35 any sort, and in my awkward posture, I could barely have gotten one hand free. It seemed inevitable that the wolves *would* attack me, for even a gopher will make a fierce defense when he is cornered in his den.   40

▲ Farley Mowat discovered a more docile side of wolves.

H   The wolves did not even growl.

I   Save for the two faintly glowing pairs of eyes, they might not have been there at all.

J   The paralysis began to ease and though it was a cold day, sweat broke out all over my body. In a fit of blind bravado, I shoved the torch forward.   45

K   It gave just sufficient light for me to recognize Angeline and one of the pups. They were scrunched hard against the back wall of the den; and they were as motionless as death.

L   The shock was wearing off by this time, and the instinct for self-preservation was regaining command. As quickly as I could, I began wiggling   50 back up the slanting tunnel, tense with the expectation that the wolves would charge. But by the time I reached the entrance, I had still not heard nor seen the slightest sign of movement from the wolves.

M   I sat down on a stone and shakily lit a cigarette, becoming aware as I did so that I was no longer frightened. Instead an irrational rage possessed   55 me. If I had had my rifle, I believe I might have reacted in brute fury and tried to kill both wolves.

N   The cigarette burned down, and a wind began to blow. I began to shiver again; this time from cold instead of rage. My anger was passing and I was limp. Mine had been the fury of resentment born of fear: resentment   60 against the beasts who had engendered naked terror in me and who, by so doing, had intolerably affronted my human ego.

O   I was appalled at the realization of how easily I had forgotten all that the summer sojourn with the wolves had taught me about them . . . and about myself. I thought of Angeline and her pup cowering at the bottom of   65 the den where they had taken refuge from the thundering apparition of the aircraft, and I was shamed.

P   Somewhere to the eastward a wolf howled; lightly, questioningly. I knew the voice, for I had heard it many times before. It was George, sounding the wasteland for an echo from the missing members of his   70 family. But for me it was a voice which spoke of the lost world which once was ours before we chose the alien role; a world which I had glimpsed and almost entered, . . . only to be excluded, at the end, by my own self.

Source: "The World We Lost" *Never Cry Wolf* (Farley Mowat)

After You Read

Recalling Vocabulary of Fear and Anger   Fear and anger are two powerful human emotions and Mowat uses many words and phrases with different shades of meaning to describe them. The words from the reading in the box on page 42 express shades of fear and anger.

3 **Recalling Vocabulary of Fear and Anger** Complete the phrases below with a word from the box. Fill in the blanks without looking back. The synonyms or definitions in parentheses give you clues.

appalled	fury	self-preservation
black	paralysis	shock
bravado	rage	terror
claustrophobia	resentment	
frightened	scrunched	

1. thinking (negative) ___*black*___ thoughts

2. to suffer from (fear of small places) _____

3. I was so (scared) _____ that (an inability to move) _____ gripped me.

4. in a fit of blind (fake courage) _____

5. they were (huddled, squeezed) _____ hard against the back wall

6. the (violent surprise, alarm) _____ was wearing off

7. the instinct for (saving your own life) _____ was regaining command

8. an irrational (violent anger) _____ possessed me

9. I might have reacted in brute (intense anger) _____

10. (repressed anger, bitterness) _____ born of fear

11. beasts who had engendered naked (intense fear) _____ in me

12. I was (horrified, outraged) _____ at the realization

Mowat was not the only one to feel emotion. Which phrase above does *not* refer to him? Circle it.

Strategy

Sequencing Events and Emotions in a Diagram

A chain diagram is used to describe the stages in an event or the step-by-step actions of the character(s) in a story. A chain diagram can help you better grasp the order in which events occurred in the story or narrative.

In Farley Mowat's true story, he describes both the *outer* and the *inner* stages of the event: the actions that occurred and also the emotions that he felt. As in many stories, this one starts with a *problem*, then moves to a *complication* (some action done because of the problem), then to a *climax* (moment of high emotion), and finally ends with a *resolution* (either a solution of the problem or, at times, a lesson learned by the character).

4 Sequencing Events and Emotions in a Diagram Work with another student and fill in the chain diagram below. On the left-hand side, tell the outer situation or action. On the right-hand side, describe the emotions the narrator feels.

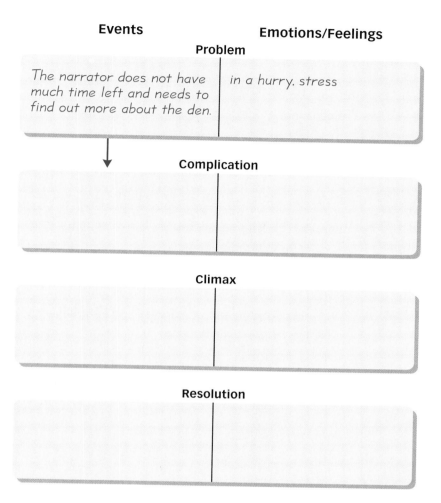

Events   **Emotions/Feelings**

Problem

The narrator does not have much time left and needs to find out more about the den.	in a hurry, stress

Complication

Climax

Resolution

5 Focusing on Words from the Academic Word List Read the following excerpt taken from the reading in Part 2. Fill in the blanks with a word from the box. Do not look back at the reading right away; instead, see if you can now remember the vocabulary. One of the words in the list will be used twice.

aware	enable	irrational	sufficient
despite	inevitable	reacted	tape

A The flashlight was so dim it cast only an orange glow—barely

_____ to _____ me to read the marks on the
       1   2

measuring _____. I squirmed onward, descending at a
              3

45-degree angle, for about eight feet. . . .

B _____ my close familiarity with the wolf family, this
          4

was the kind of situation where _____ but deeply
                          5

ingrained prejudices completely overmaster reason and experience . . .

It seemed _____ that the wolves *would* attack me, for
             6

even a gopher will make a fierce defense when he is cornered in his den . . .

C I sat down on a stone and shakily lit a cigarette, becoming

_____ as I did so that I was no longer frightened. Instead
        7

an _____ rage possessed me. If I had had my rifle, I
       8

believe I might have _____ in brute fury and tried to kill
            9

both wolves.

6 **Guided Academic Conversation** In small groups, discuss the following topics. Then summarize the group's opinions on that topic and ask if anyone has changed his or her mind. If so, this person explains why. After a time, the instructor may call on your group and ask for a summary of opinions on one of the topics.

1. **A Change of Heart** Mowat experiences a change of heart because of his experience in the den of wolves. How can you tell that Mowat has gotten to know the wolves as individuals and that he feels affection for them? Why does he become afraid and then very angry? What does he realize at the end of the story that makes him feel "shamed"? Why does he feel a sense of loss?

2. **Studying Wild Animals** Is this important or not? Why? How can it help human beings to learn about animals? Do you believe that animals have feelings? Can they make rational decisions? Explain.

3. **Interpretation of the Title** Now that you have read the whole story, how do you interpret the title?

7 **Expressing the Theme** Mowat's story was based on a real experience, but he chose, from among many true events, certain ones to tell in order to show a certain general idea, or theme. Describe in one or two sentences what you think the theme of the selection is.

_____

_____

_____

_____

8 **Thinking Your Way Out of Danger** Many times the only way to get out of a dangerous spot is with your brain. Read over the following imaginary situations. Then work together in small groups and try to figure out how you would escape from each of them. The solutions are below.

Situation A: The Windowless Prison

While participating in a revolution against an unjust tyrant, you are caught and thrown into a prison cell that has a dirt floor, thick stone walls, and no windows. There is only a skylight, very high above, to provide light and air. To prevent escape, there are no tables or chairs, only a very small mattress on the floor. Just before you are locked in, a comrade whispers to you that it is possible to escape through the skylight by digging a hole in the floor. How can you do this?

Situation B: The Cave of the Two Robots

Having entered a time machine, you have been whisked 1,000 years into the future to find yourself at the mercy of a superior civilization. These creatures of the future choose to amuse themselves by playing games with you. They set you in a cave that has two doors at the end of it: one leads back to the time machine that would transport you safely home, and the other leads to a pit filled with horrible monsters. There are also two robots in the cave. They know the secret of the doors. One always tells the truth and one always lies, and you do not know which is which. According to the rules of their game, you are allowed to ask one question to one of the robots. What question should you ask? How can you know which door to choose?

Answers:

Situation A: You simply dig a hole in the floor and use the dirt to build a ramp and then climb out through the skylight.

Situation B: You should ask the question, "Which door would the other robot tell me to take to get to the time machine?" If you are asking the robot who always tells the truth, he will tell you the wrong door, because he knows the other robot lies. If you are asking the robot who always lies, he will tell you the wrong door, too, because he knows that the other robot always tells the truth. So you simply open the opposite door, get in your time machine, and go home.

9 **What Do You Think?** Read the paragraph below and discuss the questions that follow.

Courting Danger

▲ Would you jump out of an airplane?

Many activities can be dangerous: mountain climbing, sky diving, bungee jumping, scuba diving. Even sports like downhill skiing, football, in-line skating, and horseback riding are dangerous at times.

1. Do you participate in any of these activities, or do you have friends or relatives who do? Which do you consider the most dangerous? Why?

2. In your opinion, when is it irresponsible to participate in dangerous activities? Explain.

TOEFL® iBT

Focus on Testing

Schematic-Table Questions

For each TOEFL®iBT reading passage, there is one question that is not multiple choice. This item, which always comes last in the set of questions, is either a **schematic-table** question or a **prose-summary** question. The former asks you to categorize information by completing a table. The latter asks you to complete a summary of the reading passage. Here we will focus on the schematic-table items.

A schematic-table item tests whether you have a clear understanding of the topic after reading the passage. To answer a schematic-table question correctly, you have to make connections among pieces of information throughout a reading. If the reading discusses two points of view, which ideas relate to each one? If the reading discusses two objects, which characteristics relate to one and which relate to the other?

The schematic-table item presents a grid with headings but without any information under each heading. By using your computer mouse, you choose items from a list and drag them to the appropriate spot in the table.

Practice Read the following passage. Then answer the schematic-table question that follows it.

The Psychology and Physiology of Taking Risks

A   Some people get nervous living placidly and safely. They run as surely toward danger as most people run away from it. They bungee jump, or skid down gravel roads on mountain bikes, or hang by their fingertips from minuscule cracks in the face of a cliff, or even quit secure jobs in order to take a chance on some risky venture. They are risk-takers, and scientists have long wondered why they deliberately court loss, injury, or even death. Answers to that question involve a complex interplay of psychological and physiological factors.

B   The key ingredient in the body's physiological response to danger is adrenaline. The body produces this chemical in the center of the adrenal glands atop the kidneys. When a physically or mentally stressful situation arises, a flood of adrenaline into the bloodstream prepares the body to act swiftly and forcefully to protect itself. The heart beats faster. Blood is directed away from the skin and toward such structures as the skeletal muscles and the brain—all to provide the oxygen necessary to run fast, lift heavy objects, and think quickly. This physiological reaction to risk is the well-known "fight-or-flight" response.

C   Although activated by a threat, the sudden release of adrenaline and the body's responses to it produce a distinctly pleasurable feeling once the danger has passed. Even people who are not seeking danger but who confront it accidentally will speak afterwards of an exciting "adrenaline rush." To some people, the pleasure of such an experience is so intense that they rate it among life's most desirable sensations. This hints at a likely biochemical-psychological mechanism motivating some, perhaps most, risk-seeking individuals.

D A massive release of adrenaline—and a companion chemical, norepinephrine—has its advantages, but the body cannot tolerate such high levels indefinitely. Controlling the effects of adrenaline and norepinephrine on the brain is especially important, so that relatively clear thinking can occur even in times of great stress. To help dampen arousal's effects on the brain, a chemical known as dopamine comes into play. It is one of several compounds that attach to specialized receptor sites in the brain in order to reduce pain and suppress unpleasant sensations. The action of dopamine is a very large reason for the association of an adrenaline rush with intense physical pleasure. The combination of adrenaline's excitement and dopamine's calming effect makes for an experience that many people find irresistible. Many athletes who push their bodies to great extremes speak of being "addicted" to the feeling they have during and after exercise.

E It is easy to see how this physical pleasure would become psychologically attractive. The risk-seeker likes the biological effects of the adrenaline-dopamine chain and is drawn to situations that might produce it. The physical side of the experience, the adrenaline rush, is only part of the equation. The attraction persists even in the absence of the chemical response.

F But the question remains: Why do only some of us become risk-seekers? There must be factors at work other than the adrenaline rush, which is experienced by risk-seekers and by risk-avoiders alike.

G On a very simple level, social rewards are high for risk-takers who triumph over adversity. The scientist who does cutting-edge research despite the possibility of ruining his or her career may discover the next great energy source or the long-sought cure for a disease. The civil-rights leader who perseveres in the face of threats to life or family may open new doors for millions of downtrodden citizens. Charles Lindbergh, the postal-service pilot who focused the attention of many nations on the possibilities of long-distance flight, attained immense wealth and fame. The risk-seeker, in other words, may simply be a very goal-directed person willing to take great chances to win big rewards.

H Psychologists often mention the sense of control that surviving a dangerous situation can impart. There is a great payoff for some people in facing adversity and overcoming it through superior strength and preparation. By this schema, a risk-taker is not someone who recklessly seeks trouble but someone who carefully matches himself or herself against a worthy challenge. This image fits such extreme athletes as mountain-climbers or skydivers, who spend a great deal of time preparing for a dangerous ascent or a challenging jump. It does not, however, fit the teenager who recklessly speeds down a highway or the inexperienced skier who decides to take on a black-diamond slope. What explains risk-taking of this sort, which is probably best characterized as impulsive behavior?

Psychologists in the Freudian mold would bring up the concept of a "death wish," a deep-seated impulse to flirt with personal annihilation. Physiologists pose several more-convincing possibilities. The tendency to be a risk-seeker depends, in this view, on factors such as one's brain development or one's receptivity to common brain chemicals. For example, studies of electrical patterns in the brain have shown that teenagers, as opposed to preteens and adults, exhibit more activity in the reward centers of their brains than in the planning centers. Furthermore, these reward centers are most active when the rewards appear unpredictably. This focus on instant rewards and on novelty offers a recipe for impulsive risk-taking in hopes of a chance pay-out.

Another possible factor is an enzyme called monoamine oxidase (MAO). It helps control the levels of dopamine and other chemicals in the brain so that someone whose body produces abnormally little MAO is likely to have imbalances of such chemicals in the brain. By testing individuals with a tendency toward risky behavior, researchers have established a strong correlation between low levels of MAO and living dangerously.

Directions Complete the table by classifying the phrases from the list (a–i) as either a psychological or physiological factor, according to the reading passage. Write the letter of each choice in the appropriate blank. Fill every blank in each box. One of the nine phrases will not be used.

Psychological factors	Physiological factors
▪ _____	▪ _____
▪ _____	▪ _____
▪ _____	▪ _____
▪ _____	
▪ _____	

    a. the fight-or-flight response
    b. speeding recklessly down a highway
    c. highly active reward centers in the brain
    d. a sense of control despite adversity
    e. low levels of MAO
    f. attraction to the possibility of an adrenaline rush
    g. the "death wish"
    h. impulsive risk-taking in hopes of a chance pay-out
    i. a desire to get great social rewards

1 Did You Catch That? Your instructor will write the vocabulary list below on the board. The whole class will sit in a circle. The instructor will hold a ball and read the first item from the vocabulary list, making up a sentence using this word. The instructor will then throw the ball to a student who makes up a sentence with the next item on the list, and so on. If a student does not know what a word means, the game stops until another student raises his or her hand and gives a sentence. This new student will start the chain once more. Count how many times your class can throw the ball without breaking the chain.

amputated	despite	inevitable	snapped
appalled	deteriorate	irrational	(a photo)
aware	enable	paralysis	sojourn
banal	excruciating	prejudices	spectacular
bravado	familiarity	rage	sufficient
burrow	fantasized	reacted	summit
claustrophobia	frightened	resentment	terror
compadres	fury	scrunched	throng
dallied	a gaggle	self-preservation	visibility
den	heeded	shock	

2 Making Connections Do some research on the Internet and take notes on one of the following topics. Share your results with the class or in a small group.

First to Climb Mt. Everest Who were the first people to stand on the summit of Everest? When and how did they achieve this goal? What happened to them afterward? What other famous climbers died trying before this successful attempt?

A Successful Expedition What does it take for a successful expedition up Mt. Everest? How many Sherpas must be employed? How much does it cost? What equipment is necessary? Do the Sherpas manage to make a good living this way? How do they live? What do they think about these expeditions?

Statistics of Life and Death What percentage of those who try succeed in their quest for the summit? How many people have died trying? What kinds of injuries and impairment have climbers suffered as a result of their attempts to reach the top of the world's highest mountain?

Reintroducing Wolves in Parts of the U.S. Research the attempts to re-introduce wolves into certain parts of the United States, such as Yellowstone Park, by bringing them in from Canada. What groups are in favor of these programs? What groups are against them? Why?

▲ Should wolves be reintroduced to certain parts of the U.S.?

The Book *Never Cry Wolf* by Farley Mowat
Read about the book and the movie based on it. Why do you think these have been so popular?

Traditional Stories about Wolves Look up stories about wolves found in songs and folk tales. What image is presented? Is it positive or negative? Give some examples.

Responding in Writing

WRITING TIP: FOLLOW A STRUCTURE TO WRITE LETTERS

To write a personal letter, it may help to follow a structure, beginning with your reason for writing and the main topic, then giving an example, concluding your point, and ending with a polite closing.

3 **Writing Practice** Choose one of the following topics: 1) taking risks or 2) overcoming fear. Imagine that an older aunt or uncle has written a letter to you asking about your attitude to this, as it relates to your life. Write a three-paragraph response to him or her, following the steps below.

Step 1 Begin with *Dear* _____ (your relative's name) followed by a comma.

Step 2 In the first paragraph, start by saying, "In response to your question about (taking risks, or overcoming fear), I think . . ." Then explain your general attitude toward the topic. Are you a risk-taker or are you a cautious person, fearful or brave? Do you like physical, mental, or emotional challenges? How do you respond to them? What do you think can be gained from taking risks or overcoming fear?

Step 3 In the second paragraph, give an example: describe an incident in your past life in which you took a risk or overcame fear. Tell when, where, how, and why it happened, and how you felt before, during, and after it.

Step 4 In the third paragraph, state whether you believe this event was positive or negative and why, what you learned from it, and how you see yourself taking risks or overcoming fear in the future.

Step 5 Finish your letter by saying something personal, such as, "*I hope that you are well, and look forward to hearing from you.*" Then close with one of the following: *Sincerely, Yours Truly,* or, if you are very close (emotionally) to this person: *With Affection*, or *Love*, followed by a comma and your name.

▲ Scuba diving requires swimmers to face their fears of being underwater.

Self-Assessment Log

Read the lists below. Check (✓) the strategies and vocabulary that you learned in this chapter. Look through the chapter or ask your instructor about the strategies and words that you do not understand.

Reading and Vocabulary-Building Strategies

- ❏ Previewing a reading
- ❏ Identifying more exact or colorful synonyms
- ❏ Making inferences
- ❏ Getting meaning from context: everyday phrases
- ❏ Creating a storyboard
- ❏ Recalling vocabulary of fear and anger
- ❏ Sequencing events and emotions in a diagram

Target Vocabulary

Nouns

- ❏ bravado
- ❏ burrow
- ❏ claustrophobia
- ❏ compadres
- ❏ den
- ❏ familiarity
- ❏ fury
- ❏ gaggle
- ❏ gopher
- ❏ measuring tape*
- ❏ paralysis
- ❏ prejudices
- ❏ rage

- ❏ resentment
- ❏ self-preservation
- ❏ shock
- ❏ sojourn
- ❏ summit
- ❏ terror
- ❏ throng
- ❏ visibility*

Verbs

- ❏ amputated
- ❏ dallied
- ❏ deteriorate
- ❏ enable*

- ❏ fantasized
- ❏ heeded
- ❏ snapped (a photo)

Adjectives

- ❏ appalled
- ❏ aware*
- ❏ banal
- ❏ excruciating
- ❏ frightened
- ❏ inevitable*
- ❏ irrational*
- ❏ reacted*
- ❏ scrunched

- ❏ spectacular
- ❏ sufficient*

Preposition

- ❏ despite*

Idioms and Expressions

- ❏ blanket of clouds
- ❏ into an apparent death trap
- ❏ moving at the snail's pace
- ❏ on the roof of the world
- ❏ release of emotion
- ❏ striking summit poses
- ❏ using up precious ticks of the clock

* These words are from the Academic Word List. For more information on this list, see www.vuw.ac.nz/lals/research/awl.

Gender and Relationships

In This Chapter

Down through the ages, the eternal "battle of the sexes" has been a popular topic. This chapter begins with an article about love and intimacy, in which contemporary psychologists reveal a possible explanation of why we fall in love with one person and not with another. Then a poem gives one person's view of the transforming power of love. Finally, a new problem with gender relations in China and India is examined: the sudden big decrease in the number of young women.

❝ Cold rice and cold tea are bearable; cold looks and cold words are not. **❞**

—Japanese proverb

Connecting to the Topic

1 Describe the two people in the photo. What are they doing?

2 What do you think is the relationship between these people? Why do you think so?

3 Explain the meaning of the Japanese proverb about cold rice and cold tea.

Finding Real Love

Before You Read

1 Previewing a Reading for Its Organization

The following reading is taken from the popular magazine *Psychology Today*. The word *psychology* comes from two Greek roots: *psycho*, meaning *mind* or *mental process* and *logos*, meaning *reason* or *study of.* Therefore, psychology is the science or study of the mind. An article on psychology often uses specific stories of real people to show general principles about the way the human mind works. These stories are called *case studies* or *case histories*.

Look at the following questions. Then skim the article to answer them.

1. Where does the case study begin in this article: at the beginning, in the middle, or at the end? _____

2. What are the names of the two people in the case study?

   _____

   _____

3. Judging from the title and first few sentences, the article is about people's need for intimacy, love, and companionship. Does the article provide information about how to meet people or how to have successful relationships?

   _____

In your opinion, why would people buy this magazine and read articles like this?

2 **Identifying More Exact or Colorful Synonyms** Read the phrases below from the reading. Scan the reading for the more exact, concise, or colorful synonyms of the words in parentheses. The phrases are listed in the order of their appearance in the reading.

1. Human beings (desire intensely) _____ intimacy, to love and be loved.

2. . . . four mental health professionals discuss their ideas about how we (destroy by many small acts) _____ our intimate relationships . . .

3. The various decisions we make, and our behavior toward one another, are what (help) _____ closeness or drive us apart.

4. We often choose partners who remind us of (important and meaningful) _____ people from our childhood . . .

5. . . . and we set out to (build again) _____ the patterns of our childhood.

6. She was instantly attracted to the tall, lean man with (an absent) _____ look in his eyes.

7. Abe, who had been standing alone, was delighted when Tara (came near to) _____ him . . .

8. It was not the kind of suffocating closeness he had always (feared greatly) _____ . . .

9. . . . his mother, who used to enter his room uninvited and arrange his personal belongings with no regard to his (right to independence and secrecy) _____ .

10. But occasionally, Abe would come home from work tired and (irritated) _____ .

11. . . . and he responded the way he did with his mother: by (moving away) _____ .

12. She responded in the same way she did when her father withdrew: by (hanging on tightly) _____ .

Read

Introduction

One purpose of psychology is to help us understand why we act the way we do. Psychologists examine case studies and identify patterns of behavior that occur again and again. We are often not conscious of why we are behaving in certain ways. By analyzing the patterns, we can discover the hidden causes for our actions.

- Why do we feel immediately attracted to one person but not to another?
- Why do two people in an intimate relationship often interact beautifully at first, and later develop serious problems?

▲ Why do people give gifts?

Finding Real Love

Human beings crave intimacy, to love and be loved. Why then do people feel isolated in their intimate relationships?

A   **W**e need to be close to other people as surely as we need food and water. But while it's relatively easy to get ourselves a good meal, it is difficult for many of us to create and maintain intimacy with others, particularly a romantic partner. There are many variables that affect the quality of our relationships with others; it's difficult to pin it on one thing or another. But in this article, based on a symposium recently held at the annual American Psychological Association convention in Washington, D.C., four mental health professionals discuss their ideas about how we sabotage our intimate relationships—and what we can do to fix them.

Choose to Lose?

B   Many factors influence the level of intimacy we enjoy in our relationships. The various decisions we make, and our behavior toward one another, are what foster closeness or drive us apart. These decisions are all under our control, although we are influenced by old patterns that we must work to change.

C   The first decision we make about a relationship is the partner we choose. Whom we fall in love with determines the level of intimacy in our relationships, according to Ayala Malach Pines, Ph.D., who heads the behavioral sciences in management program at Ben-Gurion University in Israel. We often choose partners who remind us of significant people from our childhood—often our parents—and we set out to recreate the patterns of our childhood. Let's look at an example:

D   Tara met Abe at a party. She was instantly attracted to the tall, lean man with a faraway look in his eyes. Abe, who had been standing alone, was delighted when Tara approached him with her open smile and outstretched hand. She was not only beautiful, but she struck him as warm and nurturing as well. The conversation between them flowed instantly. It felt comfortable and easy. Eventually, they fell in love, and after a year, they were married.

E   The intimacy between them also felt terrific to Abe. It was not the kind of suffocating closeness he always dreaded—the kind of intrusive closeness he experienced as a child with his mother, who used to enter his room uninvited and arrange his personal belongings with no regard to his privacy. But Tara was different. She did not intrude.

F But occasionally, Abe would come home from work tired and annoyed. 35 All he wanted was a drink and to sit with the paper until he could calm down and relax. Seeing him that way, Tara would 40 become concerned. "What is going on?" she would ask anxiously. "Nothing," he would answer. Sure that there was something 45

▲ Differing expectations can lead to conflict.

very wrong, and assuming that it must be something about her or their marriage, Tara would insist that he tell her. She reminded him of his mother, and he responded the way he did with his mother: by withdrawing. To Tara, this felt similar to the way her father behaved. She responded in the same way she did when her father withdrew: by clinging. The struggle 50 between them continued and became more and more intense over time, with Tara demanding more intimacy and Abe demanding more space.

Re-creating the Family

G Like Abe and Tara, people choose partners who help them re-create their childhood struggles. Tara fell in love with a man with "a faraway look in his eyes," and subsequently had to struggle for greater intimacy. Abe fell 55 in love with a woman who was "warm and nurturing," then spent a lot of energy struggling for more space.

H Tara's unresolved intimacy issues complement Abe's. For example, one partner (often the woman) will fight to break down the defenses and create more intimacy while the other (often the man) will withdraw and create 60 distance. So the "dance of intimacy" follows: If the woman gets too close, the man pulls back. If he moves too far away, she pursues, and so on.

I To achieve greater intimacy, the partners must overcome the anxiety that compels them to take their respective parts in that dance. In the example, Tara needs to control her abandonment anxiety and not pursue Abe when 65 he withdraws, and Abe needs to control his engulfment anxiety when Tara pursues him and not withdraw. Working to overcome these anxieties is an opportunity to resolve childhood issues and can be a major healing experience for both partners.

Source: "Finding Real Love" *Psychology Today* (Cary Barbor)

After You Read

Strategy

Using a Graphic Organizer to Determine the Order of Events
The order in which events are described in a reading selection is not always the order in which they actually occurred.

You can use a graphic organizer like the one in the next exercise to show the order of events. Using a graphic organizer of this type helps to organize and retain information.

3 **Determining the Order of Events** The following events are from the case study described in the article. Put them in the order in which they occurred in real life. Write one letter in each box.

1. Tara and Abe fell in love.

2. Tara began to cling to Abe.

3. Tara would become concerned and insist on talking about what was wrong.

4. Tara and Abe met at a party.

5. Abe would come home tired and annoyed.

6. Tara wanted more closeness with her father, and Abe more respect for his privacy from his mother.

7. Abe began to withdraw from Tara.

8. Tara and Abe got married.

Chain-of-Events Diagram

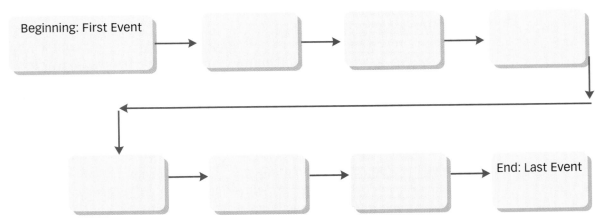

4 **Identifying Causes** The article points out common patterns in the behavior of people involved in intimate relationships. Complete each statement to show the cause for the behavior described.

1. According to Dr. Ayala Malach Pine, we often fall in love with someone because he or she reminds us of *a significant person from our childhood, such as one of our parents.*

2. Tara was first attracted to Abe because he had _____

_____ .

3. Abe was first attracted to Tara because she seemed _____

_____ .

4. Tara began to cling more and more to Abe because she felt that he

_____ .

5. Abe began to withdraw more and more from Tara because he felt that she

_____ .

 5 **Guided Academic Conversation** In small groups, discuss the following questions. Then compare your answers with those of another group.

1. In simple words, what went wrong between Abe and Tara? Do you think this is a common pattern of behavior?

2. What do you think is meant in the article by the "dance of intimacy"?

3. Do most people really look for someone to love who reminds them of one of their parents? Can it be the opposite? Explain.

4. Is it hard to find love? What is meant in the title by "real love"? What other kinds of love are there, and how do you know when love is real?

6 **Writing the Ending** What happened to Abe and Tara? Did they have children? Did they get a divorce? Did they make up and "live happily ever after"? Did their parents come to visit? Did they go to a marriage counselor? Write an ending of 10 to 15 sentences for the case study of Abe and Tara. Give it a good title. Be prepared to read it to the class, if requested to do so.

7 **Looking at Love** Read the following poem by the English poet Alfred Edward Housman (1859–1936). Listen to the poem as you read it aloud to yourself to enjoy the rhyme and rhythm.

> **Pronunciation Tip**
>
> Take care to pronounce the word *again* in the second stanza in the British way (*uh-gane*, to rhyme with *rain*) so that it will rhyme correctly. Like many English poems, this one uses rhyme, for example: *you/grew, brave/behave.*

Oh, When I Was in Love with You

A. E. Housman

Oh, when I was in love with you,

Then I was clean and brave,

And miles around the wonder grew

How well I did behave.

And now the fancy passes by,

And nothing will remain,

And miles around they'll say that I

Am quite myself again.

With a partner, discuss the following questions.

1. Do you think that love can transform a person? How? In the poem, is the transformation permanent or temporary? Do you agree with this description of love? Explain.

2. Is there a regular pattern of rhyme in the poem? Why do you think the poet used rhyme? What effect does it have on a reader?

3. How would you describe the tone of the poem? Do you think a woman would use this tone when talking about love? Why or why not?

4. Is there a song or poem about love that you like? Can you share it with the class?

▲ The average age of a bride in the U.S. is 25.3.
The average age of a groom is 26.9.

Strategy

Drawing Conclusions
You can find specifics to support generalizations or you can do the reverse: make generalizations based on specifics. The chart in the next exercise gives specific statistics.

8 Drawing Conclusions from a Chart

Read the chart on page 63, *Top 10 Months for Weddings in the U.S.* Then read the statements that follow and write *C* in front of the one generalization that correctly describes the data. Write *I* in front of the others, which are incorrect.

Top 10 Months for Weddings in the U.S.			
Month	**% of Weddings**	**Month**	**% of Weddings**
1. June	10.8%	**6.** October	9.4%
2. August	10.2%	**7.** December	7.8%
3. May	9.8%	**8.** April	7.4%
4. July	9.7%	**9.** November	7.4%
5. September	9.6%	**10.** February	7.0%

*March is at number 11 with 6.17%, and January is last with 4.7%.
Source: www.soundvision.com/info/weddings/statistics.asp

1. _____ Most Americans get married around the new year.

2. _____ Americans do not care in which month they get married.

3. _____ Americans prefer to marry in months that begin with the letter *J*.

4. _____ Americans prefer warm weather for weddings.

5. _____ Americans prefer cold weather for weddings.

Part 2   Reading Skills and Strategies

"Bare Branches" Might Snap in Asia

Before You Read

1 Scanning for Details Scan the reading to fill in the blanks on the following important points from the story. See page 9 for more on scanning. Notice that the key term *sex ratio* means the number of boy babies born for every 100 girl babies. A completely equal sex ratio, then, would be 100. That would mean that 100 boys are born for every 100 girls.

1. In China, the sex ratio for children up through age four is over _____.

2. In India, the sex ratio for children up through age six has increased over the past decade from _____ to _____.

3. In India's province of Punjab, the ratio is _____.

4. The Chinese have a term for men who will not find wives and this term translates to English as _____.

5. In China, some women have been kidnapped to provide brides for those who _____.

6. The scarcity (low number) of women means that only men with the following advantages will marry: _____, _____, and _____.

7. The number of young adult bare branches in China and India in 2020 will be between _____ and _____ percent of the young men.

8. Indian scholars have noted a very strong relationship between sex ratios and _____ rates.

9. The first generation of "bare branches" since the advent of sex identification technology was turning _____ the year this article was published.

10. Almost _____ percent of the world's population is in China and India.

2 **Getting Meaning from Word Structure and Context** Match each italicized word or phrase with the correct definition. If necessary, look ahead to where they occur in the reading to see how they are used in context.

1. __f__ the *troubling scenario* that China and India now face (line 2)

2. _____ *to weed out* . . . daughters before they are born (line 6)

3. _____ *sex-selective abortion* is illegal throughout Asia (line 7)

4. _____ a *subclass* of young men likely to have difficulty finding wives (line 26)

5. _____ bare branches . . . have played a role in *aggravating societal instability* (line 49)

6. _____ men with no *stake* in society (line 59)

7. _____ governments . . . in a *dilemma* (line 64)

8. _____ increased *authoritarianism* . . . to crack down on crime (line 66)

9. _____ *emigration* of young adult men (line 69)

10. _____ the *threshold* (line 79)

11. _____ *diminishing prospects* for democracy (line 82)

a. beginning
b. increasing the lack of stability in society
c. a difficult problem
d. leaving their country to live in another
e. to destroy or dispose of
f. situation that causes worry
g. lessening (reduction of) possibilities
h. the killing of a fetus (unborn baby) because of its gender
i. a group of people lower in status (position) than others
j. share, interest, involvement
k. strong control (by people in power)

Read

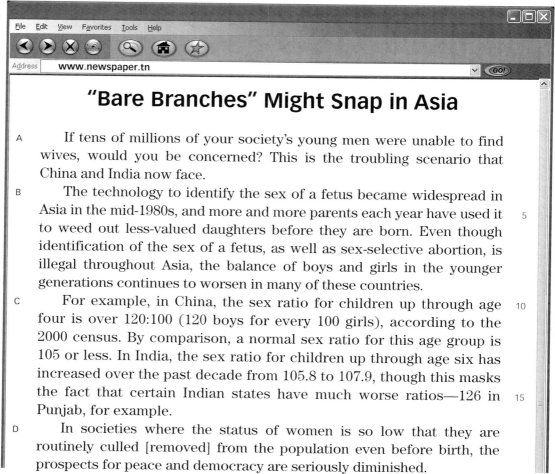

"Bare Branches" Might Snap in Asia

A   If tens of millions of your society's young men were unable to find wives, would you be concerned? This is the troubling scenario that China and India now face.

B   The technology to identify the sex of a fetus became widespread in Asia in the mid-1980s, and more and more parents each year have used it   5 to weed out less-valued daughters before they are born. Even though identification of the sex of a fetus, as well as sex-selective abortion, is illegal throughout Asia, the balance of boys and girls in the younger generations continues to worsen in many of these countries.

C   For example, in China, the sex ratio for children up through age   10 four is over 120:100 (120 boys for every 100 girls), according to the 2000 census. By comparison, a normal sex ratio for this age group is 105 or less. In India, the sex ratio for children up through age six has increased over the past decade from 105.8 to 107.9, though this masks the fact that certain Indian states have much worse ratios—126 in   15 Punjab, for example.

D   In societies where the status of women is so low that they are routinely culled [removed] from the population even before birth, the prospects for peace and democracy are seriously diminished.

E The old saying goes, "When you pick up one end of a stick, you 20 also pick up the other." When a society prefers sons to daughters to the extent found in parts of contemporary Asia, it will not only have fewer daughters but also 25 create a subclass of young men likely to have difficulty finding wives and beginning their own families. 30 Because son preference has been a significant phenomenon in Asia for centuries, the Chinese actually have a term for 35 such young men: *guang gun-er* or "bare branches"—branches of the family tree that will never bear fruit.

▲ Too many men and not enough women

F Scarcity of women leads to a situation in which men with advantages—money, skills, education—will marry, but men without such advantages—poor, unskilled, illiterate—will not. A permanent subclass 40 of bare branches from the lowest socioeconomic classes is created. In China and India, for example, by the year 2020 bare branches will make up 12 to 15 percent of the young adult male population.

G Should the leaders of these nations be worried? The answer is yes. Throughout history, bare branches in the East and South Asia have played 45 a role in aggravating societal instability, violent crime, and gang formation.

H Consider the fact that in the mid-1800s, a predominantly bare-branch rebel group in the north of China called the Nien, in combination with rebel groups farther south, openly attacked imperial troops and forts, taking control of territory inhabited by six million Chinese citizens 50 before it was quashed by the government years later.

I More recently, Indian scholars have noted a very strong relationship between sex ratios and violent crime rates in Indian states. And worldwide, more violent crime is committed by unmarried young adult men than by married young adult men. 55

J According to sociologists, young adult men with no stake in society—with little chance of forming families of their own—are much more prone to attempt to improve their situation through violent and criminal behaviour.

K Historically, governments facing a growing population of bare 60 branches find themselves in a dilemma. They must decrease the threat to society posed by these young men, but at the same time may find the cost of doing so is heavy. Increased authoritarianism in an effort to crack down on crime, gangs, smuggling, and so forth can be one result.

L At some point, governments consider how they can export their problem, either by encouraging emigration of young adult men or harnessing their energies in martial adventures abroad. 65

M Conservative estimates of the number of young adult bare branches in China in 2020 will be about 30 million, in India about 28 million. Pakistan will also have a sizable number of bare branches, as will Taiwan. When policymakers ponder the future of conflicts such as Kashmir and Taiwan, the sex ratios of the nations involved should not be forgotten. 70

N The first generation of bare branches since the advent of sex identification technology is turning 19 this year, and with every successive year, not only the number but the percentage of young adult men without wives will increase. We stand at the threshold of a time in which their presence will become a factor in policymaking. 75

O Given that almost 40 percent of the world's population is in China and India, the likelihood of diminishing prospects for democracy, stability, and peace because of the extremely low status of women in these societies will affect not only Asia but the world. 80

Source: "'Bare Branches' Might Snap in Asia" *Edmonton Journal* (Valerie Hudson and Andrea Den Boer)

▲ Fewer girls than boys are being born in some countries.

After you Read

3 **Focusing on Words from the Academic Word List** Read the excerpt below taken from the reading in Part 2. Fill in the blanks with a word from the box. Do not look back at the reading right away; instead, see if you can now remember the vocabulary.

contemporary	create	diminished
phenomenon	prospects	significant
status		

In societies where the _____ of women is so low that
1

they are routinely culled [removed] from the population even before birth,

the _____ for peace and democracy are seriously
2

_____.
3

5 The old saying goes, "When you pick up one end of a stick, you also pick

up the other." When a society prefers sons to daughters to the extent found in

parts of _____ Asia, it will not only have fewer daughters
4

but also _____ a subclass of young men likely to have
5

difficulty finding wives and beginning their own families. Because son

10 preference has been a _____ _____ in
6   7

Asia for centuries, the Chinese actually have a term for such young men:

guang gun-er or "bare branches"—branches of the family tree that will

never bear fruit.

4 **Making Inferences** Read the following sentences taken from the article or directly based on it. Then look at the options that follow and choose the one that can be inferred from the sentences. Be prepared to explain your choices.

1. Even though identification of the gender of a fetus, as well as sex-selective abortion, is illegal throughout Asia, the balance of boys and girls in the younger generations continues to worsen . . .

Ⓐ Sex-selective abortion is illegal throughout Asia because the ratio of boys to girls is getting more unequal.

B　Sex-selective abortion is illegal throughout Asia, but it is being done anyway.

C　Sex-selective abortion is illegal throughout Asia so it could not be the reason that there are fewer girl babies.

2. The old saying goes, "When you pick up one end of a stick, you also pick up the other." This saying applies to parts of contemporary Asia where parents prefer sons to daughters.

A　A society's preference for sons over daughters does harm to the girls.

B　A society's preference for sons over daughters does harm to the boys.

C　A society's preference for sons over daughters does harm to both the girls and the boys.

3. Historically, most governments facing a growing population of bare branches use increased authoritarianism to control the increase in violence.

A　In the past, when there have been many bare branches in a society, the government usually has given its citizens *more* liberty.

B　In the past, when there have been many bare branches in a society, the government usually has given its citizens *less* liberty.

C　In the past when there have been many bare branches in a society, it has made no difference to the amount of liberty the government has given its citizens.

4. At some point, where there is a great number of unmarried young men, governments often dispose of them by encouraging emigration or sending them off on martial (military) adventures.

A　The fewer young women there are in a society available to be wives, the *higher* the number of men who emigrate or leave the country for military obligations.

B　The fewer young women there are in a society available to be wives, the *lower* the number of men who emigrate or leave the country for military obligations.

C　The number of young women there are in a society available to be wives has no influence on the number of men who emigrate or leave the country for military obligations.

 5 Guided Academic Conversation In small groups, discuss the following questions:

1. Why do you think that boys are more valued in many cultures than girls? Are the reasons economic, religious, or simply traditional? Do you think this is a logical preference? Explain.

2. Who exactly are the "bare branches" that the article talks about? What has happened throughout history when there are many bare branches in a society? How do governments act then? What effect does this have on individual liberty in that society?

3. Is it a good solution to have these young single men emigrate or go off with the army to foreign lands? Why or why not?

4. Could the smaller number of girl babies born make women more valued in the long run? In your opinion, what would be the result of women having higher status?

6 **What Do You Think?** Read the paragraph below and in small groups, discuss the questions that follow.

How Men and Women Communicate

A well-known "pop (popular) psychology" book in North America is called *Men Are from Mars, Women Are from Venus*. The book talks about the differences in the styles of communication between the sexes and why they have such difficulty understanding one another. Venus (women), says author John Gray, have different values from Mars (men). "A woman's sense of self is defined through her feelings and the quality of her relationships." But "Martians (men) value power, competency, efficiency, and advancement. Their sense of self is defined through their ability to achieve results."

1. What do you think of these definitions?

2. Would they be correct for men and women in most cultures?

3. Why do you think men and women have difficulty understanding and communicating with one another?

TOEFL® iBT

Focus on Testing

Prose-Summary Questions

On the TOEFL® iBT test, summary questions do not require you to actually write anything. Instead, these prose-summary questions ask you to choose sentences from a list in order to build the best possible summary of a reading passage.

When you work with a prose-summary question, you are given the first sentence of a summary. Then out of a list of six sentences, you must choose the three that would best complete the summary. With your computer mouse, you must drag each of your choices to a blank line and place it there. If you choose the proper three, no matter what order they are in, you will get full credit for the item.

Like the schematic-table questions mentioned in Chapter 2, TOEFL® iBT summary questions test your overall understanding of a reading and your sense of how the parts of a reading work together. The three sentences you choose should express main ideas, not mere details, and should contain information that is truly in the reading passage.

Practice Read the following passage and complete the prose-summary question that follows.

Matchmaking

A   Few practices are as widespread among human cultures as the ceremonial wedding of a woman and a man. Individual impulses to ensure the survival of one's genes mesh with society's desire to establish stable family units. This may all sound very unromantic, but marriage is serious business—much too serious, some might say, to be left to extremely young men and women. Surely the elders know best. This is the impulse behind the age-old practice of matchmaking.

B   The basics of matchmaking are simple. After collecting information about marriageable men and women (or boys and girls), a matchmaker decides which would be a good match. Sometimes the matchmaker represents the male or his family and therefore assesses available females. Sometimes the matchmaker represents the female side and looks at available males. In still other cases, the matchmaker is an independent judge, representing neither side but hoping to make a choice that will satisfy both.

C   We've already hinted at one motivation for matchmaking—the belief that the people getting married are too young to make a wise decision. Especially in cultural traditions that encouraged marriages between 11- or 12-year-old children, this belief was probably true. Even with older teens or people in their early 20s, a society might encourage matchmaking in the belief that young people, blinded by the sexual attractiveness of a potential mate, cannot shrewdly choose someone who would make a good lifelong partner after the beauty of youth fades away.

D   In the main, matchmaking has historically worked to preserve the integrity of certain social groups and prevent the weakening of the group by intrusion from outsiders. This principle once guided matchmaking within strict Hindu circles. The Hindu caste system specifies distinct social roles for people based on their ancestry, a system that would become hopelessly confused if young people married freely between castes. Matchmaking, usually by the elder women of families looking to arrange a marriage, was a mechanism for ensuring that caste boundaries were observed.

E   Modern group-maintenance matchmaking still occurs in many cultures, but it usually has less to do with social caste than with other affiliations, such as religion or ethnicity. Countless religious websites and church organizations aim to keep Catholics

Catholic, Muslims Muslim, Jews Jewish, or Baptists Baptist by making it easier for them to meet and marry others of the same religion. Many young Hindus living in Europe or the Americas would reject a caste-based match in the old style but readily seek the services of matchmakers who can connect them to other marriage-minded members of the Hindu diaspora. The desire is not so much to preserve social boundaries as to seek commonalities of background and philosophy in potential mates.

F   In arranged marriages, such as those practiced in earlier centuries by European royalty or Asian nobles, the man and woman to be married have no voice. This is not, however, an essential feature of matchmaking. In 19th-century Ireland, for example, a sturdy matchmaking business grew up in the market town of Lisdoonvarna, but arranged marriages had no part in it. The main customers were bachelor farmers from the remote countryside who flocked to town in September, after their harvest had been safely gathered. They contacted well-connected locals who knew the names and circumstances of eligible females in the town, and the bachelors paid these matchmakers to set something up.

G   Few communities in highly mobile, industrialized societies could sustain an arranged-marriage system anymore, or even a freer system like Lisdoonvarna's. Such systems simply require too much knowledge of other families and their histories. This knowledge was available to matchmakers in earlier communities where families established themselves and stayed for many generations. A sense for the enduring qualities of one's neighbors is no longer the norm. Consequently, the role of family elders as matchmakers has become negligible outside remote rural areas. Instead, professional services that aim to collect and catalogue vital information have conquered the field.

H   For many years, Internet-based matchmaking services have led the way in this adjustment to less-cohesive community life. They have largely replaced earlier systems that depended on telephone contact or even on face-to-face meetings. Users of Internet matchmaking services surrender a wealth of personal information to the administrators of the system, who promise to comb similar information from other users in search of a perfect match. This is essentially what matchmakers have done in lower-tech ways for thousands of years. Internet matchmaking services can cite many successful pairings, and the business is going strong. Still, their selection practices do not always create happy customers.

Some Korean matchmaking firms, for example, have been criticized for excluding potential customers whom the firm judges to be somehow undesirable. One highly accomplished lawyer, for example, was denied a listing because of a physical disability in one leg. Complaints have also been heard from bald men and people without advanced university degrees. The matchmaking companies defend their policies by saying that their customers are picky so they must be as well. The Korean courts are likely to decide, because several rejected customers have filed lawsuits.

Practice Below is the first sentence of a possible summary of the reading passage. Following this sentence are three blanks. From the list of six sentences, choose the three that would best complete the summary. Write the letter of each choice in one of the blanks. Some sentences should not be chosen because they either express ideas that are not main points in the reading or express ideas that do not appear in the reading at all.

The practice of matchmaking, both in the past and in modern times, serves several social purposes.

- _____

- _____

- _____

(A) Matchmakers may help unmarried persons from remote, lightly populated areas find compatible mates.

(B) The concept of the "arranged marriage" is central to all matchmaking.

(C) Even Hindus who reject traditional caste-oriented matchmaking use the services of matchmakers.

(D) A religious, ethnic, or socioeconomic group may hope to promote unity and stability with the group by matchmaking among its younger members.

(E) Some Internet-matchmaking services unjustly discriminate against people who may be seen as unattractive.

(F) Matchmaking may be used as a way of keeping supposedly unwise or impulsive young people from making the important decision of whom to marry.

1 Debate

Think about the following questions and decide if your answers are *yes* or *no*.

1. Does everyone have to get married to be happy?

2. Can some people remain single and still lead a happy and complete life?

Your teacher will write "married = happiness" on one side of the board and "single = happiness" on the other side. Then you and your classmates will take a stand—literally. Walk over and stand beside the position that you consider to be most true. Once there, explain why you chose the way you did. Listen to what other students say. Did you change your mind? After you return to your seats, write an answer on a piece of paper to the questions below and have students count the votes.

1. Does everyone have to get married to be happy? Write *yes* or *no*.

2. What do you predict the majority of the students will answer?

When the votes are counted, discuss the results. Were you surprised by the results?

2 Making Connections
Do some research on the Internet and take notes on one of the following topics. Share your results with the class or in a small group.

1. **Love and Attraction** Find some information from a serious scientific or psychological perspective (not just a personal one) on why we fall in love with one person versus another or why we are physically attracted to one person versus another.

2. **Family Planning Policies** Find information on what policies China or India have at the present time or are planning to have in order to balance out the unequal sex ratio of their populations. Or you can research the family planning policies of another country.

Responding in Writing

WRITING TIP: USING A CLUSTER DIAGRAM TO ORGANIZE YOUR IDEAS

Before expressing your opinion in a written essay, use a cluster diagram to generate and organize your ideas. Below is an example of a cluster diagram. The topic, "choosing a marriage partner," is written in the center circle and the main ideas extend out from that. The details then extend out from the main ideas.

This diagram shows how you might begin to outline a composition about "choosing a marriage partner." It illustrates that the most important factors to this writer in choosing a marriage partner are the opinions of the parents, socioeconomic factors, and similarity of age.

Example Cluster Diagram

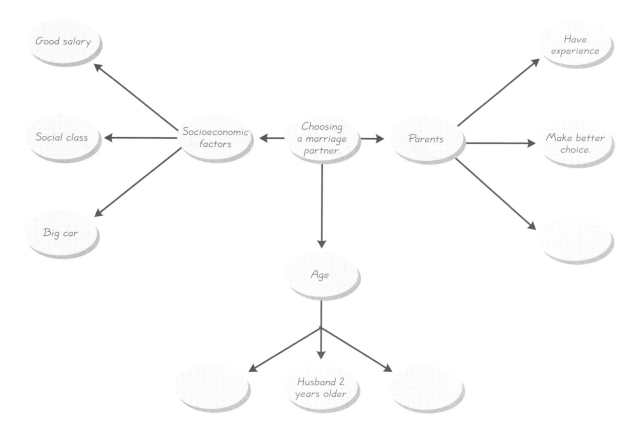

3 **Practice** Write a paragraph about your opinion on this topic, following the steps below the topic.

> **Topic** What should be the basis for choosing a marriage partner: love only, physical attraction, socioeconomic factors, personality, similar interests, being friends first, parental decision only, ethnic background, religious background, age? A mixture of these factors? Other factors?

Step 1 Choose three factors that you consider the most important and begin your composition by completing this sentence.

In my opinion, the three most important factors that are a basis for choosing a marriage partner are these: 1) _____, 2) _____, and 3) _____.

Step 2 Use a cluster diagram like the one on page 75 to outline your ideas on the topic. Put the *theme* or *topic* of your paragraph in the central circle, put one of your *main ideas* on each of the legs extending out of the circle, and put the *details* for each main idea on the lines extending out from the legs. The diagram may have as many main ideas and details as you can think of. You don't have to use them all in your paragraph.

Step 3 Write a sentence explaining your first main idea. Develop this line of argument using the details that you listed in the diagram. Then do the same for the other main ideas you listed. You may decide not to use all of your ideas in the cluster diagram if your paragraph is long enough.

Step 4 Think of an interesting way to end your paragraph. You may want to restate your main point in a different way from the first sentence, ask your reader a question, or make a joke.

Step 5 Read and revise your paragraph. Make sure that your reasons for choosing a marriage partner are clear and that there are details to support the main idea. In addition, check the spelling and punctuation. Add a good title that will make someone want to read it.

Step 6 If you have time, exchange your paper with another student. Read each others' compositions and make suggestions for improvements. Make any changes you want to. Then hand in your paper and your cluster diagram.

Self-Assessment Log

Read the lists below. Check (✓) the strategies and vocabulary that you learned in this chapter. Look through the chapter or ask your instructor about the strategies and words that you do not understand.

Reading and Vocabulary-Building Strategies

❑ Previewing a reading for its organization
❑ Identifying more exact or colorful synonyms
❑ Determining the order of events
❑ Identifying causes
❑ Drawing conclusions from a chart
❑ Scanning for details
❑ Getting meaning from word structure and context
❑ Making inferences

Target Vocabulary

Nouns

❑ authoritarianism
❑ dilemma
❑ emigration
❑ phenomenon*
❑ privacy
❑ prospects*
❑ socioeconomic classes
❑ stake
❑ status*
❑ threshold

Verbs

❑ annoyed
❑ approached*
❑ clinging
❑ crave
❑ create*
❑ diminished*
❑ disposed*
❑ dreaded
❑ foster
❑ recreate*
❑ sabotage
❑ withdrawing

Adjectives

❑ contemporary*
❑ faraway
❑ significant*

Idioms and Expressions

❑ diminishing prospects
❑ normal sex ratio
❑ sex-selective abortion
❑ troubling scenario
❑ weed out

---

* These words are from the Academic Word List. For more information on this list, see www.vuw.ac.nz/lals/research/awl.

4

Beauty and Aesthetics

In This Chapter

Aesthetics is the philosophy of beauty. So, we begin this chapter with a look at what many consider the most beautiful building in the world: the great Taj Mahal of India with its Muslim influences, mixing the traditions of Persia, India, and central Asia. Then we turn to look at current ideas about human beauty, with an article on the popularity of plastic surgery in Korea and some other Asian countries.

❝ Beauty is in the eye of the beholder. **❞**

—English proverb

Connecting to the Topic

1 Look at the photo of Da Vinci's famous painting, *The Mona Lisa*. Can you see why many people consider it an example of ideal beauty?

2 What does it mean to say that beauty is in the eye of the one who beholds (sees) it? Do you agree with this English saying? Why or why not?

3 What is the most beautiful place or thing that you have ever seen?

Taj Mahal

Before You Read

ORGANIZATION

It is not only essays, poems, and stories that have an exact organization. Even writings on architectural history, like the following selection about the famous Taj Mahal, have a particular structure carefully selected by the author to present his or her themes.

▲ The Taj Mahal in Agra, India

1 **Previewing a Reading for Its Organization** Skim the first reading on pages 83–85. Answer the questions.

1. Which of the following descriptions best describes the reading's organization?
   a. Opening paragraph, description of the Taj Mahal and its surrounding gardens, one person's description of the structure, legends surrounding the Taj Mahal.
   b. Opening paragraph, one person's description of the beauty of the structure, description of the Taj Mahal and its surrounding gardens, conclusion.
   c. Opening paragraph, legends surrounding the Taj Mahal and its construction, description of the Taj Mahal and its surrounding gardens, one person's description of the beauty of the structure.

2. Why do you think the author chose this organization for the description of this great monument?

UNDERSTANDING THE IMPORTANCE OF A GOOD OPENING
In any piece of writing, it is important to have an interesting opening to attract the
reader's attention. Then the writing should lead into the writer's main theme or point.

2 **Understanding the Importance of a Good Opening** Read the first
paragraph of the selection on the Taj Mahal on page 83, and answer the following
questions.

1. What is a proverb? Why begin with one?

2. Throughout the centuries, what human qualities have usually provided work
   for architects? Explain.

3. In what way is the Taj Mahal an exception? Why does this information attract
   the attention of most readers?

UNDERSTANDING SPECIALIZED TERMS

The selection that follows contains a number of words relating to architecture. Learning
the definitions of these words beforehand can help you read the selection more easily
and also help to build your vocabulary related to architecture.

3 **Understanding Specialized Terms Related to Architecture** Guess the
meanings of each italicized word below from its context, from the word itself, from a
synonym or explanation nearby in the text, or by consulting the picture of the Taj Mahal
(page 80). Use the hints in parentheses to help you. Choose the best definition in each case.

1. Begun in 1631, the *mausoleum* took some 20,000 workmen 22 years to build at a
   cost of 40 million rupees. (Rupees are the units of money in India.) (**Hint:** Think
   about the first paragraph you read for Exercise 2. Why was the Taj Mahal built?)
   - (A) museum which contains items of public interest
   - (B) temple to be used for religious ceremonies
   - (C) tomb in which a dead person is buried

2. Shah Jahan was apparently so pleased with the elegant mausoleum that he
   beheaded his chief architect, cut off the hands of the architect's assistants, and
   blinded the *draftsmen*, so that they would never be able to create a building to
   rival it. . . . (**Hint:** From the paragraph you read for Exercise 2, consider the
   way the Shah varies his actions to carry out his purpose.)
   - (A) people who actually put together the structures
   - (B) people who draw the plans for the structures to be built
   - (C) people who design and supervise the building of structures

3. It is a balanced and *symmetric* grouping of buildings. (**Hint:** Notice the antonym
   used in this article, *asymmetrical*—or, not symmetrical—in which one part of a
   building is higher than the other. Therefore, *symmetric* means:
   - (A) parallel and regular, with one side similar to the other
   - (B) sharp and pointed, made up only of squares and rectangles
   - (C) varied with diverse styles, sizes, and shapes

4. A harmonious synthesis of the architecture of Persia, India, and central Asia, it combines, for example, the traditional design of Mogul gardens with the characteristically Indian use of *minarets*, or towers, and a dominant dome. (**Hint:** The answer is given in the sentence itself.)
    - (A) doors
    - (B) towers
    - (C) walls

5. A harmonious synthesis of the architecture of Persia, India, and central Asia, it combines, for example, the traditional design of Mogul gardens with the characteristically Indian use of minarets, or towers, and a dominant *dome*. (**Hint:** Looking at the picture of the Taj Mahal may help you see which shape is dominant.)
    - (A) flat space that extends along the front of the building
    - (B) high stone wall with many windows
    - (C) rounded roof in the shape of a semi-sphere

6. The placement of a dome over *an arched alcove* is a characteristic of Persian architecture, successfully adapted in the Taj Mahal to a Mogul design. (**Hint:** Look at the picture of the Taj Mahal.)
    - (A) a decorated circular swimming pool containing a fountain
    - (B) a large open balcony with trees and flowers on it
    - (C) a small inner room set back under a curved ceiling

7. The placement of a dome over an arched alcove is a characteristic of Persian architecture, successfully adapted in the Taj Mahal to a *Mogul design*. (**Hint:** The first paragraph contains a clue.)
    - (A) a complicated triangular design
    - (B) a design from the Muslim group that once ruled India
    - (C) the design of an itinerant (traveling) architect from Persia

8. Flanking (on the sides of) the domed structure are a *mosque* and a second matching building, known as the "jawab," or "reply." (**Hint:** Again, remember the clue about religion in the first paragraph.)
    - (A) building in which Muslims worship
    - (B) church where Christians go to pray
    - (C) synagogue made for the ceremonies of Jewish people

9. Under the great dome, within an *octagonal* hall, are the sarcophagi (decorated boxes usually made for dead bodies) of the two lovers, enclosed by a screen of carved marble. (**Hint:** Think of the sea creature called an *octopus*.)
    - (A) five-sided
    - (B) eight-sided
    - (C) twelve-sided

10. The actual graves of the royal couple are in a small *crypt* beneath the burial hall. (**Hint:** The root of this word is from a Greek word that means *hidden*.)
    - (A) roof in the shape of a large rectangle
    - (B) idyllic square garden filled with statues, trees, and pools
    - (C) underground room used to keep treasure or the dead

Introduction

Architecture is one area where aesthetics have always been of great concern. All over the world and throughout the ages, many people have tried to build the most beautiful structures they could imagine. One such structure is India's Taj Mahal. What makes this structure so beautiful and what is the legendary history of its beginnings? The following selection from the architectural series, *The Grand Tour*, tells this story.

- What do you know of the Taj Mahal? Is it a structure that you would recognize in a picture?
- What do you consider the most beautiful architectural structures in the world and what qualities make them beautiful?

Taj Mahal, India

A   Love moves mountains, according to the proverb, but rarely does it provide work for the architect. Faith and vanity, throughout the centuries, have often been the qualities that have inspired men to build. The majestic Taj Mahal, however, is a notable exception. The famous domed building is a memorial to the fervent love of Shah Jahan, the fifth ruler of the Mogul   5 empire, for a cherished wife, who died in childbirth.

B   According to legend, the queen's last wish was that the shah build a monument so beautiful that whoever saw it could not help but sense the perfection of their love. Indeed, since its construction in the mid-17th century, the shimmering monument of white marble, set among tranquil   10 gardens and pools, has attracted many tourists and pilgrims. Visitors are as moved by the many legends surrounding its creation as they are spellbound by its serene elegance. . . .

C   Strangely enough, the architect of the Taj Mahal is unknown, although claimants to the title are legion. . . . The Indian version of the history of the   15 Taj Mahal credits Ustad Isa, an itinerant from Turkey or Persia, as being the designer. One legend tells that Ustad Isa himself was an inconsolable widower in search of an opportunity to erect a worthy monument to his own wife. Other accounts claim variously that he was from the cities of Isfahan or Samarkand or from Russia, and that he was either a Christian, a Jew, or an   20 Arab.

D   It is probable that the Taj Mahal was not the work of a single master at all but the concerted efforts of many artists and craftsmen from all over Asia. Begun in 1631, the mausoleum took some 20,000 workmen 22 years to build at a cost of 40 million rupees.

E   In one detail, however, the legends concur. Shah Jahan was apparently so pleased with the elegant mausoleum that he beheaded his chief architect, cut off the hands of the architect's assistants, and blinded the draftsmen, so that they would never be able to create a building to rival it. . . .

F   It is a balanced and symmetric grouping of buildings. A harmonious synthesis of the architecture of Persia, India, and central Asia, it combines, for example, the traditional design of Mogul gardens with the characteristically Indian use of minarets, or towers, and a dominant dome. The placement of a dome over an arched alcove is a characteristic of Persian architecture, successfully adapted in the Taj Mahal to a Mogul design.

G   At the heart of the complex stands the mausoleum itself: a massive eight-sided structure inset with arched *iwans*, or half domes, of a classically Mogul design. It is crowned by an immense, bulbous dome, which is surrounded and set off by four minarets that rise to a height of 138 feet. Flanking the domed structure are a mosque and a second matching building, known as the *jawab*, or "reply." Its sole function is to maintain the symmetry of the entire composition.

H   An idyllic square garden, divided by oblong pools, is at the front of the mausoleum. These pools, in turn, are divided into fourths by avenues, four being the number sacred to Islam. This planned and calculated reordering of nature and the severe regularity of the lines of trees are characteristic of Persian gardens and are intended to invite spiritual contemplation. Unlike the French and English gardens, the Persian garden is not a setting for recreation and pleasure but rather a retreat or sacred refuge from the disorder of temporal life.

▲ The gardens of the Taj Mahal

I   Under the great dome, within an octagonal hall, are the sarcophagi of the two lovers, enclosed by a screen of carved marble. In the exact center is the memorial tomb of Mumtaz Mahal. Next to it, but a little larger and higher, is that of Shah Jahan—the only asymmetrical element in the whole complex. However, both tombs are empty. The actual graves of the royal couple are in a small crypt beneath the burial hall.

I   The shah's tomb was not part of the original plan. Shah Jahan had planned to build another vast mausoleum for himself across the river from   65 that of his loved one. However, when he died, his son, refusing to incur the expense of another tomb, betrayed his father's last wishes and buried him beside his beloved consort.

K   Perhaps the single most alluring aspect of the Taj Mahal is the pervasive use of white marble. At different times of the day, the marble surfaces take   70 on varying and delicate casts of color. Some travelers claim that the only way to fully appreciate the Taj Mahal is by moonlight, when its surface takes on an almost incandescent glow. One of the more descriptive—and distinctly Victorian—accounts of the singular effects of light at the Taj Mahal was written by Prince William of Sweden in one of his travel books,   75 after he visited the site in 1832:

L   The sun shone so intensely on the dead-white marble that one was forced to look with half-closed eyes or to wear smoked glasses to avoid being dazzled. The many delicate details now appeared to great advantage, and the inlaid work, especially with its wealth of stones of different colors,   80 seemed to be masterly; otherwise I preferred the lovely moonlight effect of the evening before with its atmosphere of profound feeling, and it is thus that I would choose to remember this costliest gem among all the treasures of India.

Source: "Taj Mahal" *Individual Creations* (Flavio Conti, translated by Patrick Cregh)

After You Read

> The selection you have just read includes a number of adjectives that paint a very accurate description of the nouns they modify. They help describe the Taj Mahal. The next exercise looks at these adjectives and possible synonyms.

4 **Getting Meaning from Structure and Context: Identifying Synonyms for Adjectives** Read the phrases and words in the columns on page 86. Determine if the word in the second column is a correct synonym of the italicized adjective in the first column. Check the true or false box to indicate whether the word is a synonym or not. You can scan the reading for the phrase to get more context.

Vocabulary	Synonym?	True	False
1. a *notable* exception	important	❑	❑
2. *fervent* love	passionate	❑	❑
3. the *shimmering* monument	dark	❑	❑
4. *tranquil* gardens	visible	❑	❑
5. *serene* elegance	calm	❑	❑
6. an *inconsolable* widower	who cannot be comforted	❑	❑
7. a *worthy* monument	triangular	❑	❑
8. the *concerted* efforts	combined	❑	❑
9. a *harmonious* synthesis	balanced, well-proportioned	❑	❑
10. an *idyllic* square garden	boring	❑	❑
11. *oblong* pools	elongated rectangle or oval	❑	❑
12. a *sacred* refuge	quiet	❑	❑
13. *temporal* life	earthly, of this world	❑	❑
14. *incandescent* glow	shining	❑	❑
15. this *costliest* gem	most attractive	❑	❑

5 **Guided Academic Conversation** In small groups, read each item below aloud and discuss it. Then compare your opinions with those of another group.

1. **The Five W's of the Taj Mahal: When, Where, Why, Who, and What?**
   When, where, and why was the Taj Mahal built? Who built it? (**Hint:** this is not a question with a simple, easy answer.) What did it cost, both in money and in "human cost"? According to legend, what was done to the people who built the Taj Mahal after they finished, and why? What do you think of this policy? What other great structures have been built at great cost?

2. **Traditions and Fame of One of the World's Most Famous Buildings: The Taj Mahal** What types of architectural traditions does the Taj Mahal combine? Make a list with five different features that are distinctive in the Taj Mahal's design. Did Prince William of Sweden prefer the Taj Mahal at night or during the day? Why? What do you think makes the Taj Mahal so famous? What aspects of its beauty are the most important? In your opinion, is the Taj Mahal overrated? Explain.

3. **The Style and Function of a Garden** According to the article, what is the difference between Persian gardens and English or French gardens? Why does this difference exist? Which of these kinds of gardens is more similar to gardens in your culture? What other kinds of gardens have you heard of in other cultures? Write a brief description of what you would consider the perfect garden.

Illustrating Ideas

Often it is easier to imagine something if you draw a picture. In fact, drawing a picture can usually help you understand something better. Also, describing the picture with a partner or group can help you practice vocabulary related to the topic. The picture does not have to be beautiful or well done. A simple diagram or drawing can serve the purpose of understanding and of vocabulary-building just as well as a very artistic picture.

6 **Illustrating Ideas** Imagine that you are an architect and you are able to design any type of building you like. This could be a giant apartment building, a museum, a government office, a mausoleum, a gym, a church or mosque or temple, an airport, or whatever kind of building seems most interesting to you. It could be in a traditional style or what you imagine a building might look like in the future. Follow the steps below.

Step 1: Draw a diagram of the building, thinking of what kind of words you might use to describe its different parts. This diagram does not need to be elegant, and it could be a picture of the outside of the building or a floor plan of the inside, as you prefer.

Step 2: Discuss your drawing with a partner, taking turns and describing to each other the different parts of your building. Then ask and answer these questions:

1. Is this building aesthetically pleasing (beautiful)? If so, why? Or is it purely functional?

2. What words did you use to describe the building that relate specifically to architecture? Share these words with the class, so that the teacher can write all the words related to architecture on the board, making sure that everyone understands the meanings of all of them.

7 **Around the Globe: Outstanding Architecture of the World** The Taj Mahal is not the only building of outstanding beauty. Read about two more extraordinary buildings on page 88. Look at the photos, then have one partner read aloud the first paragraph and the other partner read the second paragraph. Pay attention to the words used to describe the buildings and the details of when and how they were built.

The Alhambra Palace

The Alhambra Palace (1338–90) is the most beautiful and ambitious work of Islamic architecture in Spain and perhaps in the entire world. The building is a representation of a desert oasis, guarded by high severe walls, yet inside abundant in flowing water, lush gardens, and shady alcoves. The huge citadel once enclosed mosques, gardens, prisons, seven palaces, and even the royal mint. The two main courtyards sparkle with running water and give way to garden terraces, pavilions, walkways, towers, and turrets. This Arab-planned compound is one of the finest examples of a man-made oasis, a combination of light, shadow, and outstanding architecture.

Himeji Castle

Between 1601 and 1614 a magnificent castle was built in Himeji City, Japan. The serene Himeji Castle is representative of a period in Japanese history when *shoguns* (powerful military commanders) ruled Japan. *Samurai* (warriors of the *Shogunate*) created great fortresses like Himeji to protect the *shogun* and the people in the surrounding towns. Himeji Fortress has great views across the rice fields and mountains around the castle and the *samurai* could see invaders coming for miles around. The white fairytale-like castle rises from a rocky base and has gabled roofs that look like birds in flight. The Japanese refer to the palace as The White Heron. Although the structure looks somewhat delicate, it has withstood centuries of invaders. Inside the castle is a maze of confusing courtyards and passages that throughout the ages baffled enemy intruders.

Source: Adapted from *The Story of Architecture* (Jonathan Glancey)

8 Comparing Two Buildings

1. Working together compare the two buildings using the Venn diagram below. Write words and phrases in each circle showing items (columns, fountains, gardens, towers, walls, etc.) or qualities (why, how, when, or where it was built, reaction it produces in people, etc.) of each building. Put any items or qualities that belong to both buildings in the center part where the circles overlap.

The following list represents some of the items and qualities you may wish to use for comparison. Use only the ones that apply to one or both of the two buildings you choose to compare, and feel free to add other items or qualities if you can think of any:

alcoves	delicate looking	mosque
built for defense	structure	palace
built in 1300s	desert oasis	pools
built in early 1600s	gabled roofs	prisons
built on a rocky base	gardens	running water
a castle	has withstood centuries	towers
considered a famous	of invaders	walkways
building	Islamic	white color
courtyards	maze	

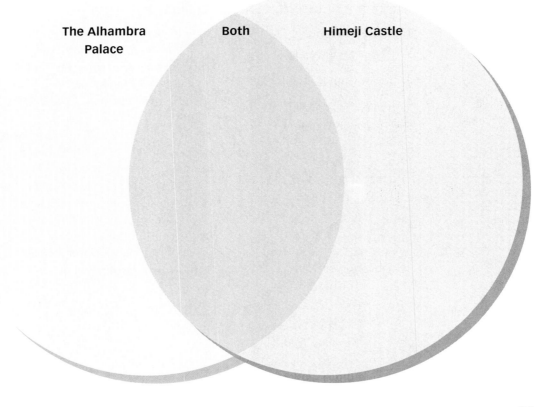

The Alhambra Palace   Both   Himeji Castle

Korea's Makeover from Dull to Hip Changes the Face of Asia

Strategy

Previewing a Reading to Identify the Key People
In an article in which a number of people are mentioned or interviewed, it is a good idea to preview in order to identify these people before you begin to read. A short identifying description of each key person mentioned will usually appear somewhere near their name.

1 **Previewing a Reading to Identify the Key People** Skim the reading on pages 93–96 to get a general idea of what it is about. Then scan it for the names of the key people listed in Column 1 below and find out the identity of each one. Some of these people are interviewed in the article, and some are just mentioned. Then put the letter of the correct description from Column 2 beside the name it describes.

Column 1

1. _____ Cate Siu
2. _____ Song Hye Kyo
3. _____ Chung Jong Pil
4. _____ Jung Dong Hak
5. _____ Lee Young Ae
6. _____ BoA
7. _____ Wang Simei
8. _____ Lee Yihsiu

Column 2

a. a Korean beauty starring in the well-known TV show *Jewel in the Palace*
b. a surgeon who runs the Cinderella Plastic Surgery Clinic in Seoul
c. a Hong Kong fan of Korean television shows
d. the vice general affairs director of the All-China Women's Federation
e. a surgeon who specializes in rhinoplasty ("nose jobs," operations to reshape a nose)
f. the head of the Taipei office of International Plastic Surgery who has had a nose job
g. a beautiful Korean star of soap operas (popular shows about romance and family)
h. a Korean pop star

2 **Understanding Specialized Terms: Personal Beauty** Many of the words and expressions in this article relate to personal aesthetics (the study of personal beauty). These are useful words to understand to be able to discuss the topic. Guess the meaning of the word or phrase in italics by breaking it apart or by finding clues in the context. Then choose the answer that best defines it.

1. Cate Siu admires a Korean actresses' *bee-stung* lips and feminine features. (**Hint:** What would your lips look like if a bee had stung them?)
   - (A) small
   - (B) white
   - (C) thick

2. Korean actresses have *prominent* and elegant noses. (**Hint:** The prefix *pro-* can mean *ahead of* in place or position.]
   - (A) tiny and rounded
   - (B) large and noticeable
   - (C) dark and thin

3. Ms. Siu decided to try to improve her looks with a *surgical makeover.*
   - (A) operation to change a person's physical appearance
   - (B) talent competition with other actresses on television
   - (C) scientifically designed diet and exercise program

4. She flew more than 1,000 miles to a clinic here for surgery to raise *the bridge* of her nose, make her eyes appear larger, and sharpen her chin. (**Hint:** Think of what a bridge looks like.)
   - (A) the highest part
   - (B) the two nostrils
   - (C) the right side

5. Korea is *redefining style.*
   - (A) returning to the fashions of the past
   - (B) paying no attention to fashion
   - (C) creating a new definition of fashion

6. The popularity of Korean stars is establishing Korean ethnic features (characteristics considered typical of Koreans) as *a standard* of beauty across the region.
   - (A) the lowest level
   - (B) an accepted model
   - (C) an unusual variety

7. This focus on beauty could result in long-term psychological damage for women who are *banking too much on their looks.* (**Hint:** The comparison here comes from the idea of going to the bank to deposit money, but this is only a comparison.)

- (A) looking around at too many others for an idea of happiness
- (B) giving too much importance to their physical appearance
- (C) working too hard to be successful and make money

8. Some sociologists see a subtext in the craze (new fad or tendency): a rebellion by Asian people against the images of *Caucasian* good looks that dominate much of the international media. (**Hint:** What kind of appearance—that isn't Asian—is the most common in international movies and advertising?)

- (A) African
- (B) European
- (C) Indian

9. Caucasians and many other ethnic groups have eyelids with a fold that allows them to *retract.* (**Hint:** The prefix *re-* often means *to go in reverse or backwards;* for example, if people *return* to a place, they go once more to a place they have already been.)

- (A) move back into the face
- (B) see clearly and track moving objects
- (C) show makeup when it is put on

10. There has been widespread speculation (many people guessing or supposing) in Asia that nearly all Korean stars have *gone under the knife.*

- (A) had plastic surgery
- (B) been attacked violently
- (C) fallen under the influence of money

11. Purported *before-and-after photos* of Korean celebrities are widely available on the Internet. (**Hint:** *Purported* photos are photos that claim to be true but may be false.)

- (A) photos of someone as a child and as an adult
- (B) photos showing a person before and after a makeover
- (C) photos of people looking their best and looking their worst

12. The number of surgeons performing *image-enhancing work* such as nose jobs and eye lifts has increased sharply.

- (A) treatments to improve someone's general health
- (B) treatments to improve someone's mental condition
- (C) treatments to improve someone's physical appearance

Introduction

In addition to appreciating beauty in the world around us, people everywhere are concerned with personal beauty. The following article from *The Wall Street Journal* looks at what is considered beautiful in some Asian cultures. It discusses the change in Korea's national image from dull to "hip" (slang for *fashionable* or *in style*) and the great popularity of plastic surgery in Korea and other Asian countries to remodel people's features so that they meet a particular Korean ideal of what is beautiful. It also raises some concerns about this popular move toward plastic surgery.

- What facial features do you consider most important to the physical attractiveness of a woman? What about a man?
- Is physical beauty as important for a man as for a woman? Explain.
- Do you think these will be the same features discussed in the article?

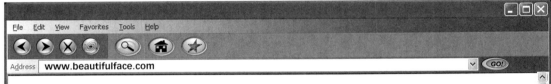

File   Edit   View   Favorites   Tools   Help

Address **www.beautifulface.com**

Korea's Makeover from Dull to Hip Changes the Face of Asia

A   . . . Cate Siu is from Hong Kong, but she's a fan of Korean television shows and she keeps up with gossip about Korean celebrities on the Internet. Her favorite is a beautiful soap-opera star, Song Hye Kyo, whose bee-stung lips and feminine

B features she admires.

"Korean actresses have prominent and elegant noses," says Ms. Siu, a 25-year-old as-

C piring actress. "They look so pretty."

So, when Ms. Siu decided she'd have a

5

10

15

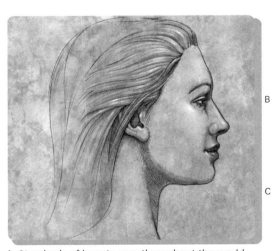

▲ Standards of beauty vary throughout the world.

▲ Some people are unhappy with their appearance.

better shot at breaking into the entertainment business after improving her looks with a surgical makeover, she knew where she wanted to go. In April, she flew more than 1,000 miles to a clinic in Seoul for operations to raise the bridge of her nose, make her eyes appear larger, and sharpen her chin.

D   Across Asia, Korea is cool. From fashion to music to film, the country of 48 million people is redefining style. And as notions of Korean beauty become popularized by the country's exploding cultural exports, women from around the region—and some men, too—are flocking to Seoul to have their faces remodeled.

E   "A lot of my patients bring a picture of a Korean star from a magazine and say, 'I want to look like that,'" says Chung Jong Pil, a surgeon who runs the Cinderella Plastic Surgery Clinic in a fashionable Seoul neighborhood.

F   Dr. Chung estimates that just under ten percent of his customers come from overseas; the rest are locals. Most of the foreign visitors come from China, Taiwan, and Hong Kong, he says. Jung Dong Hak, a surgeon who specializes in rhinoplasty, or nose jobs, at another Seoul clinic, says roughly 15 percent of his patients are foreign. That number has been rising in the past few years. "The increase has been very big since the Korean wave started," he says.

G   The trend says a lot about Korea's own image makeover. Not long ago, many people saw the country as a decidedly uncool industrial park pumping out cheap cars and appliances. But that started to change in the late 1990s, when the Korean government decided that entertainment could be an export industry. The film business in particular benefited from government help and a big influx of private capital.

H   Now, countries from Japan to Singapore are flooded with Korean hip-hop and pop acts, melodramatic soap operas, and movies from horror flicks to romantic comedies.

I   The final episode of *Jewel in the Palace*, a dramatic series about court intrigue during Korea's Chosun Dynasty, starring Korean beauty Lee Young Ae, in 2005 became the most-watched television show in Hong Kong history. More than 40 percent of the city tuned in. Korean pop star BoA outsells Britney Spears in Japan. In 2004, Chinese television stations carried more than 100 Korean shows.

J   The popularity of Korean stars is establishing Korean ethnic features as a standard of beauty across the region. Some sociologists see a subtext in the craze: a rebellion by Asian people against the images of Caucasian good looks that dominate much of the international media.

K   Others see dangers. Wang Simei, vice general affairs director of the All-China Women's Federation, says the focus on beauty could result in long-term psychological damage for women who are banking too much on their looks. "Korean culture is something worth studying," Ms. Wang says. "But we might have paid too much attention to their soap operas and pretty actresses."

L   Critics also point out that what appeals to many about Korean looks are exactly those features that make them look more Western. Koreans, related to the Mongols who once ruled the Central Asian steppes [the large flat lands of the region that is now called Mongolia], tend to have more prominent noses and, often, lighter skin than other Asians, the country's plastic surgeons say. In physical terms, the Korean ideal is a relatively small, oval face with a high-bridged nose and large eyes with Western-style eyelids. Caucasians and many other ethnic groups have eyelids with a fold that allows them to retract. Many northeast Asians lack the fold, making their eyes appear smaller.

M   Complicating the issue further, some Korean actresses have spoken openly about their own plastic surgeries. This has led to widespread speculation in Asia that nearly all Korean stars have gone under the knife. Purported before-and-after photos of Korean celebrities are widely available on the Internet . . .

N   Just how common these procedures have become is hard to track, but the number of surgeons performing image-enhancing work such as nose jobs and eye lifts has increased sharply. The Korean Society of Aesthetic and Plastic Surgery, a professional group, says its membership has risen 85 percent to 960 since 2000.

O   "All the buzz and atmosphere makes young people today think [surgery] is common," says Lee Yihsiu, who runs the Taipei office of International Plastic Surgery, which matches up foreign patients with Korean surgeons . . .

P   Ms. Lee says business is "growing amazingly." The company arranges for 15 to 20 foreigners to visit Korea for operations every month, with clients coming from Taiwan, China, and Hong Kong. The 27-year-old Ms. Lee had a nose job in Seoul herself earlier this year as part of a makeover ahead of her wedding.

Q   Korean surgeons are coy about their celebrity patients. In Dr. Chung's consulting room at the Cinderella clinic, under the glass top on the coffee table, are dozens of autographed Polaroid pictures of stylish pop musicians, actors, and actresses posing with Dr. Chung. The doctor describes the stars as friends and won't disclose which of them are also patients.

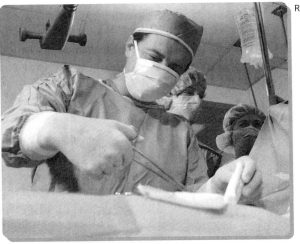
▲ Going "under the knife"

R But Dr. Chung says that beliefs about the power of surgery to transform appearances can be a mixed blessing. 110 "People come with before-and-after pictures of celebrities," Dr. Chung says. "People expect a lot because of 115 those kinds of pictures. But it's not realistic. We'll tell people they will look better, but not like the stars in the pictures." 120

Source: "Korean's Makeover from Dull to Hip Changes the Face of Asia" *The Wall Street Journal* (Gordon Fairclough)

After You Read

3 **Getting Meaning from Context: Synonym or Antonym?** Read the sentences below and write *the same as* in the blank if the word or expression is a synonym of the following word(s). Put *the opposite of* if the word or expression is an antonym of the following word(s).

1. Cate Siu keeps up with *gossip* about Korean celebrities on the Internet.

   The word *gossip* is _____ *rumors and spreading scandal.*

2. Cate Siu keeps up with gossip about Korean *celebrities* on the Internet.

   The word *celebrities* is _____ *people who are not well known.*

3. Ms. Siu is a 25-year-old *aspiring actress*.

   The expression *aspiring actress* is _____ *a woman who is trying to be a performer on TV or in plays.*

4. Across Asia, South Korea is *cool*. (Notice also the expression *decidedly uncool* to describe the international image Korea used to have in the past.)

   The word *cool* is _____ *popular, in fashion.*

5. The film business in particular benefited from government help and *a big influx of private capital*.

   The expression *a big influx of private capital* is _____ *a small amount of money going out.*

6. Now, countries from Japan to Singapore are flooded with South Korean hip-hop and pop acts, melodramatic soap operas, and movies from *horror flicks* to romantic comedies.

   The expression *horror flicks* is _____ *slow-moving films on cheerful topics.*

7. More than 40 percent of the city *tuned in* to the show *Jewel in the Palace.*

The expression *tuned in* is _____ *turned on their television to watch.*

8. "*All the buzz* and atmosphere makes young people today think [surgery] is common."

The expression *all the buzz* is _____ *all the excited talk.*

9. Dr. Chung says that beliefs about the power of surgery to transform appearances can be *a mixed blessing.*

The expression *a mixed blessing* is _____ something that *has a good side and a bad side.*

4 **Focusing on Words from the Academic Word List** Read the excerpt below taken from the reading in Part 2. Fill in the blanks with a word from the box. Do not look back at the reading right away; instead, see if you can now remember the vocabulary.

benefited	ethnic	media
dominate	export	region
establishing	image	trend

The _____ [of an increasing number of surgical
1
makeovers] says a lot about Korea's own _____ makeover.
2
Not long ago, many people saw the country as a decidedly uncool industrial park pumping out cheap cars and appliances. But that started to change in the late 1990s, when the Korean government decided that entertainment could be an _____ industry. The film
3
business in particular _____ from government help and a
4
big influx of private capital. . . .

The popularity of Korean stars is _____ Korean
5
_____ features as a standard of beauty across the
6
_____. Some sociologists see a subtext in the craze: a
7
rebellion by Asian people against the images of Caucasian good looks that

_____ much of the international _____.
8 9

5 **Guided Academic Discussion: Analyzing Facts** Read the four statements below about the reading on pages 93–96. Are these statements true or false according to the article? Circle the answers and then discuss each statement with a partner.

1. Many people in Asian countries want to look like Koreans and get plastic surgery to look this way. True or False?

2. For many years, Korean actors and actresses have been popular in many countries. True or False?

3. The Korean beauty standard is to have a round face; a short, thick nose; and small, sparkling eyes. True or False?

4. Plastic surgery can make your face look exactly like the face of your favorite movie star. True or False?

 6 **Expressing Opinions** Read the four opinions below. Do you agree or disagree with these opinions? Circle *yes* or *no* and then discuss each opinion in a group.

1. The popularity of plastic surgery to make people look more like Korean movie stars is a positive rebellion by Asian people against the Caucasian beauty standard. Yes or no?

2. It is a good thing for people to get plastic surgery to change the looks of their face whenever they want and for whatever reason. Yes or no?

3. People should get other types of surgery that are not medically necessary if it will improve their appearance. For example, if they have the money, they should get liposuction (surgery to remove body fat), tummy tucks (surgery to tighten stomach skin), or face lifts (to remove wrinkles on the face). Yes or no?

4. If someone needs any type of plastic surgery for medical reasons, or wants it to improve their appearance, their insurance should pay for it. Yes or no?

Strategy

Structuring an Argument: Weakest to Strongest Point
To be able to write an effective argument essay, it is important to know which points support your argument. It is also important to think about what order these points should come in. Several different strategies for organizing your argument exist. We will focus on one strategy here: listing them from the weakest to the strongest. One of the most common ways to organize your argument is to start with the weakest or least convincing point, and lead up to the strongest or most convincing point.

7 **Structuring an Argument: Weakest to Strongest Point** Read the two positions, or opinions, in the box below. Then read the supporting points labeled A–F following the box. Decide which three points support Position 1 and which three points support Position 2. Then decide what order you would put the points in if you were going to develop them into an argument for each position. Write the letters of the arguments in order from weakest to strongest for each position, and be ready to defend your ideas about which points are strongest.

> **Position 1**: Plastic surgery should only be done where there is medical necessity or in the case of a defacing injury, like a severe burn.
>
> Supporting points: ＿＿＿＿ ＿＿＿＿ ＿＿＿＿
>
> **Position 2**: Plastic surgery should be done whenever someone wants to change something about his or her looks and can afford it.
>
> Supporting points: ＿＿＿＿ ＿＿＿＿ ＿＿＿＿

Supporting Points

A. Plastic surgery is expensive. People could use this money to buy useful things or to donate to charity instead.

B. Our society is very focused on beauty. People who get plastic surgery will be able to get better jobs, make more money, make more friends, and basically have a better life.

C. Some people who get plastic surgery may find it easier to find romance and a husband or wife.

D. Plastic surgery has a risk of side effects. So it is possible to have an operation and be left with ugly scars, or get an infection, or even die.

E. Getting plastic surgery can improve a person's self-esteem (their feelings of how much they are worth).

F. Our society focuses too much on physical appearance. People should not get plastic surgery and just increase this focus. They should work on getting their self-esteem from within themselves or from their skills and good values.

In a small group or with the whole class together, compare your answers and your reasons for the ordering of the points.

 8 **What Do You Think?** Read the paragraph on page 100 and discuss the questions that follow.

Beauty Contests

Miss World, Miss Universe, Miss and Mrs. America. For years a steady stream of beauty contests have crossed the television channels from Hawaii to Thailand, from Brazil to Canada, and all around the globe. Some say that these contests stress physical beauty and perfection too much and give average women complexes and beauty ideals they cannot live up to. Some of the contestants in these competitions even undergo multiple plastic surgeries in order to realize their goals of ideal beauty. The promoters of the contests say they're looking for more than surface beauty and that personality and intelligence are just as important as physical beauty.

▲ Beauty contests are popular worldwide.

1. Do you think these contests are based just on physical beauty or are they a combination of factors, like beauty, intelligence, and personality? Explain.

2. If "beauty is in the eye of the beholder," how is it possible for the judges to pick the winner? Does it matter what part of the world the judges come from?

3. Is it fair to allow contestants who have had multiple plastic surgeries to compete with those who have not? Why or why not?

4. Do you think that beauty contests give women, or especially teenage women, inferiority complexes? Explain.

5. In your opinion, what is the most important attribute a woman can have, intelligence, beauty, or a good personality?

TOEFL® iBT

Focus on Testing

Vocabulary Questions

The TOEFL® iBT test places a great emphasis on understanding vocabulary in the context of a reading. Vocabulary questions are likely to constitute between 25–33 percent of all the questions within the reading section.

TOEFL® iBT vocabulary questions are all asked in the same basic way. In the body of the question, a context is named (e.g., "as used in Paragraph 2") and a target vocabulary item is presented. Then you are given four possible words or phrases from which you must choose the one closest in meaning to the target vocabulary item.

In choosing the best match, remember that a target vocabulary item may have many meanings in English. Your task is to identify its meaning in the context that the question specifies. The list of options may include other possible meanings of the vocabulary item, but you must be careful not to choose one of these distractors. Also, remember that the question asks which option is "closest in meaning" to the target item, not which item is an exact synonym. The correct choice may be similar in meaning without being an exact replacement for it in the text.

Practice Read the passage about the beauty of sound and then answer the vocabulary questions that follow.

What Makes Sound Beautiful?

A   Beauty is certainly more than skin-deep. However you might define it, beauty extends far beyond the visual to that which pleases other senses and even the mind. Prime among these other routes for the observation of beauty is the sense of hearing. Music is routinely recognized as beautiful. So are other sounds, like the whispering of wind through pines or the gentle purring of a cat.

B   Just as philosophers and scientists have struggled to pin down the definition of visual beauty, they have attempted to dissect the appeal of pleasant sounds as well. Ultimately, sonic beauty is in the ear of the beholder. Research and intuition can, however, suggest reasons why one person considers a musical piece gorgeous while another considers it a bucketful of noise.

C   The existence of noise is a clue in itself. A conventional definition of noise would include adjectives like *unwanted, annoying, disorganized, or meaningless.* Sounds that have no discernible pattern to them or that intrude on mental order are not generally considered beautiful. The relationship of sound to the situation is crucial. An assertive orchestral piece like Copland's "Fanfare for the Common Man" could be strikingly beautiful at a Fourth of July celebration yet decidedly annoying when it blares from someone else's apartment while you are trying to concentrate on a difficult task.

D   But it is the quest to discover the role of pattern that takes us beyond such obvious intuitive judgments about the beauty of sound. In the 1930s, a mathematician named George Birkhoff proposed formulas that would place a given work of art on a numerical aesthetic scale. More beautiful art would score higher than less beautiful art. He proposed different specifics for analyzing painting, or geometric figures, or poetry, or music, but his central formula is M = O / C. The symbol M stands for beauty, O for organization, and C for complexity. In other words, a work of music that is very well organized and not very complicated scores higher than a work with similarly good organization but a high degree of complexity. Organization is good, complexity is bad.

E   This aspect of Birkhoff's approach clearly oversimplifies the case. Organization and complexity do contribute to the perceived beauty of a musical piece, but not as mere opposites. They entwine and influence the piece in combination with each other and with other factors. To illustrate this, let's consider one of those other factors, the musical experience and knowledge that a listener brings to a piece of music.

F   Music critics are well-known for disliking works that become immensely popular and for praising material that the general public finds boring or even unpleasant. Why should this disparity be so common? Or why should a 40-year-old who loved bouncy pop music during his teen years now find it hard to tolerate his own teenage children's taste in music?

G   The answers probably involve a certain ideal level of complexity, a point where the complexity of a piece and the way it is organized are matched perfectly with a listener's knowledge and experience. The work presents enough of a challenge so that the listener can enjoy thinking about and deciphering its patterns, but it is not so impossibly complex that the listener remains confused. A work that falls far below this ideal level is too simple or too familiar to be interesting. A work that reaches far above the ideal level is frustrating and dissatisfying.

H   The ideal level varies with the personal knowledge and experience of the listener. Pop music may excite and entertain a teenager who has never heard anything quite like it before, yet it may bore or annoy an adult who has heard far too much like it before. It is not that the pop tune lacks pattern but that its pattern is too simple or uninventive for an adult with prior experience of such music. At the other end of the spectrum, the experimental work of composers such as John Cage seems random and pointless to many casual listeners because it draws on structural principles far beyond most listeners' experience. Again, it is not that the experimental piece lacks pattern but that the pattern is too elusive to give the listener the mental pleasure of discovering it.

1. Which of the following is closest in meaning to *pin down*, as it is used in Paragraph B?
   - (A) immobilize
   - (B) specify
   - (C) contradict
   - (D) emphasize

2. Which of the following is closest in meaning to *intrude on*, as it is used in Paragraph C?

- Ⓐ insert
- Ⓑ imply
- Ⓒ destroy
- Ⓓ disturb

3. Which of the following is closest in meaning to *scale*, as it is used in Paragraph D?

- Ⓐ ability
- Ⓑ ascent
- Ⓒ size
- Ⓓ system

4. Which of the following is closest in meaning to *disparity*, as it is used in Paragraph F?

- Ⓐ difference
- Ⓑ experience
- Ⓒ injustice
- Ⓓ opinion

5. Which of the following is closest in meaning to *deciphering*, as it is used in Paragraph G?

- Ⓐ building
- Ⓑ diminishing
- Ⓒ decoding
- Ⓓ recovering

6. Which of the following is closest in meaning to *spectrum*, as it is used in Paragraph H?

- Ⓐ set of colors
- Ⓑ range of possibilities
- Ⓒ variety of musical tastes
- Ⓓ pattern of musical notes

Part 3   Tying It All Together

1 **Making Connections** Do some research on the Internet and take notes on one of the following topics. Share your results with the class or in a small group.

The Taj Mahal Find out more facts about the Taj Mahal. For example, how did Shah Jahan meet his future wife, Arjumand Banu Begum (later given the honorary name Mumtaz Mahal) in whose honor he built the Taj Mahal? Look up the details of this legendary, romantic story. Or find some descriptions or reactions to this building from famous people.

Beautiful Architecture Is there a building that you consider one of the most beautiful architectural structures in the world? Look up information on this building and find pictures on the web.

Pros and Cons of Plastic Surgery Look up some sites in favor and some sites against plastic surgery. Find some before-and-after pictures that show good results and some that show bad results. Which position do you find more convincing after this research?

Responding in Writing

WRITING TIP: SUPPORT YOUR ARGUMENT

When writing an argument in favor of a particular opinion or point of view, select the main points that will support your argument and put them in the order of weakest (least convincing) to strongest (most convincing).

2 **Writing Practice** Write an argument of a few paragraphs about beauty. Follow the steps below.

Step 1 Choose one of the three options below to represent the position of your argument. This will be the first sentence of your essay. You can rephrase it if you wish, but make sure your point of view remains clear.

> **Option 1** Beauty (in a person, art, or nature) is something that can be universally agreed upon; there is an aesthetic standard common to all cultures the world over and throughout history.
>
> **Option 2** Beauty (in a person, art, or nature) is not something that can be universally agreed upon; individual cultures have different aesthetic standards that vary according to time and place.
>
> **Option 3** The most beautiful architectural structure in the world is
> _____. (Fill in the blank with the building or structure you think is the most beautiful.)

Step 2 Brainstorm ideas on the topic and point of view you chose above. You may use a cluster diagram, as you learned in Chapter 3, or you may just take notes, as you prefer.

Step 3 From your cluster diagram or notes, choose which will be the main points of your argument.

Step 4 Put the main points in the order of the weakest (least convincing) to the strongest (most convincing) so that your argument ends with its most convincing point.

Step 5 Write your argument beginning with the first sentence you chose and with your main points in the order you chose in Step 4.

Step 6 Read and revise your paper. Add a title. Exchange with a partner to get their comments before handing in your composition and your notes or diagram.

Self-Assessment Log

Read the lists below. Check (✔) the strategies and vocabulary that you learned in this chapter. Look through the chapter or ask your instructor about the strategies and words that you do not understand.

Reading and Vocabulary-Building Strategies

❏ Previewing a reading for its organization
❏ Understanding the importance of a good opening
❏ Understanding specialized terms related to architecture
❏ Getting meaning from structure and context: identifying synonyms for adjectives
❏ Illustrating ideas
❏ Previewing a reading to identify key people
❏ Understanding specialized terms: personal beauty
❏ Getting meaning from context: synonym or antonym?
❏ Structuring an argument: weakest to strongest point

Target Vocabulary

Nouns

❏ arched alcove
❏ aspiring actress
❏ before-and-after photos
❏ bridge (of the nose)
❏ celebrities
❏ crypt
❏ dome
❏ draftsmen
❏ export*
❏ gossip
❏ horror flicks
❏ image*
❏ image-enhancing work
❏ mausoleum
❏ media*
❏ minarets

❏ mixed blessing
❏ Mogul design
❏ mosque
❏ nose jobs
❏ region*
❏ standard
❏ surgical makeover
❏ trend*

Adjectives

❏ bee-stung
❏ Caucasian
❏ concerted
❏ cool
❏ costliest
❏ ethnic*

❏ fervent
❏ harmonious
❏ idyllic
❏ incandescent
❏ inconsolable
❏ notable
❏ oblong
❏ octagonal
❏ prominent
❏ sacred
❏ serene
❏ shimmering
❏ symmetric
❏ temporal
❏ tranquil
❏ worthy

Verbs

❏ benefited*
❏ dominate*
❏ establishing*
❏ redefining (style)
❏ retract
❏ tuned in

Idioms and Expressions

❏ all the buzz
❏ banking too much on (something)
❏ big influx of private capital
❏ gone under the knife

* These words are from the Academic Word List. For more information on this list, see www.vuw.ac.nz/lals/research/awl.

5

Transitions

Human life is a series of transitions, both ordinary and extraordinary. The first selection shows how confronting a modern urban environment for the first time causes changes in some people in developing countries. Next is the story of Inna, a Russian immigrant to Canada who left her family, native land, and culture years ago and now eagerly awaits a visit from her only brother.

❝ Life is pleasant. Death is peaceful. It's the transition that's troublesome. **❞**

—Isaac Asimov
U.S. writer (1920–1992)

Connecting to the Topic

1 How does the photo show the transition from past to present that exists in many of today's cities?

2 What differences can you imagine in the lives of the different people in the photo?

3 What is a transition you have gone through in your life?

Conversations in Malaysia

Before You Read

Strategy

Making Comparisons
Making comparisons between different genres (types) of writing can help you to understand them. By examining which elements are similar and which are different, we get a better idea of different genres. A conversation and an interview are two genres that have similarities and differences. We will explore these genres in the next exercise.

1 **Making Comparisons** Although the title of the first selection uses the word *conversations*, the reading in Part 1 is really an interview. Read the following descriptions and write *I* in the blank for interview, *C* for conversation, and *both* for any that apply to both a conversation and an interview.

1. _____ Different people share information by expressing their views about something.

2. _____ Two or more people are talking to each other.

3. _____ Person A asks Person B questions about Person B.

4. _____ Two individuals exchange ideas about a particular topic.

5. _____ Someone tries to find out information about another person by asking that person questions.

6. _____ Because Person B has information that Person A thinks is important, Person A asks B questions and records the answers.

Now answer these questions: In what ways is an interview similar to a conversation? In what ways is it different?

Strategy

Identifying Differences Between Standard English and Global English
Besides the various kinds of Standard English (spoken in Australia, Canada, England, the U.S., and New Zealand, for example), there is a new kind of English called *global English*, which is being spoken more and more all over the world by non-natives. It has its own characteristics, including the use of nonstandard grammar, and has been described as "a stripped down language . . . limited in vocabulary and cultur-ally neutral." It is not Standard English, but it communicates, and increasingly, it is becoming the common language of international business, trade, and science.

2 Identifying Differences Between Standard English and Global English In the reading that follows, the author uses standard British English to interview a young Malaysian man named Shafi. This young man, however, speaks his own form of global English. To find out more about some characteristics of Shafi's English, fill in the following blanks.

1. Shafi begins to speak in line 4 and his words are in quotation marks. His first sentence is typical of global English because it has non-standard usage of grammar. He uses a different tense of the verb at the end of the sentence when he says *is* and in Standard English he should say: _____ because _____.

2. In this same paragraph, Shafi starts out referring to himself and saying "I," and then changes to talking in general and saying _____ , and then back again to saying _____ . This is not done in Standard English without a clear reason, but Shafi does it a lot.

3. Speakers of global English often use the present participle (the -*ing* form) instead of a complete verb. Shafi does this in line 11 when he says: "*I just floating around and didn't know my direction.*" How would you say this in Standard English? _____.

4. A little later, Shafi talks about a goat in line 23 and says: "The goat would just roam anywhere he want to go without any strings." Again, Shafi uses non-standard grammar in the agreement of the subject and verb. He says *want*, but he should say _____ because _____.

5. In line 64, Shafi says: ". . . . trying to live a simpler, more meaningful life than coming to the city, where you have lots of waste and lots of things that is not real probably."
Again, there is non-standard usage with the verb *is* which should be _____ because _____.
Also, the adverb *probably* is not in the usual place. Can you guess where it should be? Rewrite the last five words of the sentence, starting with *that*:
_____

3 Getting Meaning from Word Structure and Context Choose the best meaning for the italicized words in the following excerpts taken from the reading. All of them are Shafi's words except those in number 4.

1. You see all the bright lights, you begin to sense the *materialistic* civilization around you. (**Hint:** The *bright lights* and the root word *material*, referring to stuff or objects, are clues to the meaning.) A *materialistic* civilization is a culture occupied with _____.
   - (A) building things for others
   - (B) finding spiritual values
   - (C) getting more and more things

2. "And I forgot about my religion and my *commitments*—in the sense that you had to pray."
   - (A) friends
   - (B) obligations
   - (C) pleasures

3. "But not to the extent of going out and doing *nasty* things like taking girls and drinking and gambling and drugs . . ."
   - (A) bad
   - (B) important
   - (C) unusual

4. He didn't give a straight answer. At this early stage in our conversation, *concreteness* didn't come easily to him. (**Hint:** To talk in a *concrete* way is the opposite of talking in an *abstract*, *general*, or *indefinite* way.)
   - (A) clear talk with examples
   - (B) large ideas with big words
   - (C) negative thoughts

5. "You take a goat . . . somewhere where the goat is being tied up all the time— and you release that goat . . . The goat would just *roam* anywhere he want to go without any strings."
   - (A) cry and moan
   - (B) get sick
   - (C) walk around

6. "Freedom must be within the definition of a certain *framework*." (**Hint:** Notice that a *frame* is the construction that goes around a picture and holds it up.)
   - (A) attack
   - (B) basis
   - (C) sadness

7. "Do they face the same *restrictions* of family life as I do?" (**Hint:** Pay attention to the small word *strict*, the opposite of *easygoing* or *flexible*, inside this word.)
   - (A) comforts
   - (B) hopes
   - (C) limitations

8. "You see, in the village . . . we have the bare minimum . . . In the city, you can buy a lunch at ten dollars. Or in a stall, you can have a lunch for 50 cents. That excess of nine-fifty which the city dwellers spend will be spent by us on other purposes. To us, with our framework and tradition and religion, that is *excessiveness*. (**Hint:** Take note of the prefix *ex-* which can mean *beyond* or *more so*, as in *extra*. Also, notice the context with the use of the small related word *excess*.)
   - (A) overdoing it, lack of control
   - (B) practical solution to problems
   - (C) strong action, lack of fear

9. "And whose lorries (trucks) are passing by to . . . dump the products that is manufactured by the rich at an *exorbitant* price—colour TVs, refrigerators, air conditioners, transistor radios?" (**Hint:** As in 8 above, notice the prefix *ex-*.)

- (A) too high
- (B) too low
- (C) reasonable

10. "I will tell you about *waste*. Recently the government built a skating rink. After three months, they demolished (destroyed) it because a highway going to be built over it . . ."

- (A) giving things away to people who really want them
- (B) inventing new things to replace the old ones
- (C) making or using things without need or benefit

11. "If someone passed away (died) there is an alarm in the kampong (village), where most of us would know who passed away and when he is going to be buried, what is the cause of death, and what happened to the *next of kin*—are they around?" (**Hint:** Think of the word *kindergarten*, which means a school for young children.)

- (A) close relatives
- (B) government officials
- (C) people who live next door

12. "It's not *polluted* in the village. Physical *pollution*, mental, social." (**Hint:** Remember that the speaker, Shafi, loves the village.)

- (A) contaminated, contamination
- (B) modernized, modernization
- (C) organized, organization

Read

Introduction

The following selection is taken from *Among the Believers: An Islamic Journey* by V. S. Naipaul, who was born in Trinidad and is considered one of the best writers of English of our times. It is his interview of Shafi, a young Muslim man in Kuala Lumpur, the capital city of Malaysia. Shafi used to live in a village, called a *kampong* in Malaysia, and finds that his new life as a city dweller is very different. As you read, try to understand Shafi's point of view. At the same time, notice what elements in his background give him this point of view. Before you start, think for a moment about what it would be like to move from a very small village to a large modern city.

- What aspects of the urban lifestyle do you imagine would appeal to him?
- Which aspects would disturb him or cause him trouble?

Conversations in Malaysia

A   Shafi worked for the Muslim cause. He didn't wear Arab clothes. But he understood the young men who did. Shafi had come to Kuala Lumpur from a village in the north. The disturbance of the move was still with him.

B   Shafi said: "When I was in the village, the atmosphere is entirely different. You come out of the village. You see all the bright lights, you begin to sense the materialistic civilization around you. And I forgot about my religion and my commitments—in the sense that you had to pray. But not to the extent of going out and doing nasty things like taking girls and drinking and gambling and drugs. I didn't lose my faith. I simply forgot to pray, forgot responsibilities. Just losing myself. I got nothing firm in my framework. I just floating around and didn't know my direction."

C   I said, "Where did you live when you came to Kuala Lumpur?"

D   He didn't give a straight answer. At this early stage in our conversation, concreteness didn't come easily to him. He said, "I was living in a suburb where I am exposed to materialistic civilization to which I had never been exposed before. Boys and girls can go out together. You are free from family control. You are free from society who normally criticize you in a village when you do something bad. You take a goat, a cow, a buffalo—somewhere where the goat is being tied up all the time—and you release that goat in a bunch of other animals: The goat would just roam anywhere he wanted to go without any strings."

▲ The calm life of the village.

E   "Is that bad for the goat?"

F   "I think the goat would be very happy to roam free. But for me, I don't think that would be good. If goat had brains, I would want to say, 'Why do you want to roam about when you are tied and being fed by your master and looked after? Why do you want to roam about?'"

G   I said, "But I want to roam about."

H   "What do you mean by being free? Freedom for me is not something that you can roam anywhere you want. Freedom must be within the definition of a certain framework. Because I don't think we are able to run around and get everything. That freedom means nothing. You must really frame yourself where you want to go and what you want to do."

I   "But didn't you know what you wanted to do when you came to Kuala Lumpur?"

J   "The primary aim was education. That was a framework. But the conflict of this freedom and the primary aim is there, and I consider this is the problem I faced and many of my friends face."

K   "Other people in other countries face the same problem."

L   Shafi said, "Do they face the same restrictions of family life as I do?"   45

M   "What restrictions?"

N   "Religious restrictions. You have that frame with you. Religious tradition, family life, the society, the village community. Then you come into the city, where people are running, people are free. The values contradict.   50

▲ The busy life of the city

O   "You see, in the village where I was brought up, we have the bare minimum. We have rice to eat, house to live. We didn't go begging. In the city, you can buy a lunch at ten dollars. Or in a stall, you can have a   55 lunch for 50 cents. That excess of nine-fifty which the city dwellers spend will be spent by us on other purposes. To us, with our framework and tradition and religion, that is excessiveness.   60

P   "Sometimes my wife feels that we should go back to the village, and I also feel the same. Not running away from the modern world, but trying to live a simpler, more meaningful life than coming to the city, where you have lots of waste and lots of things that is   65 not real probably. You are not honest to yourself if you can spend 50 cents and keep yourself from hunger, but instead spend ten dollars.

Q   "I will tell you about waste. Recently the government built a skating rink. After three months, they demolished it because a highway going to be built over it. They are building big roads and highways across the villages.   70 And whose lorries are passing by to collect the produce of the poor and to dump the products that is manufactured by the rich at an exorbitant price—colour TVs, refrigerators, air conditioners, transistor radios?"

R   "Don't people want those things?"

S   "In the end they are going to use the colour TVs—which the people   75 enjoy—to advertise products to draw people into wasteful living."

T   "Village life—wouldn't you say it is dull for most people?"

U   "The village? It's simple. It's devoid of—what shall I say?—wastefulness. You shouldn't waste. You don't have to rush for things. My point about going back to the *kampong* [village] is to stay with the community and not   80 to run away from development. The society is well-knit. If someone passed away there is an alarm in the kampong, where most of us would know who passed away and when he is going to be buried, what is the cause of death, and what happened to the next of kin—are they around? It's not polluted in the village. Physical pollution, mental, social." 85

V   "Social pollution?"

W   "Something that contradicts our customs and traditions. A man cannot walk with a woman who doesn't belong to his family in the kampong. It is forbidden."

X   "Why is it wrong?" 90

Y   "The very essence of human respect and dignity comes from an honourable relationship of man and woman. You must have a law to protect the unit of your society. You need your family to be protected. When the girls come from the villages to Kuala Lumpur, they don't want to be protected by the law." 95

Source: "Conversations in Malaysia" *Among the Believers: An Islamic Journey* (V. S. Naipaul)

After You Read

Strategy

Finding Support for Main Ideas
Specific details in the reading give support for the main ideas expressed. Identifying these details gives you a better understanding of the main ideas.

4 Finding Support for Main Ideas Read the pairs of statements below and check the one in each pair that expresses one of Shafi's ideas. Remember that you are looking for Shafi's ideas, not those of the author.

1. _____ City life is better than village life because it gives more freedom.

   _____ City life is not as good as village life because it lacks structure.

2. _____ People in the city are wasteful.

   _____ People in the village are dull.

3. _____ The city offers many wonderful products—color TVs, refrigerators, and so on—that improve people's lives.

   _____ The village (kampong) offers a sense of community that improves people's lives.

Now find at least two examples in the reading that support or illustrate each of the main ideas you chose above.

Paraphrasing

Paraphrasing means to state something in your own words. It could be the same length, shorter, or longer than the original. But the words used to express the idea are your own, and usually you say it in a manner that is easier to understand than the original. Paraphrasing is similar to summarizing in that you use your own words in both cases, but when you summarize, you recount just the main points, shortening the reading. When you paraphrase you don't necessarily shorten the selection.

5 **Paraphrasing** The following opinions are taken from the reading selection. In your own words, paraphrase them—rewrite in a clear way what the author or Shafi wants to say.

1. "He didn't give a straight answer. At this early stage in our conversation, concreteness didn't come easily to him."

   He didn't reply to my question in a direct way. We had just started
   talking and he still didn't feel comfortable with me so he didn't give
   examples and details from his life.

2. "You take a goat, a cow, a buffalo—somewhere where the goat is being tied up all the time—and you release that goat in a bunch of other animals: The goat would just roam anywhere he want to go without any strings."

   _____
   _____
   _____
   _____

3. "In the end they are going to use the colour TVs—which the people enjoy—to advertise products to draw people into wasteful living."

   _____
   _____
   _____
   _____

4. "It's not polluted in the village. Physical pollution, mental, social."

   _____
   _____
   _____
   _____

6 Guided Academic Conversation In small groups, discuss the following questions. Then compare your answers with those of other students.

1. What problems does Shafi have in adjusting to city life? In your opinion, what will probably happen to him and his wife if they stay in the city? What will probably happen if they go back to the village? Explain.

2. Do you agree or disagree with Shafi's ideas about the need for a framework? Do you have a framework in your life? If a person moves to a new place with very different customs, should he or she change and imitate the new customs or not? Why?

3. When Shafi gives an example of the excess and wastefulness of city life, he talks about the difference between a lunch of ten dollars and a lunch of 50 cents. He speaks as if the nine dollars and fifty cents were simply thrown away and would not benefit anyone in any way. What might a city person argue in defense of the ten-dollar lunch?

4. After reading the article, what do you think of Shafi's English? Does he communicate well or badly? Is he clear? Are there times when it is all right to speak global English (like Shafi's English that you examined more closely in Exercise 2 on page 109)?

7 Interviewing a Classmate: A Time of Transition Work with a partner and follow these steps.

Step 1 Ask your partner to identify an important transition that he or she has made—for example, a move from one place to another, a change of lifestyle, a change of job, a marriage, and so on.

▲ Transitions can be challenging.

Step 2 Write down four or five questions to ask your partner about his or her transition. Try to focus on how the other person's point of view has changed or is changing because of the transition. For example, you might write "How do you view the freedom a single person has now that you're married?"

Step 3 Ask your partner the questions. On a piece of paper, take notes on the answers. Then hand your notes in to the teacher or share them with the class.

Recognizing Regional Vocabulary Differences

The two most common types of Standard English that people learn are British or American*. Recognizing national differences in vocabulary can help you in dealing with people who have learned English in these different traditions or in reading materials from these countries.

In Naipaul's interview with Shafi could you tell which type of Standard English the author used and which type Shafi's global English is based on? Two words that immediately stand out as the British form of English are *lorries* and *honourable*. Americans do not use the word *lorry*, and many of them would not even know what it means; instead they say *truck*. *Honourable* would be spelled *honorable*— without the *u*—by an American. Can you find any other British words or spellings in the interview?

How good are you at spotting differences in vocabulary and spelling between American and British English? Do you know which of the two types has retained the longer, more old-fashioned way of spelling certain words and which one now spells them in a shorter way? You will have a chance to practice in the next exercise.

8 **Recognizing Regional Vocabulary Differences** Read the pairs of words below and determine which of the words in each pair is American and which is British. Underline the American word; circle the British word.

Vocabulary Differences

1. subway / underground
2. (electric) flex / cord
3. stove / cooker
4. (car) hood / bonnet
5. flashlight / torch

Spelling Differences

1. programme / program
2. cheque / check
3. color / colour
4. catalogue / catalog
5. behavior / behaviour

9 **What Do You Think?** Read the paragraph on page 118 and discuss the questions that follow.

---

*Of course there are other types of Standard English, too, such as Australian, Canadian, New Zealand, etc. Each of these has some of its own special words and ways of spelling.

The Refugee Problem

▲ Young refugees in Indonesia after the tsunami of December 2004

A popular definition of a refugee is a person in flight from a desperate situation, whether it be war, change of borders, political or religious persecution. According to the U.S. Committee for Refugees, there are approximately 15 million refugees and asylum seekers in the world today. In addition, 22 million persons have been forced into exile within their own countries. Women and children make up about 80 percent of the world's refugees.

1. In your opinion, what is the obligation of stable and prosperous countries towards these refugees?
2. How many should be allowed to enter prosperous nations?
3. Which refugees should be accepted and which ones turned away?

Part 2 Reading Skills and Strategies

Grisha Has Arrived

Before You Read

Strategy

Selecting Adjectives to Fit the Context
Well-chosen adjectives bring the characters and setting of a story to life. Practice noticing good adjectives when you read and then try to use them in your own English writing and speaking.

1 **Selecting Adjectives to Fit the Context** Adjectives from the story *Grisha Has Arrived* along with their definitions, are given in the chart below. Read the sentences that follow the chart and fill in the blanks with the appropriate adjectives. If you cannot guess a word from its definition and context, scan the story for that word.

Adjective	Definition
exhausted	very, very tired, completely fatigued
exquisite	unusually beautiful and fine
Herculean	very difficult (like the tasks of Hercules)
indefatigable	untiring, incapable of fatigue
inebriated	drunk, intoxicated by alcohol or emotion
marshy	swampy, soft, and wet like a swamp or marsh
mundane	ordinary, without special meaning
prosaic	dull, unimaginative, like prose (instead of poetry)
rejuvenated	brought back to youth, made young again
shabby	worn out, poor, dilapidated

1. Grandma would put on her blue-checkered apron and seem instantly ___*rejuvenated*___.

2. Their _____, sooty kitchen suddenly became bright and cheerful.

3. The stove would become the airport in the "_____ forest."

4. There was an amber brooch, perfumes, books, wooden spoons, and a small _____ box from Boris.

5. Grisha was _____ by these bright photographs and looked at his sister with admiration.

6. Grisha took childish pleasure in everything and was very enthusiastic. He was _____ in his activity.

7. The mountain of goods on the living room floor grew . . . but the shopping list hardly got shorter . . . It was a _____ task.

8. She had expected a very significant moment in her life—the family reunion—and it had turned out to be very _____, even _____.

9. Suddenly Inna felt _____.

Recognizing a Flashback

A flashback in a story is the description of a scene that happened earlier, before the time of the main story. It is important to notice the time change. Flashbacks often give us information about the characters, the setting (time and place), or the plot (events that form the action).

Remember that **scan** means to search for specific information.

2 **Recognizing a Flashback** The story begins with a flashback. Scan the first part of the story to find out when the flashback occurred to Inna, the main character. You might want to begin by scanning for the main character's name.

When did the scene described in the flashback occur?

a. in her childhood

b. late in her teens

c. when she was an adult

Read

Introduction

What is it like to leave your home and move to another country? Many people go through this transition. They often speak of being "uprooted," like a tree that has been transplanted into new ground. The following story was written by a Russian woman who left her native country and immigrated to Edmonton in western Canada. It describes her brother Grisha's visit at a time when Russia had a Communist government, and goods and commodities were very difficult to obtain. The situation has changed and many Russians now say, "Back then we had money, but there was nothing to buy; today there is plenty to buy, but we have no money!" In either case, there is a great difference in the material standard of living between Russia and Canada. Read the story to see if this creates problems for Inna and her brother Grisha.

- In your opinion, what problems can a difference in the material standard of living cause between relatives living in two different countries?

Strategy

Predicting Story Events

Predicting action in a story helps comprehension by forcing us to think ahead of what we are reading. As you read a story, try to think ahead of the plot by asking yourself, "What will happen next?"

3 **Predicting Story Events** Read the story below. It will be interrupted in a few places and you will be asked questions about what you've just read and about what you think will happen next. Check the story to confirm or correct your answers.

Grisha Has Arrived[1]

Whenever Grisha was expected in the apartment on Novosibirskaya Street, *Babushka* made some *pirozhki*[2] filled with meat and cabbage. She would put on her blue-checkered apron and seem instantly rejuvenated. Little Inna would seal these pirozhki on a wooden board while Babushka presided over the boiling oil. Their shabby, sooty kitchen suddenly became 5 bright and cheerful. In this way, Grisha's arrival became forever linked to an expectation of joyful festivity.

He would rush in, thin and pale. At once the long hallway, dimly lit by a single electric bulb, was filled with lively bustle. They played in the kitchen. It was warmer there. Babushka covered the large stove with an oilcloth. 10 The stove would become the airport in the "marshy forest." Grisha made paper airplanes and launched them skillfully from the stove towards the electric light. The small, white airplanes briefly shone against the soot-covered ceiling and fell into the dark space near the door.

Grisha would bring his tin soldiers. He was a guerrilla leader and little 15 Inna was a doctor. They always played the same war game. Inna's military hospital was located in Babushka's room. Could Inna ever forget this narrow room with the fireplace and the photograph of a young woman on the dressing table? There, among various treasures with which Inna was not allowed to play, was a carved box with letters. 20

Later she would read these yellowed sheets which Babushka had preserved so carefully. They were letters from her mother who had died in a labour camp. Inna could not remember her parents. She had been raised by Babushka, while Grisha had been adopted by relatives of their father.

Memory is a strange thing! In its vast foggy valleys one's past is kept 25 untouched. Now, when 42-year-old Inna was on the way to the airport to meet her brother coming from Moscow, the smell of the swamp grass suddenly released distant memories of frying pirozhki, of childhood, of bliss . . .

---

[1] The story has been shortened but not changed in any other way.
[2] Two Russian words are used in this sentence, *Babushka* (Grandmother) and *pirozhki* (meat pies), which many English speakers know and others would guess from the context. Later in the story, the Russian word *dacha* (country house) is used.

Stop and Predict A conflict does not always mean a problem. Sometimes it is just a change. In this case, the conflict that begins the story is the arrival of Grisha. In the flashback, what do we learn of Inna and Grisha's family? Why is he especially important to Inna? What do you think she expects from his visit? Finish the statement below to predict what happens next.

When Inna sees Grisha she will be _____.

    (A) happy to see he has not changed at all

    (B) surprised to see he is dressed in shabby clothes

    (C) sad to find he is very depressed

On the stairs of the airport, Inna came face to face with Grisha, but did not recognize him at first. His hair had gone completely grey and he seemed shorter. She was struck at once by how badly he was dressed. He was wearing a brown raincoat fit only for picking mushrooms. His worn out shoes were of an indefinable colour. Grisha was carrying a small suitcase.

They embraced, kissed, and walked slowly to her car. Grisha was telling her excitedly about the flight across the ocean, about the last days before departure, how frightened he had been that he might fall ill and be unable to come.

Inna was listening to Grisha happily and distractedly. She realized that he must be tired from lack of sleep, but why this pathetic shabbiness? Why would Yelena have allowed him to leave home in this godforsaken state? They had a marvelous apartment and *dacha* [country house]. Both were working, and Grisha earned substantial amounts from translations.

As though he had read her mind, Grisha said: "Do you know, all our acquaintances advised me to travel in my oldest clothes so that I could discard them without regret here. They said that you, my sister, anyway would clothe me and Yelena and our children."

Maybe it was because she had no family of her own that Inna was very attached to Grisha's children. She gave them expensive presents and spoiled them, especially his oldest daughter, Lyuba. Inna tolerated Yelena, no more than that. Her relationship with her brother's wife had gone wrong from the very beginning. Probably deep down Inna envied Yelena . . .

They soon reached home. Inna put a bowl with fruit on the table and a bottle of French wine which she had bought yesterday to welcome Grisha.

Grisha opened his suitcase and brought out presents from himself and Yelena, from Lyuba and Yura who had already had families of their own, and from Inna's numerous friends and relatives. There was an amber brooch, perfumes, books, wooden spoons, and a small exquisite box from Boris. He had put a sheet of paper with comical verses for Inna's birthday into the box. How many years had passed since she had seen his familiar bold handwriting?

▲ Immigrants find comfort in keeping up with their traditions.

Inna had been a young girl in Moscow when she had become involved with Boris, who was much older. On various occasions, he had left his wife to move in with Inna. At other times, he had left her to return to his family. Inna had been his friend, his mistress, his graduate student, and eventually his co-worker in the laboratory. This pattern of life had continued up to the time of her leaving Moscow.

Brother and sister sat on the balcony, smoking and talking almost till dawn. From the 12th floor, there was a view over Edmonton and the dark river valley spanned by a bridge. Below them the street lights shone moistly.

Stop and Predict Why did Grisha arrive in shabby clothing? What do we find out about Inna's relationship with Grisha's wife and children? What do we find out about Boris?

Finish this statement to predict what happens next.

Grisha will show a great interest in his sister's _____ .

- (A) thoughts and feelings
- (B) work and ambitions
- (C) possessions and appliances

Grisha walked about the apartment inspecting Inna's habitation. For a while, he remained in the bedroom where, beside the bed, there was a large desk with a computer. On the chest of drawers, he found their mother's faded photograph in its walnut frame, that had stood in Babushka's room. In the kitchen, he wanted to know how the dishwasher worked and opened the door to the microwave oven.

Inna made a bed for Grisha on the living room sofa. The following morning she got up as early as usual. She was tired from lack of sleep and took two Tylenol tablets before going into the kitchen to prepare breakfast. Grisha was up already and was doing yoga exercises on the balcony.

After breakfast they went for a walk and then to the university. Inna showed Grisha her laboratory. As it was a holiday, the university campus was deserted. They ate in a small Chinese restaurant. The evening was spent sitting on the balcony. Inna brought out albums with photographs taken on various trips: one to France and Spain, another to the Scandinavian countries, still another to South America, and finally one to Indonesia and Hong Kong.

Grisha was inebriated by these bright photographs and looked at his sister with admiration.

They were drinking tea with cake when Grisha suddenly asked:

"How much does a Lada[3] cost here?"

"I don't know, perhaps around five thousand or maybe seven. Why do you want to know?" Inna was very surprised.

"You see, it can be paid for here, and Yura would be able to get it in Moscow. Many people buy them in this way for their relatives."

"Really? They buy a whole car?"

"Of course, they can't buy it in pieces, can they?" Grisha started laughing.

The magnitude of his expectations and naïve faith in her financial prowess struck Inna like a splash of cold water. All her achievements, of which she had been so proud only yesterday, were reduced to rubble and lost their significance.

The woman in the rocking chair was suddenly middle-aged and lonely.

"For myself, I bought a secondhand car and that was almost seven years ago."

Inna cut herself short. In the depth of Grisha's eyes as in two dark mirrors she saw herself as she must have appeared to him—a rich world traveler.

Stop and Predict What do we learn about Inna's work and lifestyle? What impresses Grisha? Why does Inna suddenly feel old and lonely?

Finish this statement to predict what happens next.

Inna and her brother will spend a lot of their time _____ .

- Ⓐ talking
- Ⓑ traveling
- Ⓒ shopping

Every morning Grisha got up early and did yoga exercises frantically. Then he went to the swimming pool. The high-rise building in which Inna lived had a sauna and whirlpool in the basement. Grisha took childish pleasure in everything and was very enthusiastic. He was indefatigable. Inna took a vacation in order to devote herself completely to her brother.

She showed him the sports complex which belonged to the university. They pushed a shopping cart around the superstore which was the size of an airplane hangar. They bought groceries and Grisha had his picture taken against a backdrop of mountains of fruits and vegetables and colourful cans of cat food.

They spent a whole day at West Edmonton Mall, the world-famous shopping centre. They wandered through the shops, inspected Fantasyland,

---

[3]A type of Russian car

and, while there, took a trip in a submarine. They had lunch in a French 125 café.

The mountain of goods on the living room floor grew and threatened to become Mt. Everest, but the shopping list hardly got shorter. A sheepskin coat for Lyuba, high winter boots for Yura's wife, a waterproof coat for Yelena, a 130 videotape recorder, some kind of rings for the camera of the sister of Lyuba's husband, a Japanese walkman radio for Yura, and a mouthpiece for a trumpet belonging to some person unknown to her. It was a 135 Herculean task.

Grisha had excellent taste and an unfailing sense for what was beautiful and very expensive. He said to Inna: "We must buy this blouse for Lyuba." The blouse was 140 certainly unusually pretty. Inna would have bought it for herself if it had been on sale.

Goodness, how she had waited for him, her only brother! She would have liked to complain to him of her loneliness, 145 the fact that her job was only a temporary five-year contract, and that her future

▲ Shopping in malls like the huge Edmonton Mall is a favorite pastime of visitors.

looked extremely uncertain. After all was said and done, the trips that she had taken to conferences and seminars were all that she possessed.

His visit lasted over two weeks and, not counting the first evening, 150 when they had sat on the balcony and smoked, there had not been a free moment when they could have had a heart-to-heart talk. She wondered if such a talk was even possible. She had expected a very significant moment in her life—the family reunion—and it had turned out to be very prosaic, even mundane. 155

The gap between brother and sister was widening at an alarming rate. His trip gradually became transformed into a giant shopping expedition to North America. Each day spent wandering through stores moved them further apart into mutual incomprehension.

Once Inna took Grisha to dinner with Lyova who (amazing 160 coincidence!) had been Grisha's fellow pupil in the eighth grade of Moscow school #214. Inna's and Grisha's arrival was eagerly awaited in the elegant two-story house overlooking the ravine. Other guests were drinking cocktails on the wooden veranda surrounded by creepers. Later on, there was a barbecue on the lawn. Grisha was enthusiastic about the barbecued 165 meat, which he had never tasted before. For dessert, Lyova's wife brought out a basket carved out of a pineapple filled with large, fresh strawberries.

Grisha soaked up all this like a sponge. He committed it to memory, imagining how he would relate every minute detail in Moscow. To Grisha, Inna's new life must seem just such a fragrant pineapple-strawberry basket, which only lacked immortality to be perfect. 170

Suddenly Inna felt exhausted. She felt that she was participating in some sort of farce, that she was on stage and Grisha was viewing her from the back of a hall without being able to hear her. The loneliness became unbearable.

Stop and Predict How do Inna and Grisha spend their time together? Do you think they are enjoying themselves at Lyova's party? Why or why not?

Finish this statement to predict what happens next.

Before Grisha leaves, Inna will _____ .

- (A) have a heart-to-heart talk with him about her situation
- (B) get angry with him about his selfishness
- (C) remain silent about her true feelings

People were laughing on the veranda. In the house, Lyova demonstrated his new stereo system with the compact disk player to Grisha. Through the open window, Inna could see Grisha's forced smile and the sweat droplets on his forehead. She felt sorry for him and wanted more than anything for him to leave as soon as possible. 180

She went down from the veranda and walked along the path to the ravine. The air smelt fresh and moist. From that angle, her friend's brightly lit house seemed even grander.

"I wonder how Boris would have behaved?" she thought. "Was it possible that he, too . . . ?" 185

"*Experience determines consciousness.*" Inna remembered the long-forgotten Marxist formula.

During the last days before leaving, Grisha could talk only of the customs inspection in Moscow. He flew off on July 15th.

"Next time I will bring Yelena," Grisha promised when leaving. 190

From the airport, Inna drove straight to work. She was sad and felt like crying. The small white airplane of her childhood vanished in the empty blue sky.

Source: "Grisha Has Arrived" *Newest Review* (Tanya Filanovsky, translated from Russian by Ruth Schachter)

After You Read

Avoiding "Traps" in Standardized Vocabulary Tests

Many vocabulary tests are similar to the activity below. Each item is a sentence with a word in **bold** type, and this is followed by four choices. You must choose the best synonym or definition for the word in bold. Here are some tips to help you avoid the "traps" that often accompany this test design.

1. The choices may include a word that sounds and looks like the word in bold and begins with the same letter. It is usually but not always wrong. Do not choose a word because of its similar sound or appearance. Choose it because its meaning is similar. Five items in the following exercise have choices like this. Which numbers are they? _____

2. The choices may include an antonym of the word in bold. Because we learn by association, it is easy to fall into this trap and choose a word that means exactly the opposite of the correct one. Four of the items in the following exercise have antonyms among the choices. Which numbers are they?

   _____

3. The answer key may be in another section or on a different page. Be careful to fill in the correct circle. Sometimes it helps to say the letter in your mind until you have filled it in.

Practice Read the sentences and choose the word or phrase that best explains the meaning of the boldfaced word(s). If necessary, scan for the word(s) in the story on pages 121–126 to see them in another context. Words are given in the order they appear in the story.

1. Babushka **presided over** the boiling oil.
   - Ⓐ pressed down on
   - Ⓑ carried away, removed
   - Ⓒ lit the fire under
   - Ⓓ was in charge of, watched out for

2. At once the long hallway . . . was filled with lively **bustle**.
   - Ⓐ inactivity
   - Ⓑ games
   - Ⓒ children
   - Ⓓ movement

3. Later she would read these **yellowed** sheets . . .
   - Ⓐ colorful
   - Ⓑ mellowed
   - Ⓒ aged
   - Ⓓ sunny

4. Inna was listening to Grisha happily and **distractedly**.
- (A) absentmindedly, not carefully
- (B) noticeably, intentionally
- (C) carefully, with great attention
- (D) clearly, without hearing surrounding noises

5. Why would Yelena have allowed him to leave home in this **godforsaken state**?
- (A) God-loving country
- (B) Godless part of a country
- (C) sloppy, neglected condition
- (D) unforgiven, unpardoned way

6. Probably deep down Inna **envied** Yelena . . .
- (A) was jealous of
- (B) became tired of
- (C) watched out for
- (D) felt sorry for

7. . . . his expectations and **naïve** faith in her financial prowess struck Inna like a splash of cold water.
- (A) wise, insightful
- (B) innocent, simple
- (C) happy, smiling
- (D) negative, terrible

8. All her achievements . . . were **reduced to rubble** . . .
- (A) found in a field
- (B) examined by the police
- (C) made to seem unimportant
- (D) proudly presented

9. . . . Inna and Grisha's arrival was eagerly awaited in the elegant two-story house overlooking the **ravine**.
- (A) high mountain
- (B) small road
- (C) narrow valley
- (D) rushing water

10. She felt that she was participating in some sort of **farce**.
- (A) face lift
- (B) serious drama
- (C) ridiculous comedy
- (D) complicated dance

4 Guided Academic Conversation In small groups, discuss these questions.

1. What went wrong with Grisha's visit to his sister Inna?

2. Do you think that Inna should buy a car for Grisha's son, Yura? Why or why not?

3. What quotation of Karl Marx does Inna remember at the end of the story? Why does it seem important to her? What do you think of it?

4. The story begins and ends with the image of an airplane. What does the airplane represent in Inna's memory of childhood? What does the airplane represent at the end?

5. Which is more important to you: family feeling or material success? In your opinion, why are these two aspects of life often in conflict?

IDENTIFYING SPELLING DIFFERENCES

Just as there are vocabulary differences in the English spoken in different countries, it is important to recognize that some English words are also spelled differently in British, Canadian, and American English.

---

5 Identifying Spelling Differences Look at the differences between American and British spelling described on page 117. Americans write *labor camp, gray, color, center, colorful*. How are these words spelled in Tanya Filanovsky's story that was translated by a Canadian? Can you explain why Canadian spelling is more like British spelling than American spelling? The answer has to do more with history than with geography.

1. labor camp _____

2. gray _____

3. color _____

4. center _____

5. colorful _____

6 Summarizing a Story Write a summary from six to nine sentences of the story "Grisha Has Arrived," following these guidelines. (See Chapter 1, page 23 for more on summarizing.)

1. Identify the two main characters and setting, and state the conflict. (1–2 sentences)

2. Describe the complication, in this case involving Grisha's actions and Inna's needs and feelings. (2–3 sentences)

3. Describe the climax (crisis, or high point of the plot) that occurs at Lyova's party and brings a new insight (way of thinking) to Inna. (1–2 sentences)

4. State the resolution at the end (the part that solves or finishes the conflict and brings the story to a close). (1–2 sentences)

7 Focusing on Words from the Academic Word List Read the excerpt below taken from the reading in Part 2. Fill in the blanks with a word from the box. Do not look back at the reading right away; instead, see if you can now remember the vocabulary.

achievements	financial	inspecting
computer	found	significance
finally		

Grisha walked about the apartment _____ Inna's

  1

habitation. For a while, he remained in the bedroom where, beside the

bed, there was a large desk with a _____. On the

  2

chest of drawers, he _____ their mother's faded

  3

photograph in its walnut frame, that had stood in Babushka's room . . .

The evening was spent sitting on the balcony. Inna brought out 5

albums with photographs taken on various trips: one to France and

Spain, another to the Scandinavian countries, still another to South

America, and _____ one to Indonesia and Hong Kong . . .

  4

The magnitude of his expectations and naïve faith in her 10

_____ prowess struck Inna like a splash of cold water.

  5

All her _____, of which she had been so proud only

  6

yesterday, were reduced to rubble and lost their _____.

  7

8 Role-Playing Work with a partner. One of you plays the role of Grisha, who is visiting your city. Use your imagination to invent answers. The other one plays the role of a radio commentator interviewing Grisha with the following questions. After you finish, the radio commentator may be asked to tell the class about Grisha's impressions.

1. How are things with your wife and children in Russia now?

2. Why have you come here to visit?

3. What has impressed you most about our city?

4. What is your greatest wish?

1 Making Connections Do some research on the Internet and take notes on one of the following topics. Share your results with the class or in a small group.

Immigrating to a New Country Think of a country that you or someone you know might find interesting to immigrate to one day. Then look on the Internet to find the rules for immigrating to this country. Who can get in? How does the country decide if you can immigrate there? Does this country accept refugees? How many rules are there and what are they?

Immigrants' Stories Go to some immigrant chat rooms or other sites on the Internet where immigrants discuss their experiences. What are the problems and success stories you hear from them?

Different Kinds of English Around the World With the increased use of English in world business, information technology, science, and diplomacy, more people are learning the language than ever before. However, around the globe different kinds of English with different accents and dialects are being spoken and taught. Look up information on global English, similar to the English that Shafi speaks (also called Inter-English or WSSE for World Standard Spoken English). Or, if you prefer, look up information on one of the following types of English: Australian, Canadian, Caribbean, East Indian, Irish, Scottish, South African, or on one of the hybrid (combination) varieties, like Spanglish (Spanish and English) or Japlish (Japanese and English). When, where, and how is this kind of English used? What are its characteristics? What do people think of it?

▲ Global English is used around the world.

Responding in Writing

WRITING TIP: USING A FLASHBACK

Think back to an earlier experience (a flashback) to help you clarify in your writing the past cause for a present feeling or situation.

2 Writing on a Topic Read the topic below. Write an essay on it, following the steps below.

> **Topic**
> Describe how a transition you went through in your life affected your present situation physically, emotionally, financially, or spiritually.

Step 1 Brainstorm on the topic. You may want to use a cluster diagram (see Chapter 3, page 75) or just make a list. List how the transition you went through could have affected your physical life (your financial situation, where you live, etc.) or your emotional or spiritual situation (you are happier, more fearful, more mature, have different beliefs, etc. because of this transition). If you cannot think of any such transition in your life, feel free to invent one!

Step 2 Organize your thoughts. Decide from your list or diagram which transition you would like to discuss and which are the most important effects of this transition on your life today. You may later choose to cross out those you decide not to use.

Step 3 Find your main point. Write a sentence or two that sums up the transition you went through and your main discovery about it. You may decide later to use this at the beginning or at the ending of your composition.

Step 4 Write about who you are today, including a flashback to the transition. You may want to begin with the flashback—the description of a scene that happened earlier—explaining the transition you went through, and then turn to a discussion of who you are today because of it. Or, on the other hand, you may want to begin with who you are today, "flashback" to your transition, and then return to your situation today.

Step 5 Tie into your main point. Put your theme sentence(s) from Step 3 at the beginning or end of your composition and make sure that all your sentences relate to the theme.

Step 6 Read and revise your composition, adding a title to it. Exchange with a friend and see if you can make helpful comments on each others' compositions before handing them in along with your diagrams or lists.

Self-Assessment Log

Read the lists below. Check (✓) the strategies and vocabulary that you learned in this chapter. Look through the chapter or ask your instructor about the strategies and words that you do not understand.

Reading and Vocabulary-Building Strategies

❑ Making comparisons
❑ Identifying the difference between standard English and global English
❑ Getting meaning from word structure and context
❑ Finding support for main ideas
❑ Paraphrasing
❑ Recognizing regional vocabulary differences
❑ Selecting adjectives to fit the context
❑ Recognizing a flashback
❑ Predicting story events
❑ Identifying spelling differences
❑ Summarizing a story

Target Vocabulary

Nouns

❑ achievements*
❑ commitments*
❑ computer*
❑ concreteness
❑ excessiveness
❑ framework*
❑ next of kin
❑ pollution

❑ restrictions*
❑ significance*
❑ waste

Verbs

❑ found (find)*
❑ inspecting*
❑ roam

Adjectives

❑ exhausted
❑ exorbitant
❑ exquisite
❑ financial*
❑ Herculean
❑ indefatigable
❑ inebriated
❑ marshy

❑ materialistic
❑ mundane
❑ nasty
❑ polluted
❑ prosaic
❑ rejuvenated

Adverb

❑ finally*

---

* These words are from the Academic Word List. For more information on this list, see www.vuw.ac.nz/lals/research/awl.

6

The Mind

In This Chapter

Many scientists speak of the mind as the "new frontier," the most dynamic area of research. The first selection discusses some amazing research results by psychologists who have been studying people with an extraordinary ability to remember or memorize. Then the classical mystery writer Edgar Allan Poe provides an inside look at the disordered and diseased mind of a madman. Finally, there is a timed reading about a very unusual musical genius.

❝ Glasses are a vehicle for the eyes, the eyes are a vehicle for the mind, the mind is a vehicle for insight, and insight is a vehicle for the conscience. ❞

—M. Fethullah Gülen
Turkish scholar and writer (b. 1938)

Connecting to the Topic

1 Do you think that scientific studies of the brain like the one in the photograph are important? Why or why not?

2 What other ways are there to learn about the human mind?

3 According to the quotation, what is the purpose of the mind? Do you agree with this?

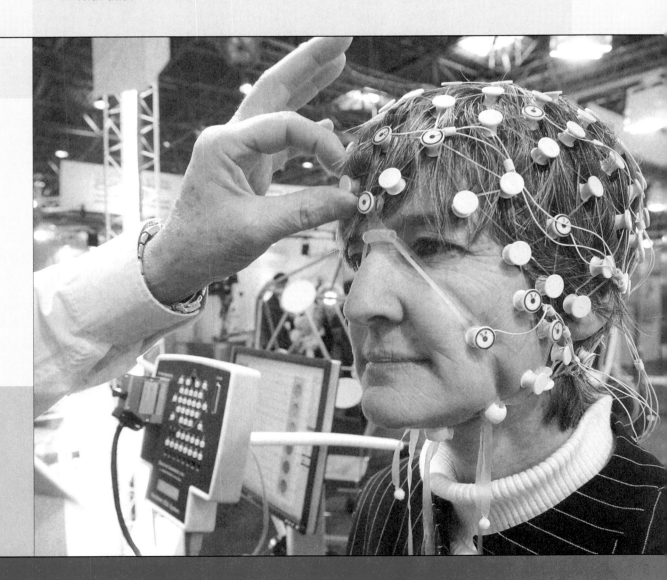

A Memory for All Seasonings

Before You Read

Strategy

Previewing and Predicting
As you learned in Chapter 2 on page 28, before beginning to read an article, it's helpful to preview it and predict what it might be about. Try to figure out the topic and main ideas. Then think about what associations or connections there are between your life and the topic. Ask yourself: What do I already know about this topic? This will improve your comprehension.

 1 Previewing and Predicting The following article is longer than the ones in previous chapters, so you should preview it and try to grasp the main ideas. Answer the following questions. Then share your answers with a partner.

1. Look at the title. What part of the mind will be discussed in this article?

_____

_____

2. Scan the article and look for these words: *psychologists, study, research.* Do you think you will get one point of view on the mind or several different ones?

_____

_____

3. Is there something practical you might learn from this reading? Where in the article do you find references to *mnemonics* or *memory tricks*?

_____

_____

4. What is the earliest event in your life that you can remember and approximately how old were you when it occurred?

_____

_____

_____

_____

5. Why do you suppose you can remember the event in question 4?

_____

_____

2 **Identifying Synonyms** Read the phrases and words in the columns below. Determine if the word in the second column is a correct synonym of the italicized word in the first column. Check the True box if the word is a synonym. Check the False box if it is not. You can scan the reading for the phrase to get more context.

Vocabulary	Synonym?	True	False
1. a *fashionable* restaurant	poor	❑	❑
2. Polson didn't think this was *exceptional*	unusual	❑	❑
3. Polson was *impressed* enough to ask	sad	❑	❑
4. he would be glad to *cooperate*	work with others	❑	❑
5. with an *extraordinary* memory	normal	❑	❑
6. have *memorized* every note	learned by heart	❑	❑
7. considered the *exclusive* gift of the genius	unique	❑	❑
8. We studied a *novice* and watched him grow into an expert.	beginner	❑	❑
9. *intellectual skills* were considered average	abilities of the mind	❑	❑
10. can be *adequately* described as	badly	❑	❑
11. he disliked being her *subordinate*	boss	❑	❑
12. just trying . . . does not *insure* that your memory will improve	guarantee	❑	❑
13. how long meat should be cooked . . . he hears "*rare*, medium, well-done,"	not very cooked	❑	❑
14. he can encode . . . fast and *effortlessly*	with difficulty	❑	❑

Read

Introduction

Memory is one of the most important functions of the mind. Without our memories, we would have no identity and no continuity from past to present to future. The following article is about a *mnemonist*, a person with an extraordinary power to remember. The title, *A Memory for All Seasonings,* includes a pun, a form of humor based on a play on words. The usual phrase to describe something constant and dependable is *for all seasons*. Here the phrase is changed to *for all seasonings* because this mnemonist happens to be a waiter. A waiter serves food, and *seasonings* is another word for spices used in food, such as salt, pepper, and curry.

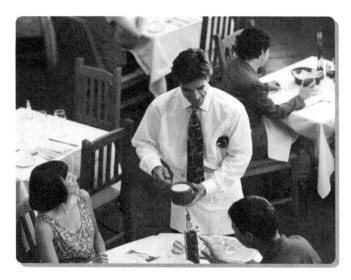

- In what way does a good memory help a waiter?
- For what other jobs is it helpful to have a good memory?
- Why do you think some people are better at remembering than others? What do you think the people who study memory have discovered on this topic?

Address www.memorizeit.net

A Memory for All Seasonings

A   One evening two years ago, Peter Polson, a member of the psychology department at the University of Colorado, took his son and daughter to dinner at Bananas, a fashionable restaurant in Boulder. When the waiter took their orders, Polson noticed that the young man didn't write anything down. He just listened, made small talk, told them that his name was John Conrad, and left. Polson didn't think this was exceptional: There were, after all, only three of them at the table. Yet he found himself watching Conrad closely when he returned to take the orders at a nearby table of eight. Again the waiter listened, chatted, and wrote nothing down. When he brought Polson and his children their dinners, the professor couldn't resist introducing himself and telling Conrad that he'd been observing him.

B   The young man was pleased. He wanted customers to notice that, unlike other waiters, he didn't use a pen and paper. Sometimes, when they did notice, they left him quite a large tip. He had once handled a table of 19 complete dinner orders without a single error. At Bananas, a party of 19 (a bill of roughly $200) would normally leave the waiter a $35 tip. They had left Conrad $85. [These days that bill would be more like $400 with a 20 percent tip of about $80.]

C   Polson was impressed enough to ask the waiter whether he would like to come to the university's psychology lab and let them run some tests on him. Anders Ericsson, a young Swedish psychologist recently involved in memory research, would be joining the university faculty soon, and Polson thought that he would be interested in exploring memory methods with the waiter. Conrad said he would be glad to cooperate. He was always on the lookout for ways to increase his income, and Polson told him he would receive $5 an hour to be a guinea pig.

▲ Conductor Arturo Toscanini had an extraordinary memory.

D   Conrad, of course, was not the first person with an extraordinary memory to attract attention from researchers. Alexander R. Luria, the distinguished Soviet psychologist, studied a Russian newspaper reporter named Shereshevskii for many years and wrote about him in *The Mind of a Mnemonist* (Basic Books, 1968). Luria says that Shereshevskii was able to hear a series of 50 words spoken once and recite them back in perfect order 15 years later. Another famous example of extraordinary memory, the conductor Arturo Toscanini, was known to have memorized every note for every instrument in 250 symphonies and 100 operas.

E   For decades, the common belief among psychologists was that memory was a fixed quantity; an exceptional memory, or a poor one, was something with which a person was born.

F   This point of view has come under attack in recent years; expert memory is no longer universally considered the exclusive gift of the genius, or the abnormal. "People with astonishing memory for pictures, musical scores, chess positions, business transactions, dramatic scripts, or faces are by no means unique," wrote Cornell psychologist Ulric Neisser in *Memory Observed* (1981). "They may not even be very rare." Some university researchers, including Polson and Ericsson, go a step further than Neisser. They believe that there are no physiological differences at all between the memory of a Shereshevskii or a Toscanini and that of the average person. The only real difference, they believe, is that Toscanini trained his memory, exercised it regularly, and wanted to improve it.

G   Like many people with his capacity to remember, Toscanini may also have used memory tricks called *mnemonics*. Shereshevskii, for example, employed a technique known as *loci*. As soon as he heard a series of words, he mentally "distributed" them along Gorky Street in Moscow. If one of the words was *orange*, he might visualize a man stepping on an orange at a precise location on the familiar street. Later, in order to retrieve *orange*, he would take an imaginary walk down Gorky Street and see the image from which it could easily be recalled. Did the waiter at Bananas have such a system? What was his secret?

H   John Conrad would be the subject of Anders Ericsson's second in-depth study of the machinations of memory. As a research associate at Carnegie-Mellon University in Pittsburgh, Ericsson had spent the previous three years working with William Chase on an extensive study of Steve Faloon, an undergraduate whose memory and intellectual skills were considered average. When Ericsson and Chase began testing Faloon, he could remember no more than seven random digits after hearing them spoken once. According to generally accepted research, almost everyone is capable of storing five to nine random digits in short-term memory. After 20 months of working with Chase and Ericsson, Faloon could memorize and retrieve 80 digits.

I   "The important thing about our testing Faloon is that researchers usually study experts," Chase says. "We studied a novice and watched him grow into an expert. Initially, we were just running tests to see whether his digit span could be expanded. For four days he could not go beyond seven digits. On the fifth day he discovered his mnemonic system and then began to improve rapidly."

J   Faloon's intellectual abilities didn't change, the researchers say. Nor did the storage capacity of his short-term memory. Chase and Ericsson believe that short-term memory is a more or less fixed quantity. It reaches saturation quickly, and to overcome its limitations, one must learn to link new data with material that is permanently stored in long-term memory. Once the associations have been made, the short-term memory is free to absorb new information. Shereshevskii transferred material from short-term to long-term memory by placing words along

Gorky Street in Moscow. Faloon's hobby was long-distance running, and he discovered that he could break down a spoken list of 80 digits into units of three or four and associate most of these with running times.

K To Faloon, a series like 4, 0, 1, 2 would translate as four minutes, one and two-tenths seconds, or "near a four-minute mile"; 2, 1, 4, 7 would be encoded as two hours fourteen minutes seven seconds, or "an excellent marathon time." When running didn't provide the link to his long-term memory, ages and dates did; 1, 9, 4, 4 is not relevant to running, but it is "near the end of World War II."

L Chase and Ericsson see individual differences in memory performance as resulting from previous experience and mental training. "In sum," they write, "adult memory performance can be described by a single model of memory."

M Not every student of psychology agrees with Chase and Ericsson, of course. "I'm very suspicious of saying that everyone has the same kind of memory," says Matthew Erdelyi, a psychologist at Brooklyn College. "In my research," he says, "I find that people have very different memory levels. They can all improve, but some levels remain high and some remain low. There are dramatic individual differences."

N It is unlikely that there will be any agreement among psychologists on the conclusions that they have thus far drawn from their research. The debate about exceptional memory will continue. But in the meantime, it is interesting to look deeper into the mind of a contemporary mnemonist.

O Ericsson and Polson, both of whom have tested Conrad over the past two years, believe that there is nothing intellectually outstanding about him. When they began testing Conrad's memory, his digit scan was normal: about seven numbers. His grades in college were average.

P Conrad himself says that he is unexceptional mentally, but he has compared his earliest memories with others' and has found that he can recall things that many people can't. His first distinct memory is of lying on his back and raising his legs so that his mother could change his diapers. As a high school student, he didn't take notes in class—he says he preferred watching the girls take notes—and he has never made a list in his life. "By never writing down a list of things to do, and letting it think for me," he says, "I've forced my memory to improve."

Q Conrad does believe that his powers of observation, including his ability to listen, are keener than most people's. Memory, he says, is just one part of the whole process of observation. "I'm not extraordinary, but sometimes people make me feel that way. I watch them and realize how many of them have disorganized minds and memories and that makes me feel unusual. A good memory is nothing more than an organized one."

R One of the first things Conrad observed at Bananas was that the headwaiter, his boss, was "a very unpleasant woman." He disliked being her subordinate, and he wanted her job. The only way he could get it was by being a superior waiter. He stayed up nights trying to figure out how to do this; the idea of memorizing orders eventually came to him. Within a year he was the headwaiter. 140

"One of the most interesting things we've found," says Ericsson, "is that just trying to memorize things does not insure that your memory will improve. It's the active decision to get better and the number of hours you push yourself to improve that make the difference. Motivation is much more important than innate ability." 145

Conrad began his memory training by trying to memorize the orders for a table of two, then progressed to memorizing larger orders.

He starts by associating the entree with the customer's face. He might see a large, heavy-set man and hear "I'd like a big Boulder Steak." Sometimes, Peter Polson says, "John thinks a person looks like a turkey 150 and that customer orders a turkey sandwich. Then it's easy."

In memorizing how long meat should be cooked, the different salad dressings, and starches, Conrad relies on patterns of repetition and variation. "John breaks things up into chunks of four," Ericsson says. "If he hears 'rare, rare, medium, well-done,' he instantly sees a pattern in 155 their relationship. Sometimes he makes a mental graph. An easy progression—rare, medium-rare, medium, well-done—would take the shape of a steadily ascending line on his graph. A more difficult order— medium, well-done, rare, medium—would resemble a mountain range."

The simplest part of Conrad's system is his encoding of salad dressings. 160 He uses letters: *B* for blue cheese; *H* for the house dressing; *O* for oil and vinegar; *F* for French; *T* for Thousand Island. A series of orders, always arranged according to entree, might spell a word, like *B-O-O-T*, or a near word, like *B-O-O-F*, or make a phonetic pattern: *F-O-F-O*. As Ericsson says, Conrad remembers orders, regardless of their size, in chunks of four. This 165 is similar to the way Faloon stores digits, and it seems to support Chase and Ericsson's contention that short-term memory is limited and that people are most comfortable working with small units of information.

One of the most intriguing things about Conrad is the number of ways he can associate material. Another is the speed with which he is 170 able to call it up from memory. Ericsson and Polson have also tested him with animals, units of time, flowers, and metals. At first, his recall was slow and uncertain. But with relatively little practice, he could retrieve these "orders" almost as quickly as he could food.

"The difference between someone like John, who has a trained 175 memory, and the average person," says Ericsson, "is that he can encode material in his memory fast and effortlessly. It's similar to the way you can understand English when you hear it spoken. In our tests in the lab, he just gets better and faster." "What John Conrad has," says Polson, "is not unlike an athletic skill. With two or three hundred hours of practice, you can 180 develop these skills in the same way you can learn to play tennis."

Source: "A Memory for all Seasonings" *Psychology Today* (Stephen Singular)

Strategy

Improving Study Skills: Underlining and Marginal Glossing

John Conrad spoke of the importance of having an organized mind for developing one's memory. In this section, two skills will be presented to help you organize materials for study: underlining and marginal glossing.

1. Underlining Material Before underlining, read the material once. Then scan the reading, underlining key words and phrases that relate to main ideas and important statistics or examples that support them. Underline no more than 20 to 30 percent of the material. Many students underline with felt pens, often using one color for main concepts and a different color for statistics and examples.

Another effective method is to underline main ideas and circle or draw rectangles around names, terms, or statistics you want to remember. Supporting ideas can be underlined with broken lines. Practice underlining a few different ways until you find a method you like.

2. Marginal Glossing Marginal glossing is another way to organize material for study. A marginal gloss is a note in the margin of your book summarizing the material next to it. When you study, these notes stand out and remind you of other points as well. This saves time because you do not reread everything, only the brief notes. You can also try to think of questions that might be asked on a test and write these questions in the margins.

3 **Underlining and Glossing** Below are the first eight paragraphs from *A Memory for All Seasonings* with underlining and marginal glosses done for the first four paragraphs. Look over the four paragraphs that have been marked. Then finish the remaining paragraphs by underlining and glossing them yourself. Afterward, compare your work with your classmates. You should find that the first part of the comprehension quiz is quite easy after this preparation.

Peter Polson, from University Colo. Psy. Dept., saw a waiter at Bananas Restaurant with an amazing memory. The waiter was John Conrad.

One evening two years ago, Peter Polson, a member of the psychology department at the University of Colorado, took his son and daughter to dinner at Bananas, a fashionable restaurant in Boulder. When the waiter took their orders, Polson noticed that the young man didn't write anything down. He just listened, made small talk, told them that his name was John Conrad, and left. Polson didn't think this was exceptional: There were, after all, only three of them at the table. Yet he found himself watching Conrad closely when he returned to take the orders at a nearby table of eight. Again the waiter listened, chatted, and wrote nothing down. When he brought Polson and his children their dinners, the professor couldn't resist introducing himself and telling Conrad that he'd been observing him.

Conrad didn't write his orders. He memorized all of them.

Polson invited Conrad to the lab for more memory study at $5/hour.

Other people with amazing memories include a Russian reporter named Shereshevskii and the conductor Arturo Toscanini.

The young man was pleased. He wanted customers to notice that, unlike other waiters, he didn't use a pen and paper. Sometimes, when they did notice, they left him quite a large tip. He had once handled a table of 19 complete dinner orders without a single error. At Bananas, a party of 19 (a bill of roughly $200) would normally leave the waiter a $35 tip. They had left Conrad $85.

Polson was impressed enough to ask the waiter whether he would like to come to the university's psychology lab and let them run some tests on him. Anders Ericsson, a young Swedish psychologist recently involved in memory research, would be joining the university faculty soon, and Polson thought that he would be interested in exploring memory methods with the waiter. Conrad said he would be glad to cooperate. He was always on the lookout for ways to increase his income, and Polson told him he would receive $5 an hour to be a guinea pig.

Conrad, of course, was not the first person with an extraordinary memory to attract attention from researchers. Alexander R. Luria, the distinguished Soviet psychologist, studied a Russian newspaper reporter named Shereshevskii for many years and wrote about him in *The Mind of a Mnemonist* (Basic Books, 1968). Luria says that Shereshevskii was able to hear a series of 50 words spoken once and recite them back in perfect order 15 years later. Another famous example of extraordinary memory, the conductor Arturo Toscanini, was known to have memorized every note for every instrument in 250 symphonies and 100 operas.

For decades, the common belief among psychologists was that memory was a fixed quantity; an exceptional memory, or a poor one, was something with which a person was born.

This point of view has come under attack in recent years; expert memory is no longer universally considered the exclusive gift of the genius, or the abnormal. "People with astonishing memory for pictures, musical scores, chess positions, business transactions, dramatic scripts, or faces are by no means unique," wrote Cornell psychologist Ulric Neisser in *Memory Observed* (1981). "They may not even be very rare." Some university researchers, including Polson and Ericsson, go a step further than Neisser. They believe that there are no physiological differences at all between the memory of a Shereshevskii or a Toscanini and that of the average person. The only real difference, they believe, is that Toscanini trained his memory, exercised it regularly, and wanted to improve it.

Like many people with his capacity to remember, Toscanini may also have used memory tricks called *mnemonics*. Shereshevskii, for example, employed a technique known as *loci*. As soon as he heard a series of words, he mentally "distributed" them along Gorky Street in Moscow. If one of the words was *orange*, he might visualize a man stepping on an orange at a precise location on the familiar street. Later, in order to retrieve *orange*, he would take an imaginary walk down Gorky Street and see the image from which it could easily be recalled. Did the waiter at Bananas have such a system? What was his secret?

John Conrad would be the subject of Anders Ericsson's second in-depth study of the machinations of memory. As a research associate at Carnegie-Mellon University in Pittsburgh, Ericsson had spent the previous three years working with William Chase on an extensive study of Steve Faloon, an undergraduate whose memory and intellectual skills were considered average. When Ericsson and Chase began testing Faloon, he could remember no more than seven random digits after hearing them spoken once. According to generally accepted research, almost everyone is capable of storing five to nine random digits in short-term memory. After 20 months of working with Chase and Ericsson, Faloon could memorize and retrieve 80 digits.

4 **Recalling Information** Based on what you have just read, choose the best way of finishing each statement.

1. The psychology professor discovered John Conrad's incredible ability to memorize _____ .
   - (A) in school
   - (B) on a test
   - (C) in a restaurant

2. Conrad agreed to let the professor study his memory because _____ .
   - (A) Conrad was interested in psychology
   - (B) Conrad wanted to increase his income
   - (C) Conrad needed to improve his memory

3. The famous Russian mnemonist Shereshevskii used a memory trick called *loci* to remember objects by _____ .
   - (A) associating them with events in Russian history
   - (B) imagining them placed along a street in Moscow
   - (C) picturing each one in his mind in a different color

4. The memory trick used by Steve Faloon was the association of certain numbers with _____ .
   - (A) running times
   - (B) important dates
   - (C) both of the above

5. Conrad had been _____ .
   - (A) a gifted student
   - (B) a below-average student
   - (C) an average student

6. Part of Conrad's motivation for developing memory tricks to aid him as a waiter was _____ .
   - (A) his desire to get his boss's job
   - (B) his great admiration for the headwaiter
   - (C) his fear of not finding any work

7. Imagine that four customers have requested that their steaks be cooked in the following way: well-done, medium, medium-rare, rare. According to John Conrad's mental graph technique, this order would be remembered as _____.

    Ⓐ a steadily ascending line

    Ⓑ a steadily descending line

    Ⓒ a mountain range

8. From this article, a careful reader should infer that _____.

    Ⓐ everyone has about the same memory capacity and can develop a superior memory through practice and motivation

    Ⓑ a good or bad memory is an ability that a person is born with and cannot change to any great degree

    Ⓒ there is still no conclusive evidence as to whether outstanding memories are inborn or developed

Strategy

Improving Study Skills: Making a Study Map

Earlier in the chapter, you were instructed to underline and gloss the important points in part of an article to help you review it. Another way to organize information for study is to make a study map.

Study mapping is a method of taking notes. It is unique in that an entire article or even a chapter of a textbook is mapped on just one page. To make a map, you must select the major and minor points of the article or chapter. Then arrange them in graph form. Students who enjoy drafting, charts, or symbols tend to like mapping. No exact method of map making is standard. Figures or shapes, lines, and arrows can be used. Some students prefer treelike designs for their maps; others use circles, octagons, or squares.

Like underlining, mapping should be done after the first reading. A study map of the preceding paragraph follows.

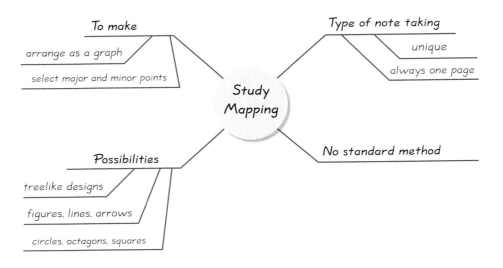

5 Making a Study Map Look at this incomplete study map for *A Man for All Seasonings*. Work with a partner and finish the map. Compare your work afterward with other pairs. Did you add too much information? Too little?

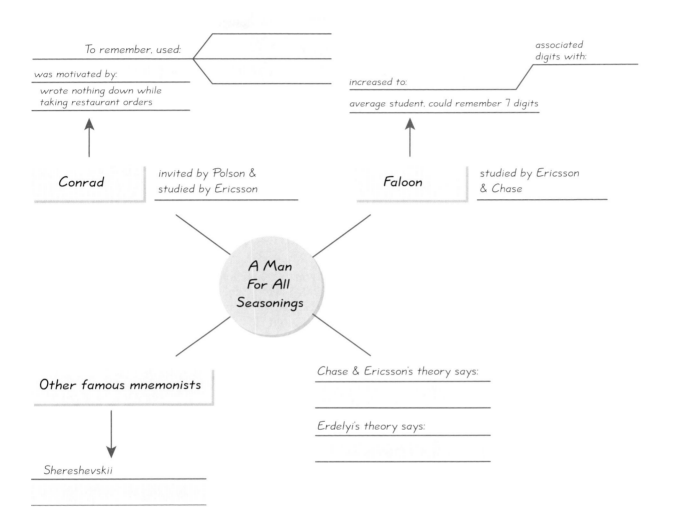

To remember, used:

was motivated by:

wrote nothing down while taking restaurant orders

Conrad

invited by Polson & studied by Ericsson

associated digits with:

increased to:

average student, could remember 7 digits

Faloon

studied by Ericsson & Chase

A Man For All Seasonings

Other famous mnemonists

Shereshevskii

Chase & Ericsson's theory says:

Erdelyi's theory says:

Strategy

Understanding Mnemonic Systems

Several different mnemonic systems (memory tricks) are described in the reading. These tricks can help you remember words and information. A list of the systems with line references is given below.

   a. *loci* (imagining objects in a familiar place), used by Shereshevskii, lines 61–67
   b. number association, used by Steve Faloon, lines 94–102
   c. physical appearance association, used by John Conrad, lines 148–151
   d. mental graph or picture, used by Conrad, lines 156–159
   e. word or sound pattern association, used by Conrad, lines 160–165

6 Understanding Mnemonic Systems Working in small groups, show that you understand mnemonic systems by applying them to the following situations. Look in the Strategy Box on page 147 for a list of the mnemonic systems discussed in the reading.

1. You want to remember the names of all the psychologists mentioned in this article: Polson, Ericsson, Luria, Neisser, Chase. How would you do this using word or sound pattern association?

2. You want to remember to buy the following items at the grocery store: apples, milk, rice, pepper, salad dressing, and olives. How would you do this, using *loci*? How would you do it using word or sound pattern association? Which system would be better for you?

3. You have just a minute or two to look at the alphabetical list of exam grades and want to remember the grades of seven of your friends. What kind of mental graph would you picture in your mind to remember them in the following order: A, D, A, D, B, C, B?

4. You want to remember the combinations for the locks you use for your bicycle, your school locker, and your gym locker: 0915, 1220, 1492. How could you do this, using number association? Can you think of any other way of doing it?

5. You are at a dinner party and want to remember the names of the four other guests: a very tall lady named Mrs. Stemski; a large, heavy-set man named Mr. Barnes; a cheerful young woman with a big smile named Miss Rich; and a sad-looking young man named Mr. Winter. How could you use physical appearance association to remember their names?

7 Guided Academic Conversation In small groups, discuss the following questions.

1. In what other professions, besides that of a waiter or waitress, is it useful to have a good memory? Why?

2. What people with extraordinary memories are mentioned in the article? What others have you heard about or met?

3. What tools, gadgets, or techniques, other than those mentioned in the preceding exercise, are sometimes used to aid memory? What do you do to help you remember things?

Reading Tip

A **hypothesis** is an explanation which has not yet been verified. (An explanation that has been verified to some degree and is believed by many is a **theory**.)

---

8 Finding Support For or Against a Hypothesis

As the article points out, some psychologists today believe that extraordinary memories are simply the result of development through hard work and the application of a system. According to their hypothesis, *an average person can achieve a superior memory if he or she tries hard enough.*

Complete the following activity. Then compare and share your work with a partner or in a small group.

1. Find evidence from the article to support this hypothesis. Write it below.

_____

_____

2. Find evidence from the article that goes against this hypothesis.

_____

_____

3. What is your opinion of this controversial (debatable) question?

_____

_____

Part 2   Reading Skills and Strategies

The Tell-Tale Heart

Before You Read

Strategy

Getting the Meaning of Words from Context
Some words and expressions in the next selection are no longer used in modern English. Many English-speaking readers would not be familiar with them. However, they would have little trouble following the story because the context provides many clues.

1 **Getting the Meaning of Words from Context** Read the following sentences from the Edgar Allan Poe story that follows and select a modern word or expression to replace the old-fashioned one in italics. Remember to use the context to help you.

1. "How, then, am I mad? *Hearken!* and observe how healthily—how calmly I can tell you the whole story." (line 5)
   a. Speak!
   b. Listen!
   c. Go away!

2. "It is impossible to say how first the idea entered my brain, but once conceived, it haunted me day and night. *Object* there was none. Passion there was none. . . . For his gold I had no desire." (line 7)

a. fear

b. purpose

c. argument

3. "Now this is the point. You *fancy* me mad. Madmen know nothing. But you should have seen me." (line 15)

    a. like

    b. imagine

    c. offend

4. "Presently I heard a slight groan, and I knew it was the groan of mortal terror. It was not a groan of pain or of grief—oh, no!—it was the low stifled sound that arises from the bottom of the soul. I knew the sound well. Many a night. . . it has welled up from my own *bosom* . . ." (line 54)

    a. house

    b. chest

    c. table

5. "I knew what the old man felt, and pitied him . . . His fears had been ever since growing upon him . . . He had been saying to himself—'It is nothing but the wind in the chimney . . .' Yes, he had been trying to comfort himself with these suppositions: but he had found all *in vain*. All *in vain*; because Death . . . had stalked with his black shadow before him, and enveloped the victim." (line 59)

    a. useless

    b. successful

    c. harmful

6. "But, for many minutes, the heart beat on with a muffled sound. This, however, did not *vex* me; it would not be heard through the wall. *At length* it ceased. The old man was dead." (line 99)

    vex

    a. delight

    b. confuse

    c. irritate

    at length

    a. soon

    b. after a while

    c. in a moment

7. "I took my visitors all over the house. I *bade* them search—search *well*." (line 132)

    a. bathed

    b. invited

    c. refused

8. "They sat, and while I answered cheerily, they chatted of familiar things. But, *ere long*, I felt myself getting pale and wished them gone." (line 141)

    a. too long, after many hours

    b. before long, in a short while

    c. immediately, right at that moment

Introduction

It is not only science that brings us a better understanding of the human mind. Throughout the ages, writers of fiction have also examined the mind. The famous American poet and short-story writer Edgar Allan Poe was born in Boston, Massachusetts in 1809. He died 40 years later after a stormy but productive life that included wild sprees and tragic romances as well as a great deal of serious journalistic and literary writing. His works are still popular today and several have served as the basis for modern plays and

▲ Edgar Allan Poe

movies. He is best known for his tales of fear and horror such as *The Tell-Tale Heart*.

The following story is told from the point of view of a madman who commits a terrible crime. Many psychologists and criminologists have felt that Poe describes with great accuracy the inner workings of a severely disordered mind.

- What do you know, from reading or from personal contact, about madness (insanity)?
- What are some of the characteristics of the thinking, perception, or speech of a person that show he or she is mad (insane)? Watch for examples of these characteristics in the story.

2 **Getting Meaning from Context** As you read the story, skip words or expressions you do not understand and then go back and reread after you see more of the context.

The Tell-Tale Heart

A   True—nervous—very, very dreadfully nervous I had been and am; but why will you say that I am mad? The disease had sharpened my senses— not destroyed—not dulled them. Above all was the sense of hearing acute. I heard all things in the heaven and in the earth. I heard many things in hell. How, then, am I mad? Hearken! and observe how healthily—how calmly I can tell you the whole story.

B   It is impossible to say how first the idea entered my brain; but once conceived, it haunted me day and night. Object there was none. Passion there was none. I loved the old man. He had never wronged me. He had never given me insult. For his gold I had no desire. I think it was his eye! Yes, it was this! He had the eye of a vulture—a pale blue eye, with a film over it. Whenever it fell upon me, my blood ran cold; and so by degrees—very gradually—I made up my mind to take the life of the old man, and thus rid myself of the eye forever.

C   Now this is the point. You fancy me mad. Madmen know nothing. But you should have seen me. You should have seen how wisely I proceeded—with what caution—with what foresight—with what dissimulation I went to work! I was never kinder to the old man than during the whole week before I killed him. And every night, about midnight, I turned the latch of his door and opened it—oh, so gently! And then, when I had made an opening sufficient for my head, I put in a dark lantern, all closed, closed, so that no light shone out, and then I thrust in my head. Oh, you would have laughed to see how cunningly I thrust it in! I moved it slowly—very slowly, so that I might not disturb the old man's sleep. It took me an hour to place my whole head within the opening so far that I could see him as he lay upon his bed. Ha!—would a madman have been so wise as this? And then, when my head was well in the room, I undid the lantern cautiously—oh so cautiously—cautiously (for the hinges creaked)—I undid it just so much that a single thin ray fell upon the vulture eye. And this I did for seven long nights—every night just at midnight—but I found the eye always closed; and so it was impossible to do the work; for it was not the old man who vexed me, but his Evil Eye. And every morning, when the day broke, I went boldly into the chamber, and spoke courageously to him, calling him by name in a hearty tone, and inquiring how he had passed the night. So you see he would have been a very profound old man, indeed, to suspect that every night, just at twelve, I looked in upon him while he slept.

D   Upon the eighth night I was more than usually cautious in opening the door. A watch's minute hand moves more quickly than did mine. Never before that night, had I *felt* the extent of my own powers—of my sagacity. I could scarcely contain my feelings of triumph. To think that there I was, opening the door, little by little, and he not even to dream of my secret deeds or thoughts. I fairly chuckled at the idea; and perhaps he heard me; for he moved on the bed suddenly, as if startled. Now you may think that I drew back—but no. His room was as black as pitch with the thick darkness (for the shutters were close fastened, through fear of robbers), and so I knew that he could not see the opening of the door, and I kept pushing it on steadily, steadily.

E   I had my head in, and was about to open the lantern, when my thumb slipped upon the tin fastening, and the old man sprang up in bed, crying out—"Who's there?"

F   I kept quite still and said nothing. For a whole hour I did not move a muscle, and in the meantime I did not hear him lie down. He was still sitting up in the bed listening;—just as I have done, night after night, hearkening to the death watches in the wall.

G   Presently I heard a slight groan, and I knew it was the groan of mortal terror. It was not a groan of pain or of grief—oh, no!—it was the low stifled sound that arises from the bottom of the soul. I knew the sound well. Many a night, just at midnight, when all the world slept, it has welled up from my own bosom, deepening, with its dreadful echo, the terrors that distracted me. I say I knew it well. I knew what the old man felt, and pitied him, although I chuckled at heart. I knew that he had been lying awake ever since the first slight noise, when he had turned in the bed. His fears had been ever since growing upon him. He had been trying to fancy them causeless, but could not. He had been saying to himself—"It is nothing but the wind in the chimney—it is only a mouse crossing the floor." Yes, he had been trying to comfort himself with these suppositions: but he had found all in vain. *All in vain*; because Death, in approaching him had stalked with his black shadow before him, and enveloped the victim. And it was the mournful influence of the unperceived shadow that caused him to feel—although he neither saw nor heard—to *feel* the presence of my head within the room.

H   When I had waited a long time, very patiently, without hearing him lie down, I resolved to open a little—a very, very little crevice in the lantern. So I opened it—you cannot imagine how stealthily, stealthily—until, at length a single dim ray, like the thread of the spider, shot from out the crevice and fell full upon the vulture eye.

I   It was open—wide, wide open—and I grew furious as I gazed upon it. I saw it with perfect distinctness—all a dull blue with a hideous veil over it that chilled the very marrow in my bones; but I could see nothing else of the old man's face or person: for I had directed the ray, as if by instinct, precisely upon the damned spot.

J   And have I not told you that what you mistake for madness is but overacuteness of the senses?—now, I say, there came to my ears a low, dull, quick sound, such as a watch makes when enveloped in cotton. I knew that sound well, too. It was the beating of the old man's heart. It increased my fury, as the beating of a drum stimulates the soldier into courage.

K   But even yet I refrained and kept still. I scarcely breathed. I held the lantern motionless. I tried how steadily I could maintain the ray upon the eye. Meantime the hellish tattoo of the heart increased. It grew quicker and quicker, and louder and louder every instant. The old man's terror must have been extreme! It grew louder, I say, louder every moment—do you

mark me well? I have told you that I am nervous: so I am. And now at the 90
dead hour of the night, amid the dreadful silence of that old house, so
strange a noise as this excited me to uncontrollable terror. Yet, for some
minutes longer I refrained and stood still. But the beating grew louder,
louder! I thought the heart must burst. And now a new anxiety seized me—
the sound would be heard by a neighbor! The old man's hour had come! 95
With a loud yell, I threw open the lantern and leaped into the room. He
shrieked once—once only. In an instant I dragged him to the floor, and
pulled the heavy bed over him. I then smiled gaily, to find the deed so far
done. But, for many minutes, the heart beat on with a muffled sound. This,
however, did not vex me; it would not be heard through the wall. At length 100
it ceased. The old man was dead. I removed the bed and examined the
corpse. Yes, he was stone, stone dead. I placed my hand upon the heart and
held it there many minutes. There was no pulsation. He was stone dead. His
eye would trouble me no more.

L　　If you still think me mad, you will think so no longer when I describe 105
the wise precautions I took for the concealment of the body. The night

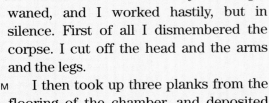

waned, and I worked hastily, but in
silence. First of all I dismembered the
corpse. I cut off the head and the arms
and the legs. 110

M　I then took up three planks from the
flooring of the chamber, and deposited
all between the scantlings. I then
replaced the boards so cleverly, so
cunningly, that no human eye—not *even* 115
his—could have detected anything
wrong. There was nothing to wash out—
no stain of any kind—no blood-spot
whatever. I had been too wary for that. A
tub had caught all—ha! ha! 120

N　When I had made an end of these
labors, it was four o'clock—still dark as
midnight. As the bell sounded the hour, there came a knocking at the street
door. I went down to open it with a light heart,—for what had I now to fear?
There entered three men, who introduced themselves, with perfect suavity, 125
as officers of the police. A shriek had been heard by a neighbor during the
night; suspicion of foul play had been aroused; information had been
lodged at the police office, and they (the officers) had been deputed to
search the premises.

O　　I smiled,—for *what* had I to fear? I bade the gentlemen welcome. The 130
shriek, I said, was my own in a dream. The old man, I mentioned, was absent
in the country. I took my visitors all over the house. I bade them search—

search *well*. I led them, at length, to his chamber. I showed them his treasures, secure, undisturbed. In the enthusiasm of my confidence, I brought chairs into the room, and desired them *here* to rest from their fatigues, while I myself, in the wild audacity of my perfect triumph, placed my own seat upon the very spot beneath which reposed the corpse of the victim.

P   The officers were satisfied. My *manner* had convinced them. I was singularly at ease. They sat, and while I answered cheerily, they chatted of familiar things. But, ere long, I felt myself getting pale and wished them gone. My head ached, and I fancied a ringing in my ears: but still they sat and still chatted. The ringing became more distinct:—it continued and became more distinct: I talked more freely to get rid of the feeling: but it continued and gained definiteness— until, at length, I found that the noise was *not* within my ears.

Q   No doubt I now grew very pale;—but I talked more fluently, and with a heightened voice. Yet the sound increased—and what could I do? It was a *low, dull, quick sound—much such a sound as a watch makes when enveloped in cotton*. I gasped for breath—and yet the officers heard it not. I talked more quickly—more vehemently; but the noise steadily increased. I arose and argued about trifles, in a high key and with violent gesticulations; but the noise steadily increased. Why *would* they not be gone? I paced the floor to and fro with heavy strides, as if excited to fury by the observations of the men—but the noise steadily increased. Oh God! what *could* I do? I foamed—I raved—I swore! I swung the chair upon which I had been sitting, and grated it upon the boards, but the noise arose over all and continually increased. It grew louder—louder—*louder*! And still the men chatted pleasantly, and smiled. Was it possible they heard not? Almighty God!—no, no! They heard!—they suspected!—they *knew*!—they were making a mockery of my horror!—this I thought, and this I think. But anything was better than this agony! Anything was more tolerable than this derision! I could bear those hypocritical smiles no longer! I felt that I must scream or die! and now— again!—hark! louder! louder! louder! *louder*!

R   "Villains!" I shrieked, "dissemble no more! I admit the deed!—tear up the planks! here, here!—it is the beating of his hideous heart!"

Source: "The Tell-Tale Heart" *The Pioneer* (Edgar Allen Poe)

After You Read

3 **Recalling Information** Choose the best way of finishing each statement, based on what you have just read.

1. The narrator believes that he suffers from acute nervousness that has _____.
   a. destroyed the power of his senses
   b. increased the power of his senses
   c. driven him mad

2. The motive for the murder was _____.
   a. a strong desire for the victim's money
   b. an intense hatred for the victim
   c. a dislike of the victim's eye

3. During the week before he killed the old man, the narrator's manner toward him was very _____.
   a. kind
   b. angry
   c. indifferent

4. Each night just at midnight, he thrust into the old man's room a _____.
   a. black cat
   b. chain
   c. lantern

5. On the eighth night, the old man awakened because of a noise and then _____.
   a. went right back to sleep
   b. began to call for help
   c. sat up waiting in terror

6. After a while, the murderer heard a sound that increased his fury and that he thought was _____.
   a. a watch enveloped in cotton
   b. the neighbors coming to enter the house
   c. the beating of his victim's heart

7. The murderer disposed of the old man's body by putting it _____.
   a. in the garden
   b. under the floor
   c. into the chimney

8. At four in the morning, three police officers arrived because neighbors had complained of _____.
   a. the lights
   b. some knocking
   c. a shriek

9. The officers found out the truth because _____.
   a. the murderer confessed
   b. a neighbor had told them
   c. there was a bloodstain on the floor

4 Guided Academic Conversation In small groups, discuss the following questions.

1. Give three statements the narrator makes to prove he is sane. Then show how the author indicates to us that these claims are not true.

2. We are not told what relationship the murderer had to the old man or why they lived together. What did you imagine about this?

3. To whom do you think the murderer is telling this story and for what reason?

4. What do you think the author means by the term "evil eye"? Have you ever heard of people who believe in the "evil eye"? According to this belief, you can suffer bad luck or illness if you are looked at by someone who has this power. What do you think is the origin of this belief? Why do you think the narrator of the story was so disturbed by the old man's eye?

5. Various interpretations have been given to explain the loud beating that the narrator hears during the police visit. Do you agree with any of the following interpretations? Or do you have some other interpretation? Explain.

   a. It is simply a clock or other normal sound that seems louder to him because of his guilt.

   b. It is really the beating of his own heart, which becomes stronger as he gets more and more nervous.

   c. It is the old man's ghost taking revenge on him.

5 Focusing on Words from the Academic Word List Read the excerpt below taken from the reading in Part 2. Fill in the blanks with a word from the box. Do not look back at the reading right away; instead, see if you can now remember the vocabulary. One word is repeated.

ceased	distinct	removed
convinced	found	secure
detected	labors	

A   In an instant I dragged him to the floor, and pulled the heavy bed over him. I then smiled gaily, to find the deed so far done. But, for many minutes, the heart beat on with a muffled sound. This, however, did not vex me; it would not be heard through the wall. At length it _____.

1

The old man was dead. I _____ the bed and examined the   5

2

corpse. Yes, he was stone, stone dead . . .

B   I then took up three planks from the flooring of the chamber, and deposited all between the scantlings. I then replaced the boards so cleverly, so cunningly, that no human eye—not *even* his—could have _____ anything wrong . . .   10

         3

C   When I had made an end of these _____, it was four

                                             4

o'clock—still dark as midnight. As the bell sounded the hour, there came a knocking at the street door. . .

D   I smiled,—for *what* had I to fear? I bade the gentlemen welcome. The shriek, I said, was my own in a dream. The old man, I mentioned, was ab- 15 sent in the country. I took my visitors all over the house. I bade them search—search *well*. I led them, at length, to his chamber. I showed them his treasures, _____, undisturbed . . .

                                           5

E   The officers were satisfied. My *manner* had _____

                                           6

them. I was singularly at ease. They sat, and while I answered cheerily, they 20 chatted of familiar things. But, ere long, I felt myself getting pale and wished them gone. My head ached, and I fancied a ringing in my ears: but still they sat and still chatted. The ringing became more _____ :—it

                                           7

continued and became more _____ : I talked more freely 25

                                         8

to get rid of the feeling: but it continued and gained definiteness—until, at length, I _____ that the noise was *not* within my ears . . .

                                    9

SUMMARIZING FROM A DIFFERENT POINT OF VIEW

An author chooses one point of view, the position of one of the characters or an outside observer, on what happened. But other points of view might be different from the one chosen, so summarizing from a different point of view can help you see what really occurred and how the narrator's character is influencing the telling of the story.

What really happened when the three police officers came to search the narrator's house? What did he do or say to make them so suspicious that they stayed to chat with him? The events are presented from his point of view (lines 126–174), but we must read "between the lines" in order to see what really happened. We must take into account the narrator's character and pinpoint the places in which he describes events incorrectly.

6 Summarizing from a Different Point of View

Pretend you are one of the police officers in the story. Summarize what you think really happened. Write your summary on the following lines. After you finish, compare your notes with those of two other "police officers" (classmates). Then share your work with the class.

_____

_____

_____

_____

Strategy

Identifying Narrative Elements
Most horror stories focus on certain narrative elements in order to provoke terror. Very often an author will use a special description of a character or of the setting to frighten the reader. Of course, the plot or story line is primarily about horror. The story you read on page 151 is a classic horror story; over the years it has frightened many people.

7 Identifying Elements in a Story
Listen to or read the story again to determine what elements make this a classic horror story. Fill in the information requested below. After you finish, compare your work with a partner and then with the class.

1. Something the main character says that could frighten someone:

_____

_____

_____

2. Something from the setting that could frighten someone:

_____

_____

_____

Mental Illness

Mental illness in many ways remains a mystery to us. Some scientists think that it is hereditary, passed down from parents to children in the genes. Others think it is caused by a chemical imbalance in the body. Other factors considered are a person's environment or perhaps an injury to the brain. Experts have differing opinions as to what causes mental illness and different ideas on how to treat it. One method is to place mentally ill people in hospitals and even prisons to separate them from society. Another method is to give medications under the supervision of a psychiatrist to modify behavior. Mentally ill persons under medication often live in supervised housing, or even in their own homes. Another method of treatment, pioneered by Sigmund Freud (1856-1939) is psychoanalysis, whereby the patient receives many hours of counseling and talk therapy at a psychiatrist's office. The above treatments are often combined.

▲ Sigmund Freud

1. What do you think is the most likely cause of mental illness?

2. What do you think is the best method of treatment?

Focus on Testing

Reading for Speed and Fluency

Skimming and Scanning Most tests have a time limit, so good reading speed can be a great asset. Understanding what you read, however, is critical to reading quickly. As you learned in Chapter 1, two ways to read for speedy comprehension are **skimming** or **scanning** the text. For example, if all you want to find out is a general idea of what the reading is about, skim the text by letting your eyes quickly roam across the page or even down the middle of it, looking for clues. If you need specific information, like a description of a particular character or date, you can scan for it—that is, run your eyes quickly through the passage until you find the character's name or the date. For both types of reading, remember not to read every word and sometimes, not even every phrase or sentence.

Practice

Read the three questions below and then scan the reading *May's Boy* to find the answers.

1. Who is May? _____

2. Who is Leslie Lemke? _____

3. Why is he famous? _____

Next, skim the article to get the main ideas and answer the two questions that follow.

May's Boy

A   Oshkosh, WI (AP)—It was only fitting that this concert be held in a church. After all, it had to do with miracles. Leslie Lemke, whose name has become synonymous with the savant syndrome*, meaning an "island of genius," has come to be even more associated with the term "miracle of love."

B   Blind, retarded, palsied, Leslie, who has to be led to the piano by his sister, Mary Parker, can play any piece of music he's ever heard.

C   Last Sunday, his genius came through more strongly than ever. This day he was playing for a special lady—his mother, May—who was celebrating her 93rd birthday and her last scheduled public appearance with him.

D   It was she who had taken him in and told her own children, "God has something special in mind for Leslie." But even she could not have known what "May's boy," as Leslie has come to be known, could accomplish.

E   Walter Cronkite used May and Leslie as his "Christmas miracle" years ago. Since then, Leslie has appeared on *That's Incredible, Donahue, 60 Minutes*, and finally, served as a prototype for the film *Rain Man*. He's played the piano for the

---

*The "savant syndrome" is the name given to the condition of certain people who are mentally ill but have a special genius for one subject or skill, often for mathematics or music. Their general intelligence is usually so low that they cannot lead independent lives, but in their one area of genius, they show extraordinary aptitude that is far above the average.

King of Norway and appeared in Japan. Japanese television sent a crew to film Leslie for its Discovery program at the concert held both at the Seventh-Day Adventist Church in Neenah and St. John Lutheran Church in Oshkosh. "There Was a Lady May Who Prayed for a Miracle," a song written especially for May, was sung by Leslie as his mother, now suffering from Alzheimer's disease, was wheeled next to the piano.

F "Day by day and year by year, she stuck by his side. Others thought it hopeless, but he never even cried," he sang in the presence of May's children, grandchildren, great-grandchildren, and even a few great-great-grandchildren.

▲ Leslie Lemke plays the piano from memory.

G A spark of recognition lit May's eyes as the song continued, and her family came up to embrace her, though the years when she actually out-talked Donahue on the program are gone. All that is left is the loving glance she casts toward Leslie, as he plays the piece that has become his theme song, Tchaikovsky's Piano Concerto No. 1.

H It was that piece May and Joe Lemke heard in the night a decade and a half ago when they were awakened by beautiful music and discovered their profoundly handicapped boy at the piano. It was the miracle May had told her family would come. From that night on, Leslie has been researched, lauded, filmed.

I His ability to hear any piece of music just once, imprint it in his brain, and repeat it on the piano on command and in its entirety has brought him fame. No one knows how many pieces are forever locked in his memory. He can play and sing hundreds of songs at will—spirituals, ballads, arias, marches, ragtime, folksongs, and the classics. And yet, seconds before he appears before the crowd, he sits in a chair, head bowed, eyes shut, hand gnarled, unaware of his surroundings, waiting for his sister, Mary, to come and take him to the piano.

As soon as he sits down at the piano bench and lifts his head heavenward, his palsied fingers spread across the keys and praise the Lord with "How Great Thou Art." In the front pew, May's own hands lift in adoration.

Source: "May's Boy" *The Post Crescent* (Maya Penikis)

1. May is Leslie Lemke's _____.
   - (A) teacher
   - (B) mother
   - (C) doctor

2. Leslie Lemke is _____.
   - (A) a mentally challenged man with the ability to sing, dance, and play classical music on television and in the movies
   - (B) a piano player of very low intelligence who can play from memory any song he has ever heard
   - (C) a genius who has learned to play many different musical instruments with near perfection

 9 **Guided Academic Conversation** In small groups, discuss the following questions about the Focus on Testing section.

1. In your opinion, how important was May in Leslie's success?

2. What lesson can most people learn from the case of Leslie Lemke?

3. When do you like to read fast? When and why do you like to read slowly?

Part 3 Tying It All Together

 1 **Test Your Own Memory** Choose a favorite email address that you haven't memorized yet. Try memorizing it by using one of the mnemonic tricks you learned about in this chapter. Next choose a favorite Internet web site URL (address) beginning with www. Use another mnemonic trick to memorize it. Share your experiences with a partner and with the class.

2 Making Connections Do some research on the Internet and take notes on one of the following topics. Share your results with the class or in a small group.

Mnemonics Look up *mnemonic tricks, memory techniques* or *memory devices* or other synonyms for this concept on the Internet. Read a few of the mnemonic tricks you find and be ready to explain at least two of them that are different from the ones mentioned in *A Memory for All Seasonings*. Which seem to be the most popular mnemonic tricks that you found?

Biography on Edgar Allan Poe Look up information on the biography of Edgar Allan Poe. You may want to find out what other works he wrote, whom he influenced, or information about his scandalous marriage, mysterious death, and an enemy's attempt to ruin his reputation after his death. As well as being a great writer, Poe had a very interesting life. Find some interesting stories or details to share.

Responding in Writing

WRITING TIP: USE EXAMPLES

Use strong examples to illustrate an argument, and tie them clearly back to your main point. You can take examples from your life, from history, or from any source that illustrates the point.

Using Examples in Writing Choose one of these two topics. Then write an argument of a few paragraphs following the steps after the topics.

Topic 1
Is it important to develop a good memory through steps like those described in *A Memory for All Seasonings* in Part 1? What benefits could a good memory bring to your life? Or does following these steps just take too much time that could be better spent on other areas of education or skill development?

Topic 2
What causes insanity or madness? Do you think that there must be a genetic disposition for someone to become insane? Or can the experiences in one's childhood or adult life lead to madness? What sort of traumatic experiences would lead one to insanity?

Step 1 Brainstorm on the topic, using a cluster diagram or another form of note taking.

Step 2 Develop your main thesis or argument by writing a sentence to describe the main focus of your argument. You may want to use this as part of your introduction, perhaps adding a couple of sentences before or after it to open your composition.

Step 3 Develop at least three strong examples to illustrate your point of view. These examples can be from your experience or from something you have read or seen in a movie or on TV.

Step 4 Make sure that these examples all tie back into supporting your argument. If the connection of the example to your main point is not completely clear, write a sentence explaining how it proves your point.

Step 5 Write a conclusion and a title for your composition. Revise, and exchange with a friend for help with revision. Hand in your composition, rough copy diagram, and notes.

Self-Assessment Log

Read the lists below. Check (✓) the strategies and vocabulary that you learned in this chapter. Look through the chapter or ask your instructor about the strategies and words that you do not understand.

Reading and Vocabulary-Building Strategies
- ❑ Previewing and predicting
- ❑ Identifying synonyms
- ❑ Improving study skills: underlining and marginal glossing
- ❑ Recalling information
- ❑ Improving study skills: making a study map
- ❑ Understanding mnemonic systems
- ❑ Finding support for or against a hypothesis
- ❑ Getting the meaning of words from context
- ❑ Summarizing from a different point of view
- ❑ Identifying elements in a story
- ❑ Reading for speed and fluency: skimming and scanning

Target Vocabulary

Nouns
- ❑ bosom
- ❑ hypothesis*
- ❑ intellectual skills
- ❑ labors*
- ❑ novice
- ❑ subordinate*

Verbs
- ❑ bade

- ❑ ceased*
- ❑ convinced*
- ❑ cooperate*
- ❑ detected*
- ❑ fancy
- ❑ found*
- ❑ insure
- ❑ memorized

- ❑ removed*
- ❑ vex

Adjectives
- ❑ distinct*
- ❑ exceptional
- ❑ exclusive*
- ❑ extraordinary
- ❑ fashionable

- ❑ impressed
- ❑ rare (describing meat)
- ❑ secure*

Adverbs
- ❑ adequately*
- ❑ at length
- ❑ effortlessly
- ❑ in vain

* These words are from the Academic Word List. For more information on this list, see www.vuw.ac.nz/lals/research/awl.

" Everyone has been made for some particular work, and the desire for that work has been put in every heart. **"**

—Jalalu'l-Din Rumi,
Persian poet (1207–1273)

Connecting to the Topic

1 Who are the people in the photo? Where might they be going? What thoughts are in their minds?

2 Would you like to work in a big city and be part of a crowd like this? Explain.

3 Do you agree with the quotation by Jalalu'l-Din Rumi? Why or why not?

The San Francisco Sculptor Who Created Nicolas Cage's "Dreadful Dragon"

Before You Read

1 **Previewing a Reading: Predicting** Look at the title and illustrations of the article. Is there any part you don't understand? Which of the items in the following list do you *not* expect to find in the article? Explain.

❑ a description of movies that the Hollywood star Nicolas Cage has acted in

❑ a description of various pieces of sculpture in San Francisco

❑ information about the life and work of a sculptor

❑ information about the habits of dragons, lizards, and salamanders

2 **Scanning for Specific Words** Read each definition or description below. Then scan the reading to find the word that matches it, using the line number to guide you.

1. A compound word for a place where things are stored (line 1) __*warehouse*__

2. A word for the projecting shelf or ledge above a fireplace that serves as a place to put things (line 9) _____

3. An adjective describing the style popular during the times of Queen Victoria of England, 1837–1901 (line 10) _____

4. A synonym for *choices* (line 11) _____

5. Two words describing a style of the 1930s that used curves and ornaments (line 20) _____

6. A compound word for the outstanding features that mark a particular place (line 24) _____

7. A word starting with *u* that means *decorative vases or jars* (line 29) _____

8. A synonym for *carved* or *sculpted* (line 51) _____

9. The name of the machine used for lifting very heavy objects (line 59) _____

10. A word that means *a journey to a holy place or a place of inspiration* (line 86) _____

Read

Introduction

Manuel Palos spends most weekends working alone in his studio in San Francisco, but he doesn't mind. He feels very lucky: "I really enjoy my life. There are people who are born to be something and who find out early enough to enjoy the rest of their lives doing what they want. That's the trick." Palos is a sculptor. He carves statues and other objects out of stone or marble, makes castings in bronze, and restores historic buildings. He also runs a school for sculptors in Puerto Vallarta, Mexico, where the art and craft of sculpting stone is passed on to people from all over the world. The article that follows from the *San Francisco Chronicle* presents Palos's story.

- What do you imagine it is like to work as a sculptor?
- How would someone get started in this line of work?
- What advantages and disadvantages do you think there are to being a sculptor?

File   Edit   View   Favorites   Tools   Help

Address www.manuelpalos.com

The San Francisco Sculptor Who Created Nicolas Cage's "Dreadful Dragon"

A   In an old warehouse in an industrial section of town, San Francisco sculptor Manuel Palos takes the plebeian [common] fireplace and turns it into a monumental work of art.

▲ Manuel Palos in his studio

B   Plaster molds representing 5 many periods and styles line the walls of his shop. Pinned on one wall is a sketch of a mantel for a restored Victorian house. "I will give 10 the owner two options," says Palos, who wears jeans and a black T-shirt covered with white plaster dust. A green beret partially hides his curly, 15 gray-flecked hair. "One will be traditional, the other softer and rounder in scale."

C   Over the course of his 30-year career, Palos has designed many fireplaces for businesses and private residences. Two are in San Francisco hotels: The Galleria Park has an eight-foot by eight-foot art nouveau style with undulating curves, while the Villa Florence has a traditional European design . . . Another fireplace is in the First Interstate Bank, and he counts among his personal clients the Gallo family and Donald Trump.[1]

Worked on Many San Francisco Landmarks

D   Palos also has worked on many of the city's famous landmarks. He resculpted six life-sized mythological figures at the California Palace of the Legion of Honor in Lincoln Park and made eight 13-foot-tall eagles for Pacific Bell's San Francisco headquarters. He worked on the old City of Paris building when Neiman Marcus[2] moved in and restored friezes and urns at the Academy of Sciences in Golden Gate Park. He is working on a bronze medallion to go outside San Francisco's Hall of Justice.

E   But it is the "Dreadful Dragon" fireplace for actor Nicolas Cage's Pacific Heights home that is his most memorable piece. "Every time I talk about it, I get excited," says Palos. "It was challenging, but it was also a labor of love."

F   Cage stopped by Palos' studio one morning last year wearing a baseball hat and ripped jeans. "I didn't know who he was," Palos says. "He told me he wanted a fireplace made out of stone."

G   "I asked him if he had a design and he said he wanted a dragon. I thought he was kidding, so I played along. I told him I could make a huge dragon from the floor to the ceiling with the mouth as the opening. He looked at me and said, 'That's exactly what I want.'" Cage left a deposit and that's when Palos got "scared"—"I had to make the dragon I proposed."

By the Book

H   Using a children's book about dragons, Palos sketched a design. When it was approved, he made a clay model before casting the real thing in stone.

I   For nearly five months, Palos labored over the sculpture. Cage wanted black limestone and the 13-foot-tall-by-ten-foot-wide piece required four and a half tons; Palos moved to a studio in Mexico because that was the only place he could find big enough.

J   "Every line had to match," says Palos of the bends and sinewy coils. He chiseled the dragon's nostrils to flare and created fiery-looking eyes. He used pneumatic tools to carve the hooked beak, scales, and fang-like teeth for maximum control. "If any part of the

---

[1]The Gallos are a successful family of California wine makers. Donald Trump is a wealthy U.S. businessman.
[2]Neiman Marcus is the name of a chain of expensive department stores in the U.S.

face broke, I would have to start over." When finished, the sculpture was loaded on a truck, and Palos drove it back to the United States himself. 55

Heavy-duty Installation

K   Cage's San Francisco house is a Victorian and before the fireplace could be installed, the walls and the foundation had to be reinforced to hold the weight. It took a crane to lift the fireplace from the street to the house. 60

L   Palos and four assistants rolled it up a ramp and in the front door. It had been shipped in 13 pieces and was reassembled using a special scaffold and pulley system. Stainless steel pins and epoxy secured it while Palos carved and 65 shaped it to fit the entire living room wall. At the end of three weeks, everything was in place.

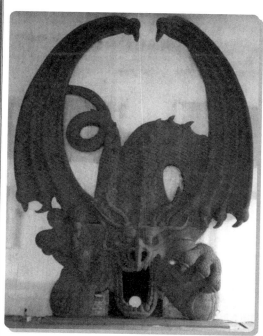

▲ The "Dreadful Dragon" fireplace

M   The son of a shoemaker, Palos moved to San Francisco from 70 Zacatecas, Mexico, while in his early 20s to learn how to sculpt. He took a job making molds and models, studying English at night. "My teachers encouraged me to 75 travel," he says, so he spent several months visiting museums and galleries throughout Europe. "I learned from the masters, but I developed my own style." 80

N   Palos opened his own studio in San Francisco 26 years ago. Eight people work for him, including his daughter, Alexandra, who helps in the office. He prefers to sculpt on weekends when things are quiet and he can "really produce." 85

They Think I Am Sicilian

O   Every year Palos makes a six-week pilgrimage back to Europe to the small town of Carrara, Italy, known for its marble, which Michelangelo[3] used to sculpt the *Pietà*.

P   "They think I am Sicilian," says Palos, who is fluent in Italian.

Q   A showroom adjoins his studio where much of his artistic work— 90 torsos, fountains, statues, and urns—is on display.

---

[3]Michelangelo (1475–1564) was a superb Italian sculptor, painter, and architect, in the period known as the Renaissance. The *Pietà* is a famous sculpture he created in 1499 for St. Peter's Basilica in Rome.

R   Not everything is classical in style. A scale model of the "Dreadful Dragon" leans against one wall and a woman's head carved out of sleek black Belgian marble is in the contemporary mode.

S   When asked about his favorite, it is still the "Dreadful Dragon," he   95
says. "Cage came to my studio and shook my hand when it was all over," Palos recalls. "He said, 'You are an artist.'"

T   "I told him it takes two."

Source: "The San Francisco Sculptor Who Created Nicholas Cage's 'Dreadful Dragon.'" *San Francisco Examiner* (Kristine M. Carber)

After You Read

Strategy

Forming Adjectives from Nouns

In English, nouns are often used as adjectives with no change, for example, the *shoe* salesman or the *book*store. However, there are also many suffixes (endings) that can be added to nouns to change them into adjectives. Learning the relationships of different parts of speech (like adjectives and nouns) from the same word family can help you build your vocabulary in English.

3 Forming Adjectives from Nouns Read the sentences below. Fill in each blank with an adjective that is related to the noun in italics. If you need help, scan the article for the missing word.

1. A section of town where there is a lot of *industry* is an ___*industrial*___ section.

2. A work of art that is large and important like a *monument* is a _____ work of art.

3. Hair that is full of *curls* is _____ hair.

4. A mantel made according to *tradition* is a _____ mantel.

5. A design that comes from *Europe* is a _____ design.

6. Statues of figures from Greek and Roman *mythology* are _____ statues.

7. A piece of art that stays in your *memory* is a _____ piece.

8. A job that presents a *challenge* is a _____ job.

9. A house built in the style of Queen *Victoria* is a _____ house.

10. A person who is from *Sicily* is a _____ person.

11. Marble that is from *Belgium* is _____ marble.

4 **Recalling Information** Choose the best way of completing each statement, based on what you have just read.

1. Manuel Palos designs and builds works of art for _____.
   - (A) hotels and other businesses
   - (B) private residences
   - (C) San Francisco landmarks
   - (D) all of these

2. He found inspiration for the dragon design of Nicolas Cage's fireplace in _____.
   - (A) the Legion of Honor
   - (B) the Academy of Sciences
   - (C) a children's book
   - (C) the public zoo

3. In order to find a studio big enough to work on the "Dreadful Dragon," Palos had to move temporarily to _____.
   - (A) Italy
   - (B) Mexico
   - (C) Greece
   - (D) Arizona

4. If any part of the face of the dragon had broken, Palos would have had to _____.
   - (A) pay a lot of money to have it fixed
   - (B) start over from the beginning
   - (C) give up the whole job
   - (D) find a new design

5. As a young man, Palos immigrated to the United States from his native country, _____.
   - (A) Mexico
   - (B) Ireland
   - (C) Germany
   - (D) Italy

6. He opened up his own studio many years ago and now _____.
   - (A) still works completely alone
   - (B) works with one other sculptor
   - (C) has eight people working for him, including his daughter
   - (D) has given up the sculpting and only works on the designs

7. Every year Palos returns for inspiration to _____.
   - (A) Italy
   - (B) France
   - (C) Greece
   - (D) South America

Finding the Basis for Inferences

In Chapter 2, you learned that inferences are ideas or opinions that are not stated but that can be *inferred* or concluded from the information given. In many readings, you can make inferences from what is written. The details in the reading give you the basis for the inferences you make.

5 **Finding the Basis for Inferences** The following sentences are not stated directly in the article; they are inferences. In small groups, scan the reading to find and explain the basis for the following inferences about Manuel Palos.

1. Palos's sculpture is well known in San Francisco.

2. He has a sense of humor.

3. He is emotional about his work.

4. He is a perfectionist.

5. He is not afraid to take risks.

6. He works hard to please his clients.

6 **Guided Academic Conversation: How Our Work Affects Our Life** With a partner, discuss the following questions. For questions 3–5, take turns interviewing each other. One of you reads the question out loud and the other answers; then change roles.

1. Manuel Palos immigrated to the United States from Mexico as a young man. What factors do you think helped him to achieve success?

2. Why do you think he loves his work so much? Is this common? Why do some people dislike what they do for a living or feel indifferent to it?

3. What is your idea of the perfect kind of work? Explain.

4. Which is more important for your future happiness: where you will live or what work you will do? Why?

5. What kind of people would you like to work with? Or would you prefer to work alone? Look at the cartoon on page 175. What inferences can you make about the employees and the management of that office?

"The computer system is down again."

Source: CLOSE TO HOME ©1993 John McPherson. Reprinted with permission of UNIVERSAL PRESS SYNDICATE. All rights reserved.

7 **What Do You Think?** Read the paragraph below and discuss the questions that follow with a partner.

Home Offices

▲ Working in a home office

With our society's contemporary technology of instant communications such as cell phones, blackberries, computers, fax machines, scanners, chat rooms, web cams, and email, many people have chosen to set up their work office at home. Around the world, millions of people have their main office in their homes. They work as consultants, writers, editors, and business people.

1. Would you like to have a home office if your profession allowed? Why or why not?

2. What are the advantages and disadvantages of a home office?

A Lifetime of Learning to Manage Effectively

Before You Read

Strategy

Understanding Idiomatic Phrases from the Context
An idiomatic phrase is a group of words that have a special meaning when used together. Native speakers typically use many idiomatic phrases but they may be difficult for non-native speakers to understand. Sometimes you recognize every word in the phrase but still do not understand the meaning of the whole phrase in the special idiomatic way it is being used. Usually, if you keep reading, you will find a clue to the meaning—an example, an explanation, or a contrasting phrase.

1 **Understanding Idiomatic Phrases from the Context** All the following phrases from the selection have clues to their meanings given in the reading except the first one. Scan the article for each phrase and write a definition or explanation; then write the words that provided clues to the meaning.

1. raw brain power (line 3) (**Hint:** In this case there are no clues. You have to think of the more common usage of *raw* when applied to foods and extend the meaning.)
   definition:

   _____

   _____

2. broad human beings (line 21)
   definition:

   _____

   _____

   clue:

   _____

   _____

3. sense of integrity (line 33)
   definition:

   _____

   _____

   clue:

4. cut corners (line 45)

definition:

_____

_____

clue:

_____

_____

5. in the short run (line 46)

definition:

_____

_____

clue:

_____

_____

6. hard knocks (line 74)

definition:

_____

_____

clue:

_____

_____

Read

Introduction

Have you ever worked for someone you really liked and admired? Have you had the opposite experience—working for someone you disliked and did not respect? Either way, you know that a manager or boss can make a great difference in the quality of an employee's work. The following article is written by Ralph Z. Sorenson, president and chief executive officer (CEO) of Barry Wright Corporation, a manufacturer of computer accessories and other products. He gives his opinion on the kind of person who makes a good manager and explains how his views on this subject have changed over the years.

- What qualities do you think make a good manager?
- What would you guess is the number one most important quality for a manager? (You may be surprised by the answer given in the article.)

A Lifetime of Learning to Manage Effectively

A   Years ago, when I was a young assistant professor at Harvard Business School, I thought that the key to developing managerial leadership lay in raw brain power. I thought the role of business schools was to develop future managers who knew all about the various functions of business—to teach them how to define problems succinctly, analyze these problems, and   5 identify alternatives in a clear, logical fashion, and, finally, to teach them to make an intelligent decision.

B   My thinking gradually became tempered by living and working outside the United States and by serving seven years as a college president. During my presidency of Babson College, I added several additional traits or skills   10 that I felt a good manager must possess.

C   The first is the *ability to express oneself* in a clear, articulate fashion. Good oral and written communication skills are absolutely essential if one is to be an effective manager.

D   Second, one must possess that intangible set of qualities called   15 *leadership skills*. To be a good leader, one must understand and be sensitive to people and be able to inspire them toward the achievement of common goals.

▲ Good communication skills are essential for managers.

E   Next, I concluded that effective   20 managers must be *broad human beings* who not only understand the world of business but also have a sense of the cultural, social, political, historical, and (particularly today) the international   25 aspects of life and society. This suggests that exposure to the liberal arts and humanities should be part of every manager's education.

F   Finally, as I pondered the business and   30 government-related scandals that have occupied the front pages of newspapers, it became clear that a good manager in today's world must have *courage and a strong sense of integrity*. He or she must know where to draw the line between right and wrong.   35

G   That can be agonizingly difficult. Drawing a line in a corporate setting sometimes involves having to make a choice between what appears to be conflicting "rights." For example, if one is faced with a decision whether or not to close an ailing factory, whose interests should prevail? Those of stockholders? Of employees? Of customers? Or those of the community in which the factory is located? It's a tough choice. And the typical manager faces many others.

H   Sometimes these choices involve simple questions of honesty or truthfulness. More often, they are more subtle and involve such issues as having to decide whether to "cut corners" and economize to meet profit objectives that may be beneficial in the short run but that are not in the best long-term interests of the various groups being served by one's company. Making the right choice in situations such as these clearly demands integrity and the courage to follow where one's integrity leads.

I   But now I have left behind the cap and gown of a college president and put on the hat of chief executive officer. As a result of my experience as a corporate CEO, my list of desirable managerial traits has become still longer.

J   It now seems to me that what matters most in the majority of organizations is to have reasonably intelligent, hard-working managers who have a sense of pride and loyalty toward their organization; who can get to the root of a problem and are inclined toward action; who are decent human beings with a natural empathy and concern for people; who possess humor, humility, and common sense; and who are able to couple drive with "stick-to-it-iveness" and patience in the accomplishment of a goal.

K   It is the *ability to make positive things happen* that most distinguishes the successful manager from the mediocre or unsuccessful one. It is far better to have dependable managers who can make the right things happen in a timely fashion than to have brilliant, sophisticated, highly educated executives who are excellent at planning and analyzing, but who are not so good at implementing. The most cherished manager is the one who says "I can do it," and then does.

L   Many business schools continue to focus almost exclusively on the development of analytical skills. As a result, these schools are continuing to graduate large numbers of MBAs and business majors who know a great deal about analyzing strategies, dissecting balance sheets, and using computers—but who still don't know how to manage!

M   As a practical matter, of course, schools can go only so far in teaching their students to manage. Only hard knocks and actual work experience will fully develop the kinds of managerial traits, skills, and virtues that I have discussed here.

N   Put another way: The best way to learn to manage is to manage. Companies such as mine that hire aspiring young managers can help the process along by:

- providing good role models and mentors 80
- setting clear standards and high expectations that emphasize the kind of broad leadership traits that are important to the organization, and then rewarding young managers accordingly
- letting young managers actually manage

O   Having thereby encouraged those who are not only "the best and the 85 brightest" but *also* broad, sensitive human beings possessing all of the other traits and virtues essential for their managerial leadership to rise to the top, we just might be able to breathe a bit more easily about the future health of industry and society.

Source: *Wall Street Journal* (Ralph Z. Sorenson)

After You Read

2 **Recalling Information** Choose the best way of finishing each statement, based on what you have just read.

1. The author's work experience includes _____.
- (A) college teaching and administration
- (B) working outside the United States
- (C) business management
- (D) all of the above

2. Since he believes managers should be broad human beings, he would like to see their education focused on business and also on _____.
- (A) the humanities and liberal arts
- (B) computers and high technology
- (C) accounting and finance
- (D) none of the above

3. For him, a manager should have leadership skills; a good leader is one who _____.
- (A) defines problems succinctly
- (B) understands and inspires people
- (C) expresses his or her ideas clearly
- (D) none of the above

4. One of the experiences that convinced him of the need for a sense of integrity in managers was _____.

- (A) a conversation with a high government official
- (B) the discovery of dishonesty among students
- (C) reading about scandals in the newspapers
- (D) working for a corrupt business in another country

5. According to Sorenson, when facing a decision about the possible closing of a factory that is not profitable, a manager should consider the interests of

_____.

- (A) the stockholders and customers
- (B) the employees
- (C) the community
- (D) all the above

6. He thinks that managers should think not just of what is profitable in the short run but also of _____.

- (A) how to "cut corners" to meet objectives
- (B) the long-term interests of those involved
- (C) the fastest way to make money for the company
- (D) the best way to advance their own careers

7. In his view at present, the trait that distinguishes the successful manager from the mediocre is _____.

- (A) high academic achievement
- (B) the ability to get things done
- (C) a critical and analytical mind
- (D) a knowledge of several languages

8. Companies that hire young managers ought to _____.

- (A) let them manage right away
- (B) put them under the authority of an older manager
- (C) give them a training course
- (D) make them wait a few years before managing

3 **Guided Academic Conversation: Applying Inferences to a Situation**
Now that you have read Sorenson's article, imagine that he is looking for a new manager for a department of his company and has received the following descriptions of three candidates for the position. Based on what he says in the article, what can you infer about his reaction to these candidates? Working in small groups, decide which candidate he would probably hire and why. Support your opinion for or against each candidate with specific statements from the reading. Then discuss whether you as a group would agree with this choice or not, and why.

> **Reading Tip**
>
> From what you read or learn of one person's views, you can often **infer** what they would think of a new situation as well.

Candidate A

- graduated with high honors from a top private university
- majored in business, minored in computer science
- won two prizes for inventing new computer programs
- was chess champion of the university for two years
- received a medal for highest academic achievement in her senior year
- was described by her teachers as "brilliant, analytical, clear-thinking"

Candidate B

- graduated with above-average marks from a large public university
- majored in history, minored in business
- spent two summers traveling through Europe and Asia
- won a national essay contest
- was secretary of a debate club
- was active in community activities—for example, neighborhood cleanup drive, fund-raising for new senior citizens' center
- worked part time for three years as assistant manager of the school bookstore in order to finance his education
- was described by his teachers as "well-liked, honest, industrious"

Candidate C

- graduated with honors from a well-known private university
- had a joint major in political science and business and a minor in economics
- is fluent in three languages
- spent his junior year at an international school in Switzerland
- was president of the music society and treasurer of the drama club
- was editor of the campus humor magazine
- organized and successfully ran (for two years) a small mail-order company that sold tapes and records of local singers
- was suspended from the university for six months for cheating on an accounting exam but was later reinstated without penalties
- was described by his teachers as "highly intelligent, ambitious, a natural leader"

1. Candidate most likely to be hired by Sorenson: _____

2. Reasons: _____

_____

_____

_____

4 **Focusing on Words from the Academic Word List** Read the excerpt below taken from the reading in Part 2. Fill in the blanks with a word from the box. Do not look back at the reading right away; instead, see if you can now remember the vocabulary.

achievement	cultural	goals	occupied
aspects	exposure	integrity	
concluded	finally	liberal	

Second, one must possess that intangible set of qualities called *leadership skills*. To be a good leader, one must understand and be sensitive to people and be able to inspire them toward the _____ of ₁

common _____. ₂

Next, I _____ that effective managers must be *broad* 5 ₃

human beings who not only understand the world of business but also have a sense of the _____, social, political, historical, and ₄

(particularly today) the international _____ of life and ₅

society. This suggests that _____ to the ₆

_____ arts and humanities should be part of every 10 ₇

manager's education.

_____, as I pondered the business and government- ₈

related scandals that have _____ the front pages of ₉

newspapers, it became clear that a good manager in today's world must have courage and a strong sense of _____. He or she 15 ₁₀

must know where to draw the line between right and wrong.

5 **Around the Globe: Women Moving to the Top** Read the articles below, taking notes or underlining important points, and then complete the activity that follows.

▲ Women and men increasingly share leadership positions in many businesses today.

Introduction

Not only are women moving into higher-paying technical jobs, they're moving into executive positions that formerly were unavailable to them. This is a world-wide trend from North America to South America, from Asia to Europe. Among those who have moved into executive positions are the following three women from Japan, Korea, and Mexico.

IZUMI KOBAYASHI, President, Merrill Lynch Japan Securities

When Izumi Kobayashi took charge of Merrill Lynch Japan Securities Co. in December 2001, the brokerage firm was in disarray. That year, the Merrill Lynch & Co. unit had a loss of nearly $550 million.

Four year later, Ms. Kobayashi had steered the firm out of its darkest days; by fiscal 2003, Merrill had become the most profitable stock firm in Japan, turning a nearly $130 million profit.

Since becoming both the first woman and the first Japanese to run the Japan unit of Merrill Lynch, Ms. Kobayashi, 46, has shown a willingness to make tough decisions and carry them out quickly. She has been able to identify areas of growth and build them out to get in front of the competition.

After college, Ms. Kobayashi embarked on a typical Japanese woman's path. She joined a chemical company, making copies and pouring tea for male colleagues. But after four years, she got fed up and joined Merrill. In 2000, she became chief administrative officer of the company.

Source: *Wall Street Journal* (Andrew Morse)

KIM SUNG JOO, Sungjoo International, Sungjoo Design Tech and Distribution, Korea

When Kim Sung Joo founded a company to sell luxury goods in Korea in 1990, her biggest problem wasn't uncooperative suppliers or restrictive government regulations. It was family opposition to her being a businesswoman.

Ms. Kim's father was the owner of a huge conglomerate, Daesung Group, and was so conservative that he wouldn't even let the female members of his family set foot in his office. Ms. Kim was expected to follow her sisters' examples to get married and have children.

But Ms. Kim balked at tradition and after schooling in the U.S. and United Kingdom, went into business for herself. Today she heads the country's largest luxury-goods retailers. Her companies have exclusive rights to sell many luxury brands. In 2003, the companies had sales of $54 million, a work force of 350 people, and 90 outlets in Korea.

Despite her financial success, Ms. Kim still finds resentment from the male members of her family. After her father's death, her three brothers took over the family business. They still refuse to accept Ms. Kim's business career, she says. She sees them just once or twice a year.

Source: *Wall Street Journal* (Seah Park)

MARÍA ASUNCIÓN ARAMBURUZABALA, Vice Chairman, Grupo Modelo SA, Mexico

▲ María Asunción Aramburuzabala

Every time someone around the world squeezes a sliver of lime into a Corona beer, a fraction of that money goes to María Asunción Aramburuzabala, Mexico's richest woman.

Ms. Aramburuzabala, 41, is the granddaughter of a penniless immigrant from Spain who founded Mexico's leading beer company, Grupo Modelo SA, in the wake of the 1910–1917 Mexican Revolution. She owns 10% of Modelo and is its vice-chairman.

Unlike many other heiresses in Latin America, Ms. Aramburuzabala felt uncomfortable sitting on her fortune when her father died in 1995. So she set out to build on it, taking an active role in Modelo, buying a stake in Mexico's biggest media company, and funding Internet start-ups and real-estate ventures.

With much success in business, Ms. Aramburuzabala is now starting a campaign to get Mexican women more involved in politics. "Mexican women need to get involved and realize we can change things," she says.

Source: *Wall Street Journal* (David Luhnow)

Strategy

Using a Chart for Comparison

Sometimes a chart can help you remember and clearly see distinctive traits, similarities, and differences between people or items you wish to compare.

6 **Using a Chart for Comparison** Based on what you read on pages 184–186, put a checkmark under the name of the woman executive or executives who fits each of the descriptions in the column on the left.

Description	Izumi Kobayashi	Kim Sung Joo	María Asunción Aramburuzabala
Has had to put up with opposition from her family or society	✓	✓	
Is the richest woman in her country			
Is the head of a company			
Sells luxury goods			
Sells beer			
Heads a securities firm			
Wants to help women in her country get ahead in politics			
Family started with no money and built a big company			
Started her own company which now has many outlets in her country			
Brought her company from a loss to a big profit			
Invests in a media company, Internet start-ups, and real estate			
Father wanted her to focus on getting married and having children			
Started out making copies and pouring tea for male colleagues in a chemical company			
Family still opposes her career, despite her success			
Works in the family business			

Strategy

Reading for Speed and Fluency: Concentrating
To improve your reading speed and fluency, pay attention when you are reading. Try not to get distracted. When we are distracted, we tend to reread lines. That slows down our reading speed.

7 **Timed Reading: Reading for Speed and Fluency** After reading the introduction in the box on the next page, try to finish the reading and comprehension exercises in eight minutes. Remember to concentrate as you read. Try not to get distracted by other thoughts or what is happening around you.

Your beginning time: _____

The Worst That Recruiters Have Seen

A   Let's face it: It's a jungle out there, and you can use all the help available to avoid the mistakes that can doom a promising job candidacy.

B   Perhaps you can draw some lessons from these fatal *faux pas*, gleaned from veteran corporate and executive recruiters. They consider them the worst mistakes they've seen.

Red-Handed

C   During his interview with me, a candidate bit his fingernails and proceeded to bleed onto his tie. When I asked him if he wanted a Band-Aid, he said that he chewed his nails all the time and that he'd be fine. He continued to chew away.

—Audrey W. Hellinger, Chicago office of
Martin H. Bauman Associates, New York

Let's Be Buddies

D   In his first meeting with me, a candidate made himself a little too comfortable. Not only did he liberally pepper his conversation with profanities, he also pulled his chair right up to the edge of my desk and started picking up and examining papers and knickknacks.

—Nina Proct, Martin H. Bauman Associates, New York

Deep Water

E   One of the top candidates for a senior vice presidency at a big consumer-products company was a young man under 35 who had grown up in a small town in the Midwest. As I frequently do, I asked about his years in high school. He said he'd been a star swimmer—so good that he'd even won a gold medal in the Olympics. It hung in his high-school gymnasium. The client liked him very much and was preparing to make him an offer. But when I checked his references, I discovered he hadn't gone to the college he'd listed, and he had never even swum in the Olympics.

—John A. Coleman, Canny, Bowen Inc., New York

Loser's Circle

F   I walked into the reception area to pick up my next applicant, Sarah B., a recent college graduate.

G   Once in my office, I glanced at her well-written résumé and wondered how much time and money she had spent preparing it. She was obviously intelligent and articulate. How, I wondered, could she misjudge our corporate climate this way?

H   The sad fact was that I could never send her out to be interviewed by our administrators or physicians. They might forgive her sandals, her long billowy skirt and her white peasant blouse—but never, ever, the large gold ring through her nose.

—Janet Garber, Manager of Employment-
Employee Relations, Cornell University
Medical College, New York

Bon Voyage

I   It was a million-dollar job, and he was a top-notch candidate. My client had decided to hire him, and he was having dinner with the chief executive officer. He asked the CEO, "How do we travel?" The response was: "We're being careful of costs these days. We travel business class internationally and back-of-the-bus domestically." Without thinking, the candidate said, "I'm used to traveling first class."

—Tony Lord, New York office of
A. T. Kearney Executive Search, Chicago

It's Not Always the Candidate

J   It isn't always the job candidate who's the disaster. Consider what happened to the top aspirant for a senior position at one of Richard Slayton's client companies. As related by the Chicago executive recruiter, the candidate was set for a full day of interviews with senior executives, including a final session over dinner with the CEO.

K   At lunch with the candidate, the senior vice president of human resources broke a bridge and lined up the pieces of broken teeth on a napkin in front of him. And, finally, the CEO was called away unexpectedly and never met with the candidate.

L   But, says Mr. Slayton, the day from hell had a happy ending. "My client said that if he could survive all that with good humor, he was worth serious consideration. He got the job."

Source: "The Worst That Recruiters Have Seen" *Wall Street Journal*

Put an X in front of the mistakes made by the job applicants described in the article.

1. _____ acting too casual

2. _____ acting too formal

3. _____ arriving 30 minutes late for the appointment

4. _____ biting fingernails

5. _____ dropping papers and personal items on the floor

6. _____ forgetting the company's name

7. _____ not carrying a business card

8. _____ not leaving a tip

9. _____ showing a gold medal won in swimming class

10. _____ showing an unwillingness to economize

11. _____ telling lies

12. _____ using swear words and bad language

13. _____ wearing a nose ring

14. _____ wearing inappropriate clothing

15. _____ breaking his teeth

Choose the best way of finishing each statement, based on what you have just read.

1. The job candidates described in the article are _____.
   - Ⓐ all men
   - Ⓑ all women
   - Ⓒ mostly men
   - Ⓓ mostly women

2. In the article, there is only one job candidate who gets the job. He gets the job because _____.
   - Ⓐ his father works for the company
   - Ⓑ he doesn't make any mistakes
   - Ⓒ he acts like an old buddy
   - Ⓓ he shows patience and humor

Word count in reading: <u>530</u>

Your time for completing the reading and exercises: _____

Part 3   Tying It All Together

 1 Making Connections Do some research on the Internet and take notes on one of the following topics. Share your results with the class or in a small group.

A Classic Sculptor Read about the life and work of a great classical sculptor, like the Italian master Michelangelo whose famous statue, the *Pietà*, is referred to in the article, or the French sculptor Auguste Rodin, or a famous sculptor from your culture.

A Contemporary Sculptor Research work being done now by Manuel Palos and his associates in San Francisco and Puerto Vallarta, or by other contemporary sculptors from other places.

Alternative Decorating Find information about a style for decorating homes and public buildings that is different from the classical style generally used by Palos. Possible styles include postmodern, art nouveau, art deco. Or research the influence of the Asian philosophy of Feng Shui.

Women Executives Around the World What kinds of barriers do women executives face? What kinds of organizations exist to support them? Can you find another example of an impressive female executive like the ones in the "Around the Globe" segment of this chapter (page 00)?

Tips on Being a Good Manager What does it take to be a good manager? (Remember to look up all the forms of the word, such as *management* and *manage effectively*, etc.) Are the tips you find similar to or different from those in the article in Part 2?

What to Do in a Job Interview The timed reading gave some good examples of what not to do in a job interview. But what *should* you do? Look up some tips on what to do in a job interview (other key words include *job interview advice* or *job interview etiquette*.) Are the tips different when they come from different countries, or are they all just about the same?

Focus on Testing

Grammar-Oriented Reading Questions

In the TOEFL® iBT reading section two types of questions specifically target the effect of grammar on the meaning of a passage.

Reference questions focus on pronouns and other elements that refer backward or forward within the passage. Sentence-rephrasing questions test your ability to understand the core meaning of a statement without being distracted by less-important sentence parts.

Practice Read the passage about management consultants. Answer the reference and sentence-rephrasing questions that follow. Shaded parts of the text are referred to in the questions.

Before the Consultants Arrive

A   Management consultants are advisers hired by a company to help improve overall operations. They do not usually focus on one or two functions within the company they advise. Rather, they aim to see a bigger picture and assess the interrelationship of all. Their arrival presents both great opportunity and great risk. Advance steps taken by the management of the client company play a big role in determining which it will be.

B   The greatest value of external consultants is the perspective of a group of informed outsiders. They must be familiar with the basic standards of quality within the client's field without being immersed in the firm's internal rivalries, social cliques, or unexamined corporate traditions. One possible pitfall here would be a lack of true independence, perhaps because of personal or business relationships with someone inside the client company. A consultant who is an old college buddy of the accounting manager is not likely to fairly evaluate the accounting department. Such connections are not hard to screen for, but the screening has to be done thoroughly and out in the open before the consultants even set foot on site.

C   Making sure the management consultants are adequately informed is a harder problem. One assumes they have the professional qualifications to do the job, but their specialized knowledge of the firm is only as good as what they discover once they begin their interviews among company employees. If an employee sees the management consultants as a threat, whatever he or she says is unreliable. The team's questions may be seen as a means of discovering what that particular employee has done wrong. Full candor, the thinking goes, could cause me to lose some of my privileges, my stature, or (at worst) my job. My solution: Manipulate the truth so I look really good.

D   To head off such unhelpful sentiments, any company contracting with management consultants should begin talking up the enterprise at least two months in advance. The message should be, "This is an opportunity, not an investigation." Convince employees that the outside review is their chance to influence the future direction of the company. Lay out in advance a set of rules for protecting the anonymity of employees. Supervisors should not be able to link any individual to any particular point of view unless he or she wants. Since distortions of the truth could also include unfair negative statements about one's "enemies" within the firm, the system must also protect employees from grudge-bearing colleagues. Most management consultants have calibrated their data-gathering tools to weed out vengeful attacks, but the company should emphasize in advance that the consultants' report will contain no references to individuals. Furthermore, the consulting team must be reminded to apply a strict standard of evidence, so that no apparent weakness in the company even shows up in the report unless multiple, independent sources point to it.

E   Ultimately—and this should be central to what any company tells its employees about an upcoming review—decisions about the team's findings rest with upper management in the client firm. The consultants' report is a piece of advice, not a court ruling. Any policies that result from the outside review will be enacted, in the full light of day, by managers who must come to work and face the consequences of their decisions. If employees understand this, the visiting consultants are less likely to be seen as hired assassins or as a firewall behind which managers can make unpopular changes without taking the heat.

F   Clearly, the buy-in of all managers at the client firm is vital to the success of the process. Even a single holdout could torpedo the entire exercise. Especially within a very large company, such unanimity is dauntingly difficult to achieve. It calls for an exceptional level of cooperation throughout the higher strata of the company. Many firms have discovered, though, that the effort to achieve it is, in itself, a valuable experience. Intensely competitive managers are drawn into a group endeavor that promotes a unity of purpose and a new collegiality, strengthening the company even before the first outside consultant knocks on the door.

1. Which of the statements below best expresses the most important information in the shaded sentence in Paragraph A? Incorrect choices either change the basic meaning of the original or fail to express important information.

    Ⓐ A consulting review moves forward in several steps.

    Ⓑ A company takes a big risk by hiring management consultants.

    Ⓒ The success of a consulting review depends on how well a company prepares for it.

    Ⓓ The client company must decide beforehand on a suitable group of management consultants.

2. The word they in Paragraph B refers to _____

    Ⓐ consultants

    Ⓑ clients

    Ⓒ rivalries

    Ⓓ standards

3. The word here in Paragraph B means _____

    Ⓐ in a tradition

    Ⓑ in a company

    Ⓒ in a field

    Ⓓ in a relationship

4. The word their in Paragraph C refers to _____

    Ⓐ consultants

    Ⓑ employees

    Ⓒ qualifications

    Ⓓ questions

5. Which statement best expresses the most important information in the shaded sentence in Paragraph D? Incorrect choices either change the basic meaning of the original or fail to express important information.
   - (A) A consultant review focuses on interpersonal problems among employees.
   - (B) During a review, employees should be kept safe from personal attacks by other employees.
   - (C) Consultants must know they are safe from attacks by employees.
   - (D) Some employees might use a review as a chance to say negative things about others.

6. The word this in Paragraph E refers to _____
   - (A) management's responsibility for decision-making
   - (B) an apparent weakness in the company
   - (C) a strict standard of evidence
   - (D) what a company tells its employees

7. The word itself in Paragraph F refers to _____
   - (A) cooperation
   - (B) effort
   - (C) experience
   - (D) unanimity

Responding in Writing

WRITING TIP: WRITE A SENTENCE TO COVER EACH OF THE MAIN POINTS

To write a summary of a reading, first write a summary sentence as an introduction, then identify the main points of the reading and write a sentence covering each one of the main points. Headings can often help you identify the main points.

2 **Writing Practice** In Chapter 1, you wrote a summary statement in the Responding in Writing section, and in Chapters 5 and 6, you did some short, directed exercises on summarizing. Now you will write a summary of the whole reading.

Topic

Write a one- or two-paragraph summary of any one of the three longer readings in this chapter *The San Francisco Sculptor Who Created Nicolas Cage's "Dreadful Dragon," A Lifetime of Learning to Manage Effectively,* or the timed reading *The Worst Recruiters Have Seen.*

Step 1 Choose which reading you would like to summarize.

Step 2 Write a summary statement for the reading, as you did in Chapter 1. This statement will be the first sentence of your longer summary. Remember that to write a summary statement, put down the main idea in one sentence. Try to express this in *your own words*, not in the same words that were written. Use the most important details from the whole piece, not just from the beginning.

Step 3 Find the main points of the reading. Notice that each of the three longer readings in this chapter include headings. These headings provide useful markers, dividing the reading into main points. Write one sentence for each main point in the reading (one sentence for each section that begins with a new heading). Try to express the main point in your own words. Make sure it is a *main* point you are describing and not just a minor detail related to one point.

Step 4 Write a concluding sentence if you think it is necessary.

Step 5 Revise your summary. Then exchange with a partner. Has your partner captured the meaning of the whole piece in the first sentence? Do each of the other sentences capture one main point of the work?

Self-Assessment Log

Read the lists below. Check (✓) the strategies and vocabulary that you learned in this chapter. Look through the chapter or ask your instructor about the strategies and words that you do not understand.

Reading and Vocabulary-Building Strategies
- ❏ Previewing a reading: predicting
- ❏ Scanning for specific words
- ❏ Forming adjectives from nouns
- ❏ Recalling information
- ❏ Finding the basis for inferences
- ❏ Understanding idiomatic phrases from the context
- ❏ Applying inferences to a situation
- ❏ Using a chart for comparison
- ❏ Reading for speed and fluency: concentrating

Target Vocabulary

Nouns
- ❏ achievement*
- ❏ art nouveau
- ❏ aspects*
- ❏ crane
- ❏ exposure*
- ❏ goals*
- ❏ integrity*
- ❏ landmarks
- ❏ mantel
- ❏ options*
- ❏ pilgrimage
- ❏ urns
- ❏ warehouse

Verbs
- ❏ chiseled
- ❏ concluded*
- ❏ occupied*

Adjectives
- ❏ Belgian
- ❏ cultural*
- ❏ curly
- ❏ European
- ❏ industrial
- ❏ liberal*
- ❏ memorable
- ❏ monumental
- ❏ mythological
- ❏ Sicilian
- ❏ traditional*
- ❏ Victorian

Adverb
- ❏ finally*

Idioms and Expressions
- ❏ broad human beings
- ❏ cut corners
- ❏ hard knocks
- ❏ in the short run
- ❏ a labor of love
- ❏ raw brain power
- ❏ sense of integrity

* These words are from the Academic Word List. For more information on this list, see www.vuw.ac.nz/lals/research/awl.

Breakthroughs

In This Chapter

In the last 20 years, technological breakthroughs have profoundly advanced the way we communicate, bringing us computers, cell phones, and the Internet. Equally amazing, but less easily seen, are recent social breakthroughs. First, we look at an extraordinary woman who fought against great odds to turn a simple idea into an ecological movement of far-reaching benefits for planet Earth. Then we examine a remarkable achievement that will forever change medical treatment throughout the world: the mapping of the entire human genome. Finally, we consider the creation of a new territory, owned and governed by the native peoples who live there.

❝ If at first you don't succeed, try, try again. ❞

—English proverb

Connecting to the Topic

1. What is the woman in the photo doing? How might she be involved in an important breakthrough?

2. What breakthroughs in technology, politics, or economics do you think have brought the most benefit to humanity?

3. Describe a situation where persistence, as expressed the the English proverb at left, has paid off for you.

Trees for Democracy

In 2004, Wangari Maathai became the first woman from the African continent to receive the famous Nobel Peace prize. Because of her work, she was chosen that year as the one person out of the whole world who contributed the most to the cause of peace.

1 Previewing a Speech

The following reading is the speech that Wangari Maathai gave when she accepted the Nobel Peace prize. Scan it for these important clues to her identity, and fill in the blanks in the sentences below.

1. The native language of the speaker is _____.

2. Her country of origin is _____; this is on the continent of _____.

3. When she heard what women wanted, her response was to plant _____.

4. She did this to help heal the land and break the cycle of _____.

5. This idea has become a movement called the _____ Movement.

Strategy

Building New Words with Prefixes and Suffixes
Word building can greatly extend your English vocabulary. In the last chapter, you practiced forming adjectives from nouns by adding suffixes to the roots of words. Now extend this strategy and practice finding the root in a verb, noun, adjective, or adverb and adding prefixes and suffixes to make related forms.

Examples
connect, disconnect, connection
month, monthly, semimonthly
prove, disprove, approve, proven

---

2 Building New Words with Prefixes and Suffixes Look at each italicized word and the comments about it. Add a suffix or prefix to the root of that word to form the new word which belongs in the sentence taken from the reading. If you need help, scan the reading on pages 201–203 for the sentence.

1. **suit** The verb *suit* means to be fitting or good for something. For example, you can say, "This house suits our needs; I like it." Add the suffix *-able* and you get the adjective *suitable* meaning "fitting, appropriate," as in "This room is suitable for the meeting." Add to this a prefix that means *not,* and you will get the adjective that belongs in this blank.

   But today in Nyeri . . . the soil is parched (very dry) and ___*unsuitable*___ for growing food.

2. **nutrition** The noun *nutrition* means "taking in things to eat that are nourishing (beneficial to health)." Take off the suffix *-tion* and you get the root *nutri-*. Add the correct suffix to this, and you will get the adjective to describe something that is nourishing and beneficial.

   I listened as women related (told) what they wanted . . . clean drinking water

   and _____ food.

3. **erode** The verb *erode* means "to break apart, wear down, or wash away." It is often used to describe the washing away of the soil (ground, land). Add the correct suffix to the root *ero-*, and you get the noun that refers to this action.

   Trees stop soil _____ . . .

4. **conserve** The verb *conserve* means almost the opposite of *erode*; it means "to keep, preserve and protect." Change the *e* at the end of *conserve* to an *a* and add the right suffix to get the noun that refers to this action and finish the sentence from question 3 above.

   . . . leading to water _____ .

5. **ecology** The noun *ecology* means "the study of the relationship between living beings and their environment." Change the *y* to *i* and add the correct suffix to get the adjective describing this action.

   As household managers . . . women are the first to encounter the effects of

   _____ stress.

6. **primary** Here's your chance to build an adverb from the adjective *primary*, meaning "main, most important, predominant." Change the *y* to *i* and add the suffix, which almost always indicates an adverb.

   My idea evolved into the Green Belt Movement, made up of thousands of

   groups, _____ of women . . .

7. **degrade** The verb *degrade* means "to lower, bring down, make worse." Turn it into a noun by changing the *e* to *a* and adding a suffix.

   . . . I came to see that environmental _____ . . . was both a source of their problems and a symptom.

8. **deteriorate** The verb *deteriorate* is similar to *degrade* since it means "to go down in value or become worse." Use the same process you used in question 7 to change *deteriorate* into a noun.

   Growing crops on steep mountain slopes leads to . . . land

   _____ .

9. **forest** Start with the word *forest*, which means "a group of trees." (In the second sentence of the reading, the adjective *forested* is used to describe land with trees on it.) Now you want a word that refers to the action of losing trees. Begin with a prefix that means to *take away, make worse.* (**Hint:** Look at questions 7 and 8 above.) Add that to *forest,* and then add a suffix to make it a noun that describes the action of losing trees.

Similarly, _____ causes rivers to dry up . . .

10. **advocate** The noun *advocate* refers to a specific person who supports and works for an idea or belief. Change the last two letters, *te,* to two different letters to form the more general noun that refers to the words and actions of these people.

Through public education, political _____ , and protests, we also sought to protect open spaces . . .

11. **harass** The verb *harass* means "to annoy, bother, or attack." Change it to a noun by adding the right suffix.

Mr. Moi's government strongly opposed advocates for democracy and

environmental rights; _____ , beatings, death threats, and jail time followed . . .

12. **desert** A *desert* is an extension of dry land that is infertile (not capable of producing crops or providing for animals). In recent years, much of the fertile land on Earth has become desert. A new word with a rather long and unusual ending has appeared in English to refer to this recent phenomenon. Can you guess what this word is and fill in the blank? (You will probably have to scan for this one or look it up on the Web.)

. . . community efforts to restore the Earth at a time when we face the ecological

crises of deforestation, _____ , water scarcity, and a lack of biological diversity.

Read

Introduction

Great journeys often begin with one small step. Wangari Maathai's Green Belt Movement is based on a simple idea, planting trees. Because of the place she was born and the fact that she was a woman, she had to face immense obstacles to put her idea into practice. Her speech, which follows, describes her work, the reasons that make it effective, and some of the difficulties she had to overcome.

- Do you know of any environmental movements?
- How do you think planting trees might help a country?
- What kind of obstacles would you guess a woman like Maathai might face in starting an environmental movement?

Trees for Democracy

A   When I was growing up in Nyeri in central Kenya, there was no word for *desert* in my mother tongue, Kikuyu. Our land was fertile and forested.

▲ Wangari Maathai

But today in Nyeri, as in much of Africa and the developing world, water sources have dried up, the soil is parched and unsuitable for growing food, and conflicts over land are common. So it should come as no surprise that I was inspired to plant trees to help meet the basic needs of rural women. As a member of the National Council of Women of Kenya in the early 1970s, I listened as women related what they wanted but did not have enough of: energy, clean drinking water, and nutritious food.

B   My response was to begin planting trees with them, to help heal the land and break the cycle of poverty. Trees stop soil erosion, leading to water conservation and increased rainfall. Trees provide fuel, material for building and fencing, fruits, fodder, shade, and beauty. As household managers in rural and urban areas of the developing world, women are the first to encounter the effects of ecological stress. It forces them to walk farther to get wood for cooking and heating, to search for clean water, and to find new sources of food as old ones disappear.

C   My idea evolved into the Green Belt Movement, made up of thousands of groups, primarily of women, who have planted 30 million trees across Kenya. The women are paid a small amount for each seedling they grow, giving them an income as well as improving their environment. The movement has spread to countries in East and Central Africa.

D   Through this work, I came to see that environmental degradation by poor communities was both a source of their problems and a symptom. Growing crops on steep mountain slopes leads to loss of topsoil and land deterioration. Similarly, deforestation causes rivers to dry up and rainfall patterns to shift, which, in turn, result in much lower crop yields and less land for grazing.

E   In the 1970s and 1980s, as I was encouraging farmers to plant trees on their land, I also discovered that corrupt government agents were responsible for much of the deforestation by illegally selling off land and trees to well-connected developers. In the early 1990s, the livelihoods, the rights, and even the lives of many Kenyans in the Rift Valley were lost when elements of President Daniel arap Moi's government encouraged ethnic communities to attack one another over land. Supporters of the ruling party got the land, while those in the pro-democracy movement were displaced. This was one of the government's ways of retaining power; if communities were kept busy fighting over land, they would have less opportunity to demand democracy.

F   Land issues in Kenya are complex and easily exploited by politicians. Communities needed to understand and be sensitized about the history of land ownership and distribution in Kenya and Africa. We held seminars on human rights, governing, and reducing conflict.

G   In time, the Green Belt Movement became a leading advocate of reintroducing multiparty democracy and free and fair elections in Kenya. Through public education, political advocacy, and protests, we also sought to protect open spaces and forests from unscrupulous developers, who were often working hand in hand with politicians. Mr. Moi's government strongly opposed advocates for democracy and environmental rights; harassment, beatings, death threats, and jail time followed, for me and for many others.

H   Fortunately, in 2002, Kenyans realized their dream and elected a democratic government. What we've learned in Kenya—the symbiotic relationship between the sustainable management of natural resources and democratic governance—is also relevant globally.

I   Indeed, many local and international wars, like those in West and Central Africa and the Middle East, continue to be fought over resources. In the process, human rights, democracy, and democratic space are denied.

J   I believe the Nobel Committee recognized the links between the environment, democracy, and peace and sought to bring them to worldwide attention with the Peace Prize that I am accepting today. The committee,

▲ Successful African women selling their products at a market

I believe, is seeking to encourage community efforts to restore the Earth at a time when we face the ecological crises of deforestation, desertification, water scarcity, and a lack of biological diversity.

K   Unless we properly manage resources like forests, water, land, minerals, and oil, we will not win the fight against poverty. And there will not be peace. Old conflicts will rage on and new resource wars will erupt unless we change the path we are on.   85

L   To celebrate this award, and the work it recognizes of those around the world, let me recall the words of Gandhi: My life is my message. Also, plant a tree.   90

Source: "Nobel Prize Acceptance Speech" *The New York Times* (Wangari Maathai)

After You Read

Strategy

Finding Evidence to Disprove False Arguments
No matter how good a person's work is or what prize he or she wins, there will always be people who will say negative things. In such cases, that person may want to disprove those negative or false things.

If you have understood a reading well, you should be able to find evidence from it to disprove arguments about it that are false. Disproving false arguments with evidence helps you practice your skills for argumentation and persuasion.

3 Finding Evidence to Disprove False Arguments Imagine that a person made the following untrue comments. Find evidence (facts and direct quotations) from the article to disprove these false arguments.

1. "There is no new problem with the land in central Kenya or any place else. It is just the same now as it was 30 or 40 years ago. The Earth doesn't change."

    _____

    _____

2. "Trees? Who cares about trees? Women like trees because they are beautiful but they serve no practical use at all. You can't eat a tree."

    _____

    _____

3. "The lady who wrote this speech sounds like a troublemaker. Back in the 1990s, they said in the newspapers that she was put in jail and beaten by the police, so she must have done bad things."

    _____

    _____

4. "Why is this Green Belt Movement pushing for democracy? They are supposed to be an ecological movement, so they should keep their noses out of politics. What does politics have to do with ecology?

_____

_____

 4 **The Word Builder Challenge** Work in groups of three to five students. The object of the game is to build (and write down) as many *new* related words as possible in the time allowed from the list of 20 words given below.

> **Rules**
>
> To be considered new, a word must be spelled differently from the word on the list and be *either* a different part of speech or have a different meaning. So, if the list word is the verb *celebrate,* you can not say that *celebrates* is a new word, but *celebration* is a new word because it is a noun. The word *celebrated* could also be considered a new word since it can be used as an adjective, e.g., *the celebrated author. Celebrating* can be used as a noun, so that would also be correct, e.g., *Celebrating birthdays is fun!*
>
> However, someone on the team *must know what the word means* and be able to use it in a good sentence, if asked to do so. When the teacher calls time, the team with the most new words wins. If there is a difference of opinion, the decision of the teacher is final. The winning team should take a bow and get a round of applause.

corrupt	education	global	protest
democracy	encourage	improve	recognize
develop	energy	inspired	responsible
disappear	environment	manage	scarce
ecology	fertile	protect	wood

Strategy

Identifying Compound Words Remember that compound words are words made up of two smaller words. Some have a hyphen, but most do not. Usually, it is not hard to guess their meaning if you know what the smaller words mean. An example of a compound word is *rainfall*.

5 **Identifying Compound Words** Read the definitions below that describe compound words taken from the reading. Scan the reading for the words and write them in the chart. The definitions are in the order of the words' appearance in the reading.

	Definitions	Compound Word
1.	people living in a home	
2.	dirt on the highest part of the ground	
3.	what comes down from the sky	
4.	having powerful friends	
5.	all across the globe	

6 **Guided Academic Conversation: Analyzing the Author's Point of View** Discuss at least three of the following topics with another student. Try to think about them from the point of view of the speech by Wangari Maathai. After you finish, compare your ideas with those of the rest of the class.

1. **Breaking the Cycle of Poverty** A *cycle* means a complete set of events that occurs over and over again in the same order. What does Maathai mean by "the cycle of poverty"? Why does she say that she wants to "heal the land" in order to break this? Are there people in cultures you know well who are in a cycle of poverty? Explain.

2. **Paying for Planting** The Green Belt Movement has planted 30 million trees across Kenya and the women are paid for each seedling they grow. What do you think about that? Is it a good idea to pay them? Would it be better if they did this for free? Where do you think that the money comes from?

3. **Deforestation and Desertification** Why are trees disappearing and deserts growing larger? Is this happening only in Africa or in other places, too? What problems will this cause and what can be done about it?

4. **Sustainable Management** What does this mean? The verb *sustain* means "to maintain, support, or keep something in existence." Maathai speaks about the sustainable management of natural resources (water, land, minerals, plants, animals, etc.). How could this be done? Why is it necessary?

5. **The Relationship Between Democracy and Sustainable Management** Maathai refers to a "symbiotic" relationship between these two. *Symbiosis* is a term from biology that refers to two organisms (plants or animals) that can only live together and will die if they are apart. Why would democracy be necessary for sustainable management of resources, and vice versa? Do you agree with this?

A Revolution in Medicine

Before You Read

Strategy

Previewing: Reading Diagrams
When you preview a reading that contains diagrams, be sure to read them. A clear grasp of the diagrams will help you better understand the reading.

1 **Previewing: Reading Diagrams** The following article talks about the enormous changes occurring in the field of medicine as a result of the recent decoding of the human genome by scientists. A good way to prepare for this article is to read the diagram on page 210, called "What Is the Human Genome?" Then alone or with a partner, answer these questions:

1. What does the word *code* mean? When and where are codes used?

2. What does the genetic code determine? Where is it located?

3. What is DNA?

4. What is a gene?

2 **Understanding Idiomatic Phrases in Context** Read the sentences and parts of sentences taken from the article and select the best explanation for the phrase in italics. Line numbers are given so that you can check the context.

1. Ann Miscoi . . . was lucky to be living . . . The trouble was, she felt *half dead*. (line 3)
   - (A) healthy
   - (B) sickly
   - (C) pale
   - (D) unfortunate

2. As Miscoi read about it, everything *started making sense*. (line 11)
   - (A) became easy to understand
   - (B) became hard to understand
   - (C) began to bother her
   - (D) began to make her happy

3. So she found a doctor who would *take her concerns more seriously.* (lines 12–13)

   (A) charge her less money

   (B) not make jokes about her illness

   (C) assure her that she was in good health

   (D) pay attention to her problems

4. Until recently, diagnosing the condition required a liver biopsy—*not a procedure to be taken lightly.* (line 14)

   (A) not a difficult or complicated course of action

   (B) not a course of action to be worried about

   (C) a course of action to take when you are old

   (D) a course of action to think about seriously

5. But Miscoi didn't have to *go that route.* (line 15)

   (A) go out by that door

   (B) have that done to her

   (C) take that medicine

   (D) drive home on that highway

6. Scientists . . . developed a test that *can spot* it in a drop of blood. (line 16)

   (A) is able to find

   (B) is able to form a circle

   (C) sometimes weakens

   (D) sometimes cures

7. . . . she should live *a normal life span.* (line 21)

   (A) an ordinary life with some bad health

   (B) a life filled with common experience

   (C) the usual difficulties between doctors' appointments

   (D) the typical number of years before dying

8. Meanwhile, genetic discoveries will *trigger a flood* of new pharmaceuticals . . . (line 30)

   (A) cause problems for many liquid medicines

   (B) bring about the production of a large number

   (C) stop the arrival of many

   (D) destroy the promotion

9. . . . but Collins believes even that *will be routine* within a few decades. (line 38)

   (A) is going to become a common practice

   (B) is going to get boring and unnecessary

   (C) will be governed by new rules and regulations

   (D) will be impossible to continue

10. *Only a handful* of clinics are using gene tests to guide drug therapy. (line 67)

   (A) a selected group

   (B) an unusual combination

   (C) a small number

   (D) a large number

Introduction

Fifteen years ago, most people said it couldn't be done. No one would ever be able to decode, map out, and sequence (put in order) the entire human genome, the 3.1 billion genes that make up a human being. Genes are the building blocks of life. So learning what each gene is made of could give us the ability to control our own health. Even biologists and scientists thought that this was an impossible dream.

Nevertheless, just in time for the new millennium, two separate scientific groups announced that they had completed the task. One of these groups is the Human Genome Project sponsored by the U.S. National Institutes of Health, and the other is a private company called Celera Genomics.

- This is a great achievement, but how do you think it might be able to help us?
- Do you know, or can you imagine, how this breakthrough is already having an effect on health?

A Revolution in Medicine

A   **A**nn Miscoi had seen her father and her uncle die of organ failure in their mid-40s. So she figured she was lucky to be living when she turned 50 last year. The trouble was, she felt half dead. Her joints ached, her hair was falling out, and she was plagued by unrelenting fatigue. Her doctor assured her that nothing was seriously wrong, even after a blood test revealed un- 5 usually high iron levels, but Miscoi wasn't so sure. Scanning the Internet, she learned about a hereditary condition called hemochromatosis, in which the body stores iron at dangerous concentrations in the blood, tissues, and organs. Hemochromatosis is the nation's most common genetic illness, and probably the most underdiagnosed. As Miscoi read about it, everything 10 started making sense—her symptoms, her blood readings, even her relatives' early deaths. So she found a doctor who would take her concerns more seriously.

B   Until recently, diagnosing the condition required a liver biopsy—not a procedure to be taken lightly. But Miscoi didn't have to go that route. 15 Scientists isolated the gene for hemochromatosis a few years ago, and developed a test that can spot it in a drop of blood. Miscoi tested positive, and the diagnosis may well have saved her life. Through a regimen of weekly blood lettings, she was able to reduce her iron level before her organs sustained lasting damage. She's now free of symptoms, and as long as she gives blood every few months she should live a normal life span. "Without the DNA test, I would have had a hard time convincing any doctor that I had a real problem."

C Hemochromatosis testing could save millions of lives in coming decades. And it's just one early hint of the changes that the sequencing of the human genome could bring. By 2010, says Dr. Francis Collins of the National Human Genome Research Institute, screening tests will enable anyone to gauge his or her unique health risks, down to the body's tolerance for cigarettes and cheeseburgers.

D Meanwhile, genetic discoveries will trigger a flood of new pharmaceuticals—drugs aimed at the causes of disease rather than the symptoms—and doctors will start prescribing different treatments for different patients, depending on their genetic profiles. The use of genes *as* medicine is probably farther off, but Collins believes even that will be routine within a few decades. "By 2050," he said recently, "many potential diseases will be cured at the molecular level before they arise."

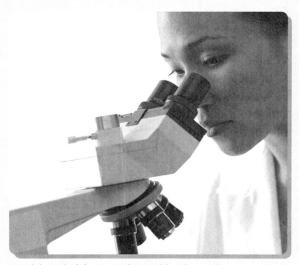

▲ A lab technician examines a blood sample.

E That may be a bit optimistic, but the trends Collins foresees are already well in motion. Clinical labs now perform some four million genetic tests each year in the United States. Newborns are routinely checked for sickle cell anemia, congenital thyroid disease, and phenylketonuria, a metabolic disease that causes retardation. Like hemochromatosis, these conditions are catastrophic if they go undetected, but highly manageable when they're spotted early. Newer tests can help people from cancer-prone families determine whether they've inherited the culpable mutation. "My mother died of colon cancer at age 47," says Dr. Bert Vogelstein, an oncologist at Johns Hopkins and the Howard Hughes Medical Institute. "If we had known she was [genetically] at risk, we could have screened for the disease and caught it early."

F Early detection is just the beginning. Genes help determine not only whether we get sick but also how we respond to various treatments. "In the past," says Dr. William Evans of St. Jude Children's Research Hospital in Memphis, Tennessee, "the questions were 'How old are you and how much

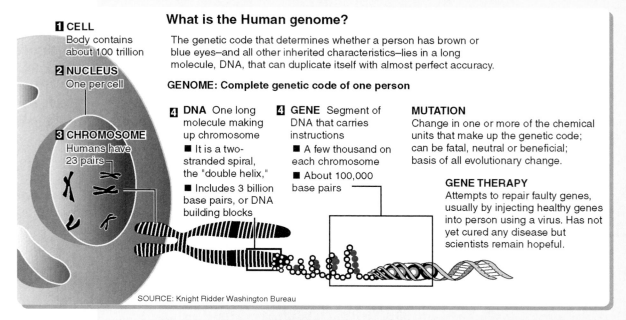

What is the Human genome?

The genetic code that determines whether a person has brown or blue eyes—and all other inherited characteristics—lies in a long molecule, DNA, that can duplicate itself with almost perfect accuracy.

GENOME: Complete genetic code of one person

1 CELL
Body contains about 100 trillion

2 NUCLEUS
One per cell

3 CHROMOSOME
Humans have 23 pairs

4 DNA One long molecule making up chromosome
■ It is a two-stranded spiral, the "double helix,"
■ Includes 3 billion base pairs, or DNA building blocks

5 GENE Segment of DNA that carries instructions
■ A few thousand on each chromosome
■ About 100,000 base pairs

MUTATION
Change in one or more of the chemical units that make up the genetic code; can be fatal, neutral or beneficial; basis of all evolutionary change.

GENE THERAPY
Attempts to repair faulty genes, usually by injecting healthy genes into person using a virus. Has not yet cured any disease but scientists remain hopeful.

SOURCE: Knight Ridder Washington Bureau

do you weigh?' Now, thanks to recent genetic discoveries, physicians can sometimes determine who stands to benefit from a given drug, and who might be harmed by it." 65

G   Only a handful of clinics are using gene tests to guide drug therapy, but the practice (known as *pharmacogenetics*) is spreading fast. Researchers are now learning to predict reactions to treatments for asthma, diabetes, heart disease, and migraines—and firms like Incyte Genomics are 70 developing chips that can analyze thousands of genes at a time. "My vision is that everyone will be sequenced at birth," says Dr. Mark Ratain of the University of Chicago. "Parents will get a CD-ROM with their child's genetic sequence. When physicians prescribe drugs, they'll use it to optimize treatment."

Source: "A Revolution in Medicine" *Newsweek* (Geoffrey Cowley and Anne Underwood)

Strategy

Separating Fact from Opinion

The difference between fact and opinion is not always clear, but some general rules can help you distinguish between them.

1. General statements that can be checked online or in a reference book about past or present events are usually facts; statements about the future are generally opinions, since the future is uncertain.

2. Statements that include the modals *may, might*, or *could*, or qualifiers such as *perhaps, maybe, possibly*, or *probably* are opinions.

3. Statements based on evidence (research, case studies, experiments, questionnaires) need to be evaluated. If they are based on only one person's research, they should be considered opinions. If they are based on a great deal of research and if most experts agree, then they can be considered facts.

4. The line between fact and opinion is sometimes open to discussion. Time, place, and culture influence these limits for all societies. For example, several decades ago, medical science thought commercial baby formula was better for babies than their mother's milk; later the guidelines were revised to recommend breastfeeding for one year. Now the World Health Organization strongly recommends breastfeeding babies for at least two years if at all possible because of the great benefits over formula.

3 **Separating Fact from Opinion** Write whether each of the following statements based on the article is a fact (F) or an opinion (O). You might need to look at its context. Since some statements are not presented exactly as they appear in the text; the line numbers are given.

1. _____ Hemochromatosis is the most common genetic illness in the United States. (line 9)

2. _____ Hemochromatosis is probably the most undiagnosed genetic illness. (line 10)

3. _____ Scientists isolated the gene for hemochromatosis a few years ago and developed a test that can spot it in a drop of blood. (lines 16–17)

4. _____ If the blood tests had been available earlier, the lives of Ann Miscoi's father and uncle would have been saved. (line 24)

5. _____ Genetic discoveries will trigger a flood of new pharmaceuticals. (line 30)

6. _____ By 2050, many potential diseases will be cured at the molecular level before they arise. (lines 42–45)

7. _____ Clinical labs now perform some four million genetic tests each year in the United States. (line 48)

8. _____ Newborn babies in the United States are routinely checked for sickle cell anemia and other diseases. (line 50)

9. _____ Certain terrible diseases can be highly manageable if they are detected early. (line 53)

10. _____ Genes help determine not only whether we get sick but also how we respond to various treatments. (lines 60–61)

11. _____ Soon parents will get a CD-ROM with their child's genetic sequence as soon as he or she is born. (line 73)

4 Focusing on Words From the Academic Word List Read the excerpt below taken from the reading in Part 2. Fill in the blanks with a word from the box. Do not look back at the reading right away; instead, see if you can now remember the vocabulary.

analyze	predict	sequence
benefit	researchers	sequenced
detection	respond	vision

Early _____ is just the beginning. Genes help determine not only whether we get sick but also how we _____ to various treatments. "In the past," says Dr. William Evans of St. Jude Children's Research Hospital in Memphis, Tennessee, "the questions were How old are you and how much do you weigh?' Now, thanks to recent genetic discoveries, physicians can sometimes determine who stands to _____ from a given drug, and who might be harmed by it."

Only a handful of clinics are using gene tests to guide drug therapy, but the practice (known as *pharmacogenetics*) is spreading fast. _____ are now learning to _____ reactions to treatments for asthma, diabetes, heart disease, and migraines—and firms like Incyte Genomics are developing chips that can _____ thousands of genes at a time. "My

_____ is that everyone will be _____ at
                7   8

birth," says Dr. Mark Ratain of the University of Chicago. "Parents will get a

CD-ROM with their child's genetic _____. When
                                                              9

physicians prescribe drugs, they'll use it to optimize treatment."

Strategy

Scanning a Timeline
A timeline is a chart that shows a sequence of events and when they occurred. It is presented in chronological order. You can scan it like you would a story or a graph to extract the information you are looking for.

5 **Scanning a Timeline** Scan the timeline on the top of page 214 to answer the following questions. See who can find the correct answers first.

1. What is the structure of DNA that Watson and Crick discovered? When did they discover it?
2. What is the name of the Austrian monk who started the science of genetics?
3. What plants did he use to establish the rules of inheritance?
4. What did scientists use in the 70s to put DNA into and produce the genetic function?
5. Where are the genes carried?
6. What year was this discovered?
7. When was the Human Genome project started? When was it finished?
8. Who showed that DNA carries genetic information?
9. Can DNA testing be used to help solve crimes?
10. When was DNA testing used to determine family relations?

 6 **Guided Academic Conversation: Expressing Your Opinion** Answer *yes* or *no* to the first four questions that follow. Complete the sentence in question five, filling in the blank with as many breakthroughs as you can think of. Then discuss and justify all of your answers with a partner.

1. Notice that in the first paragraph, Ann Miscoi found help from the Internet when her doctor could not help her. The Internet is the best place to go for reliable health information. Yes or no?
2. If I were experiencing pain, the only place I would go would be to a conventional family doctor. There are no other possibilities. Yes or no?

1865	1910	1944	1953	1973	1990	2000	2001–2006
Genetic inheritance was discovered by Gregor Mendel, an Austrian monk who used generations of peas to unravel the mystery.	Researchers studying fruit flies show that genes are carried on chromosomes inside the cell's nucleus.	Oswald Avery shows that DNA carries genetic information.	The now familiar double helical structures of DNA are described by James Watson and Francis Crick.	Scientists use a restriction enzyme to cut animal DNA. They then splice the DNA into bacteria where the gene's function is carried out.	The Human Genome Project, a publicly funded consortium of scientists, sets out to map the human genome.	Scientists complete sequencing the three billion or so letters that spell out the human genome, nearly five years sooner than anticipated.	DNA testing is used to find genealogical (or family) roots DNA testing used to prove innocence or guilt based on evidence at crime scenes.

3. If Dr. Francis Collins is right, screening tests will soon enable people to judge their tolerance for cigarettes or cheeseburgers. This will be 100 percent a good thing. Yes or no?

4. If you were from a family with a history of serious disease, you should absolutely take a genetic test to find out if you will some day suffer from it. Yes or no?

5. In my opinion, the most important breakthroughs that have occurred in the

field of health and medicine are _____

_____.

▲ One sheep cloned from another

Speaking in Front of People

Sometimes you are given an oral exam or asked to speak during an interview or at a meeting. Whether the question is completely unexpected or whether you've thought a lot about it, the tips below can help you speak well in public.

1. If you feel nervous, take a deep breath. Then take another.

2. Think for a moment about what you want to say. Then say the best or strongest idea first.

3. Stand firmly with both feet on the ground. Do not shuffle.

4. Keep your hands at your sides or your arms slightly bent, whichever feels more comfortable.

5. Look at your audience, but not just at one person. Change the directions of your eyes from time to time.

6. Don't talk too long. Prepare a good "exit line" (something to say at the end) and when you want to finish, say it. Then smile and sit down.

7. Practice with friends and in small groups at first. Talk with them afterwards and get their suggestions. Practice makes perfect. Good luck!

Practice Practice speaking in a group with two or three others. Take turns with each person giving a short talk for one or two minutes on a topic from the list below. Afterwards, give advice to each other on how to improve.

A breakthrough in technology that I like

A breakthrough in technology that I don't like

The idea of the "mad scientist"

My relationship with my computer

What I think about pills and medicines

Why go to a doctor?

_____ (write your own topic)

7 **What Do You Think?** Read the paragraph below and discuss the questions that follow.

Stem Cells

Perhaps the greatest scientific achievement of the late-20th and early-21st centuries is the ability of scientists to create basic human cells, or stem cells, in the laboratory. In 1998, Dr. James Thompson, a researcher at the University of Wisconsin, became the first person to develop stem-cell lines that can be differentiated and transformed into specific-type cells. Stem cells could be the beginning of the end of many deadly diseases by allowing medical science to form custom-made tissues and organs, such as hearts, lungs, livers, and skin that would replace or repair damaged ones. This gives hope to people with diseases such as Alzheimer's, Parkinson's, type 1 diabetes, heart disease, cancer, even some types of paralysis. Stem-cell research has also led to the asexual cloning of animals from the cells of like animals; sheep, cattle, cats, mice, and several other species have already been cloned. The possibility of human cloning lies ahead. Much controversy, especially among religious groups, has developed in regards to stem-cell research.

1. Do you think the reproduction of stem cells in a laboratory is a great discovery? Why or why not?
2. What are the positive and negative consequences of stem-cell research?
3. What do you think of the cloning of animals? Of human beings?
4. In the future, if human cloning is accomplished, would you like to have yourself cloned? Why or why not?

Strategy

Reading for Speed and Fluency: Viewing Words in Groups or Clusters
For this timed reading, try out a skill that can help you to read faster: viewing words in groups or clusters. Try not to read word by word, but instead to see groups of words at once.

So instead of reading this sentence one word at a time, like this:

> The—topic—of—*thought*—is—one—area—of—psychology, —and—many—observers—have—considered—this—aspect—in—connection—with—robots—and—computers.

Try to read the sentence in four sections like this:

> The topic of *thought* is one area of psychology, and many observers have considered this aspect in connection with robots and computers.

Introduction

The following selection discusses what many people view as the most recent extension of the human mind: the computer. Is it simply a tool, or can we speak of it as an intelligent being that "thinks"? Read the selection to find out the author's point of view on this question. Concentrate on reading quickly, without vocalizing the words as you read.

Time you began to read: _____

Are Computers Alive?

A The topic of *thought* is one area of psychology, and many observers have considered this aspect in connection with robots and computers: Some of the old worries about AI (artificial intelligence) were closely linked to the question of whether computers could think. The first massive electronic computers, capable of rapid (if often unreliable) computation and little or no creative activity, were soon dubbed "electronic brains." A reaction to this terminology quickly followed. To put them in their place, computers were called "high-speed idiots," an effort to protect human vanity. In such a climate, the possibility of computers actually being alive was rarely considered: It was bad enough that computers might be capable of thought. But not everyone realized the implications of the high-speed idiot tag. It has not been pointed out often enough that even the human idiot is one of the most intelligent life forms on Earth. If the early computers were even that intelligent, it was already a remarkable state of affairs.

B One consequence of speculation about the possibility of computer thought was that we were forced to examine with new care the idea of thought in general. It soon became clear that we were not sure what we meant by such terms as *thought* and *thinking*. We tend to assume that human beings think, some more than others, though we often call people *thoughtless* or *unthinking*. Dreams cause a problem, partly because they usually happen outside our control. They are obviously some type of mental experience, but are they a type of thinking? And the question of nonhuman life forms adds further problems. Many of us would maintain that some of the higher animals—dogs, cats, apes, and so on—are capable of at least basic thought, but what about fish and insects? It is certainly true that the higher mammals show complex brain activity when tested with the appropriate equipment. If thinking is demonstrated by evident electrical activity in the brain, then many animal species are capable of thought. Once we have formulated clear ideas on what thought is in biological creatures, it will be easier to discuss the question of thought in artifacts. And what is true of thought is also true of the many other mental processes. One of the immense benefits of AI research is that we are being forced to scrutinize, with new rigor, the working of the human mind.

c   It is already clear that machines have superior mental abilities to many life forms. No fern or oak tree can play chess as well as even the simplest digital computer; nor can frogs weld car bodies as well as robots. The three-fingered mechanical manipulator is cleverer in some ways than the three-toed sloth. It seems that, viewed in terms of intellect, the computer should be set well above plants and most animals. Only the higher animals can, it seems, compete with computers with regard to intellect—and even then with diminishing success. (Examples of this are in the games of backgammon and chess. Some of the world's best players are now computers.)

Source: *Are Computers Alive?* (Geoff Simons)

Choose the best way of finishing each statement, based on what you have just read.

1. The first electronic computers were _____.
   a. slow and reliable
   b. creative and accurate
   c. large and fast

2. The author feels that by calling these early computers "high-speed idiots," people were really implying that computers _____.
   a. would never be capable of thought
   b. were already somewhat intelligent
   c. can never work as rapidly as people

3. The author believes that such words as *thought* and *thinking* _____.
   a. are terms that are not clear and will never be exactly defined
   b. might come to be better understood because of research into artificial intelligence and computers
   c. have precise biological meanings that refer only to human mental processes

4. In the author's view, mental activities are characteristic of _____ .

    a. all plants and animals

    b. some animals

    c. human beings alone

5. The author's opinion regarding the possibility of machines thinking seems to be that _____ .

    a. there are already machines that think

    b. this is somewhat possible

    c. this is totally improbable

Word count in reading: 530

My time for completing the reading and exercise: _____

9 **Around the Globe** Examine the map below, read the passage on page 220, and discuss the questions that follow.

▲ The new Canadian territory of Nunavut

Nunavut, a Breakthrough in Social Justice

In April, 1999, a new territory of Canada was formed and became a separate political entity. This new territory is called Nunavut, which means "Our Land" in the Inuit language of Inuktitut. It includes the central and eastern portions of what used to be the Northwest Territories, and covers 1,994,000 square kilometers, or almost the equivalent of one-fifth of the size of Canada.

▲ An Inuit fishing in Nunavut

By creating this new territory, the Canadian government has given clear ownership of both the land and its resources to the people who live there, including control of the rich deposits of oil, gas, and minerals. Most of the inhabitants of Nunavut are native Inuit whose ancestors first came there thousands of years ago.

In most places in the world, native populations live in poverty, without their own land, so the creation of Nunavut is considered by many people to be a significant breakthrough in the field of social justice. The territory is vast and rich in resources and valuable also for the development of tourism. Now the people who live there have reclaimed their ancestral homeland.

1. What do you think about this breakthrough? Was this a good idea for Canada?

2. What other countries in the world have groups of natives who are descendants of the first inhabitants? Are some of them working to receive land or rights from the countries in which they live?

3. Do you think that other governments should follow the example of Canada and give land to native people? Why or why not?

1 Making Connections Do some research on the Internet and take notes on one of the following topics. Share your results with the class or in a small group.

The Human Genome Find recently-updated information on the Internet about the human genome. Has anything new developed since this article on it was written in your textbook? If so, what has happened?

Genetic Testing "By 2010," says Dr. Francis Collins of the National Human Genome Research Institute, "screening tests will enable anyone to gauge his or her unique health risks, down to the body's tolerance for cigarettes and cheese-burgers." Look up *genetic screening test* and variations on this phrase on the Internet. Were the predictions from the article for the year 2010 accurate? What kinds of things are people doing genetic testing for? Make a list of places that are using gene therapy and what diseases they are treating.

Wangari Maathai and the Green Belt Movement Find more information on the internet on Wangari Maathai and the Green Belt Movement she started in Kenya.

Environmental Programs Look up other environmental programs similar to the Green Belt Movement, but in other parts of the world. You might look up such terms as *environmental conservation, soil erosion, political advocacy, ecology, cycle of poverty, sustainable management,* and *desertification* among others.

Responding in Writing

WRITING TIP: CLEARLY SEPARATE A SUMMARY FROM YOUR OPINION

It is important to distinguish between the summary of a reading and your opinion of the reading. A summary or summary statement goes over the main points that an author makes without expressing an opinion. Often a summary statement can be a good lead-in to writing about your opinion on the author's point, but the summary itself should not include your opinion.

2 **Writing Practice** Write a couple of paragraphs giving a summary and then expressing your opinion about an idea that appears in one of the two selections in this chapter, following these steps:

Step 1 Choose a small section (maybe just one sentence or else a paragraph or two) in one of the two readings in this chapter that you have a strong opinion about. The section you select should say something that makes you want to respond. Maybe you agree or disagree strongly with it, maybe you have some comment or examples you want to add to it, or maybe you think it is an example that should be followed in another situation.

Step 2 Write a one-sentence summary statement [see Chapter 1, page 18] describing what is said in the passage that you selected. Make sure that you are expressing *only* the main point of what is said and *not* your opinion in this summary statement. Use a format similar to this for your summary statement:

> "Near the beginning of the article, *Trees for Democracy* the author argues that . . ."

Step 3 Next, take some notes in point form on your opinion about what the author says. (*In point form* means not writing full or correct sentences, but only writing small phrases or whatever you need to write to remember the thoughts you have on the topic.)

Step 4 Following the summary statement you wrote, now write what you think of what the author has stated or argued in the section you chose, using your notes as a guide.

Step 5 Revise your writing. Make sure that the first sentence is a summary without any of your opinion expressed and that what follows expresses *your* opinion and doesn't just repeat the author's opinion.

Self-Assessment Log

Read the lists below. Check (✔) the strategies and vocabulary that you learned in this chapter. Look through the chapter or ask your instructor about the strategies and words that you do not understand.

Reading and Vocabulary-Building Strategies

- ❏ Previewing a speech
- ❏ Building new words with prefixes and suffixes
- ❏ Finding evidence to disprove false arguments
- ❏ Identifying compound words
- ❏ Analyzing the author's point of view
- ❏ Previewing: reading diagrams
- ❏ Understanding idiomatic phrases in context
- ❏ Separating fact from opinion
- ❏ Scanning a timeline
- ❏ Reading for speed and fluency: viewing words in groups or clusters

Target Vocabulary

Nouns

- ❏ advocacy*
- ❏ conservation
- ❏ degradation
- ❏ desertification
- ❏ detection*
- ❏ deterioration
- ❏ erosion*
- ❏ harassment
- ❏ rainfall
- ❏ researchers*
- ❏ sequence*

- ❏ topsoil
- ❏ vision*

Verbs

- ❏ analyze*
- ❏ benefit*
- ❏ predict*
- ❏ respond*

Adjectives

- ❏ nutritious
- ❏ sequenced*

- ❏ unsuitable
- ❏ worldwide

Adverb

- ❏ primarily*

Idioms and Expressions

- ❏ a handful
- ❏ a normal life span
- ❏ go that route
- ❏ half dead
- ❏ not (a procedure) to be taken lightly

- ❏ spot
- ❏ started making sense
- ❏ take (her concerns) more seriously
- ❏ trigger a flood
- ❏ be routine

---

* These words are from the Academic Word List. For more information on this list, see www.vuw.ac.nz/lals/research/awl.

Art and Entertainment

In This Chapter

North America is often called a "melting pot," a place where people from many countries and races have joined together to form a new culture. The arts reflect the uniqueness of this combination with powerful novels by writers of Asian, European, and native ancestry, and the far-reaching musical styles created by Americans of African descent: jazz, gospel music, rock, and the blues. The first part of this chapter explores the strikingly original painting of Georgia O'Keeffe, whose grandparents came from four different countries; the second part examines the moving Chicano poetry of Mexican-Americans. Finally, a timed reading looks at Jackie Chan, one of the world's best-loved movie stars who spends a lot of time in a city called Hollywood.

❝ The true work of art is but a shadow of the divine perfection. ❞

—Michelangelo
Italian painter, sculptor, and architect (1475–1564)

Connecting to the Topic

1 Where do you think the photo below was taken? What is the woman thinking? What is your opinion of the painting? What do you think about "modern" art?

2 Do you enjoy art? What kinds do you like? Do you have a favorite artist?

3 Music is an important part of many people's lives. What role does music play in your life?

To Paint Is to Live

Before You Read

1 Previewing Look at the title of the reading and the photograph of Georgia O'Keeffe on page 229. Skim the first two paragraphs of the article. Then make inferences about this famous artist and answer the following questions. Afterwards, read the article to find out if you were right.

1. What kind of person do you think she was?

_____

_____

2. Why did she paint?

_____

_____

3. What kinds of problems do you imagine she had in her life? Why?

_____

_____

2 Getting Meaning Through Word Structure and Context: Verbs Verbs carry the action of a piece of writing. Choose the best synonym or definition for each of the italicized words in the following sentences taken from the reading selection. Use word structure, context, and/or the hints in parentheses to help you.

1. Tough, sparse, lean, she *embodied* the rugged individualistic nature of the American pioneer. (**Hint:** Notice the word *body* inside the verb. The pioneers were the first people who came to what is now North America to settle, and usually to farm, the land.)
- (A) followed
- (B) liked
- (C) planned
- (D) represented

2. But instead of *tilling* the soil, her strides were made in the field of contemporary American art. (**Hint:** Think of what farmers do to the soil before planting vegetables.)
- (A) buying
- (B) digging
- (C) getting rid of
- (D) selling

3. From the summer of 1929, when she made her first visit to New Mexico, the starkness of the desert *fascinated* her. (**Hint:** Scan for this sentence in the reading and see what she does after this first visit.)
   - (A) attracted
   - (B) bothered
   - (C) disgusted
   - (D) meant nothing to

4. After summering in New Mexico . . . she finally moved permanently to Abiquiu, . . . where she continued to paint until her eyesight *faltered* in the late 1970s. (**Hint:** Think of the principle of cause and effect.)
   - (A) became better
   - (B) became worse
   - (C) changed color
   - (D) changed direction

5. Teachers recognized her talent but often *criticized* the larger-than-life proportions that she liked to paint. (**Hint:** Notice the word *but* which indicates a contrast, so the second part of the sentence is in some way the opposite of the first part.)
   - (A) analyzed
   - (B) praised
   - (C) talked about
   - (D) talked against

6. At an early, age she was already moving away from realistic copying of objects to things she *perceived* with her own eyes, mind, and soul.
   - (A) controlled
   - (B) forgot
   - (C) understood
   - (D) waited for

7. In 1908, perhaps *disappointed* with the rigidity of American art education at the time, she gave up painting . . . (**Hint:** The verb *to disappoint* means to be worse than expected. Here, this is the past participle of the verb used as an adjective. Pay attention to the second part of the sentence.)
   - (A) dishonest
   - (B) pleased
   - (C) surprised
   - (D) unsatisfied

8. In 1912, she began to teach in Amarillo, Texas, and was *stunned* by the barren southern landscape.
   - (A) amazed
   - (B) crowded
   - (C) frightened
   - (D) sickened

9. It was at this point that the determined young woman . . . decided *to reject* the rigidity of the realism that she had been taught for a style all her own . . . (**Hint:** The word *for* is important here.)

- (A) accept
- (B) believe in
- (C) try out
- (D) throw away

10. The friend was so impressed with them that she *ignored* the request [to not show the prints to anyone] and took them to a famous photographer and promoter of modern artists, Alfred Stieglitz.

- (A) began the process of
- (B) completed the work for
- (C) did not pay attention to
- (D) attempted to understand

11. Without O'Keeffe's knowledge or consent, Stieglitz *exhibited* these prints in his gallery.

- (A) bought
- (B) gave away
- (C) looked at carefully
- (D) placed on view

12. Stieglitz . . . *immortalized* her through many beautiful and unusual photographs. . . . (**Hint:** To be *immortal* means to live forever.)

- (A) changed completely
- (B) damaged the image of
- (C) gave permanent meaning to
- (D) improved with technical skill

13. As art critic Lloyd Goodrich said, "Her art presents a rare combination of austerity and deep seriousness . . . The forms of nature are *translated* into forms of art." (**Hint:** This is the passive voice of the verb *translate* which usually refers to taking words from one language and expressing them in another.)

- (A) changed
- (B) destroyed
- (C) made more beautiful
- (D) reduced greatly

14. ". . . The abstraction is often the most definite form for the intangible thing in myself that I can only *clarify* in paint." (**Hint:** These are the words of the artist, trying to explain her art. Look for a relationship between this verb and an adjective within it that is a bit changed.)

- (A) discover for myself
- (B) make clear
- (C) mystify
- (D) show the complexity of

Introduction

Painting, like music, is one of the fine arts. American and Canadian painting has been influenced by many traditions from different parts of the world, especially by those from Europe. However, the 20th century witnessed an opposite trend: the development of particularly North American painting styles that have become international. One American painter who exerted an influence on Europe with a unique and independent style was a woman from Wisconsin named Georgia O'Keeffe. Three of O'Keeffe's grandparents were immigrants—from Ireland, Hungary, and Holland—and the fourth was descended from one of the earliest European colonists in America. These ancestors came to start a new life in a new world, but O'Keeffe was destined to become a pioneer of a different sort. The following article discusses her life and work.

- What famous artists have you heard of? What kind of art do they do? Who is one of your favorite artists?
- Who are the best-known artists in your culture? What do you know about them? Are any of them women? In your opinion, is it more unusual for a woman to become an artist than a man? Why or why not?

To Paint Is to Live: Georgia O'Keeffe, 1887–1986

A   Georgia O'Keeffe was truly an American original. Tough, sparse, lean, she embodied the rugged individualistic nature of the American pioneer. But instead of tilling the soil, her strides were made in the field of contemporary American art.

B   Born on a 600-acre farm in Sun Prairie, Wisconsin, on November 15, 1887, O'Keeffe throughout her long life preferred vast plains and open spaces to city living. From the summer of 1929, when she made her first visit to New Mexico, the starkness of the desert fascinated her. After summering in New Mexico for many years, she finally moved permanently to Abiquiu, New Mexico, in 1949, where she continued to paint until her eyesight faltered in the late 1970s. From this region the themes of some of her finest works evolved.

▲ Georgia O'Keeffe

C   O'Keeffe's strictly American art education began with private lessons at the age of ten. Teachers recognized her talent but often criticized the larger-than-life proportions that she liked to paint. At an early age, she was already moving away from realistic copying of objects to things she perceived with her own eyes, mind, and soul. 20

D   O'Keeffe's formal high school education continued at a private school in Madison, Wisconsin, and after a family move, she graduated from a Williamsburg, Virginia, high school in 1903. In 1905–06 she studied at the Art Institute in Chicago, and in 1907–08, at the Art Students' League in New York. 25

E   In 1908, perhaps disappointed with the rigidity of American art education at the time, she gave up painting and became a commercial artist, drawing advertising illustrations in Chicago. However, in the summer of 1912, she decided to take another art course in Virginia under Alon Bemont, and her interest in creative painting came alive again. 30

F   Self-supporting since graduation from high school, O'Keeffe had to find jobs to sustain her through her developing years as an artist. In 1912, she began to teach in Amarillo, Texas, and was stunned by the barren southern landscape. "That was my country," she said, "terrible wind and wonderful emptiness."

G   After art courses in 1915–16 in New York under the more liberal art teacher 35 Arthur Dow, O'Keeffe accepted a position as an art teacher at a small college in South Carolina. It was at this point that the determined young woman isolated herself, took stock of her painting, and decided to reject the rigidity of the realism that she had been taught for a style all her own: "Nothing is less real than realism—details are 40 confusing. It is only by selection, by elimination, by emphasis, that we get the real meaning of things." From this revival came black and white abstract nature forms in all shapes and sizes, the beginning of her highly individualistic style. 45

▲ O'Keeffe's *Yellow Calla*

H   O'Keeffe sent some of her prints to a friend in New York and told her not to show them to anyone. The friend was so impressed with them that she ignored the request and took them to a famous photographer and promoter of modern artists, 50 Alfred Stieglitz. His reaction was immediate: "At last, a woman on paper!" Without O'Keeffe's knowledge or consent, Stieglitz exhibited these prints in his gallery. Infuriated, she went to New York to insist that he take her drawings down. 55 Stieglitz, however, convinced her of their quality, and she allowed them to remain on exhibit. Subsequently, Stieglitz became the champion of O'Keeffe's works and helped her gain the

prominence she deserved. For Stieglitz, Georgia O'Keeffe was an unusually 60
talented American female artist. She was unspoiled by studies in Europe and
painted with a direct, clear, strong—even fierce—force.

I   The relationship between Stieglitz and O'Keeffe developed into a passionate
love affair, which eventually led to a 22-year marriage. Stieglitz, his wife's senior
by many years, died in 1946. He immortalized her through many beautiful and 65
unusual photographs—the lady in black, with piercing eyes, tightly pulled-back
hair and the artistic elongated hands of a princess.

J   Strength, clarity, and strong physical presence are words that are often used
to describe O'Keeffe's paintings. As art critic Lloyd Goodrich said, "Her art
presents a rare combination of austerity and deep seriousness . . . Even at her 70
most realistic, she is concerned not with the mere visual appearance of things,
but with their essential life, their being, their identity. . . . The forms of nature
are translated into forms of art." Or, as O'Keeffe herself put it, "A hill or a tree
cannot make a good painting just because it is a hill or a tree. It is lines and
colors put together so that they say something. For me, that is the very basis for 75
painting. The abstraction is often the most definite form for the intangible thing
in myself that I can only clarify in paint."

Source: "To Paint Is to Live" (Miki Knezevic)

After You Read

3 **Recalling Information** Based on what you have just read, choose the best
ending for each statement.

1. Georgia O'Keeffe was born _____.
- Ⓐ in New York City
- Ⓑ in a town in New Mexico
- Ⓒ on a farm in Wisconsin

2. Her art education consisted of _____.
- Ⓐ studies in schools and institutes in the United States
- Ⓑ training in the best art academies of Europe
- Ⓒ only her own efforts and experimentation at home

3. The landscape with which she identified in particular was _____.
- Ⓐ rugged mountains
- Ⓑ lush forests
- Ⓒ barren deserts

4. Alfred Stieglitz's comment when he first saw O'Keeffe's prints was, "At last, a
woman on paper!" From this we can infer that _____.
- Ⓐ there was a great deal of discrimination against women then
- Ⓑ women artists were not very common in those days
- Ⓒ he did not really like the prints very much

5. Stieglitz was important in the life of Georgia O'Keeffe because _____.

    (A) he became both her husband and champion

    (B) he bought many of her paintings at good prices

    (C) he photographed her prints and gave titles to them

4 **Paraphrasing** Paraphrase the following excerpts from the article. State the main idea of what is written in your own words. See Chapter 5, page 115 for more on paraphrasing.

1. Tough, sparse, lean, she embodied the rugged individualistic nature of the American pioneer. But instead of tilling the soil, her strides were made in the field of contemporary American art.

Georgia O'Keeffe is similar to an American pioneer. She has a slim figure and is tough, like the individualistic pioneers, and she also helped "grow" the field of American art just like pioneers grow crops.

2. Self-supporting since graduation from high school, O'Keeffe had to find jobs to sustain her through her developing years as an artist.

3. "Nothing is less real than realism—details are confusing. It is only by selection, by elimination, by emphasis, that we get the real meaning of things."

4. "Even at her most realistic, she is concerned not with the mere visual appearance of things, but with their essential life, their being, their identity . . ."

 5 **Guided Academic Conversation: Art** In small groups, discuss the following questions. Then compare your answers with those of another group of students.

1. Artist and Mother Do you think it was more difficult for a woman to be an artist in the 1920s than now? Why? Georgia O'Keeffe did not have children. Should women artists decide not to have children? Why or why not?

2. A Favor or a Betrayal? What do you think of the friend in New York who did not obey O'Keeffe's wishes? Did she betray O'Keeffe when she showed her art prints to Stieglitz? Or did she do her a favor? Why?

3. **You, the Artist** If you could be an artist, what kind of art would you like to do? Big? Small? Painting? Sculpture? Architecture? Some other kind?

4. **Abstract Art** Look at the cartoon about abstract art. Why is it funny that the artist wins first prize? The woman does not appreciate abstract art. What do you think of it?

Source: From *Bound & Gagged* by Dana Summers. © Tribune Media Information Services, Inc. All Rights Reserved. Reprinted with permission.

6 **Expressing Ideas** Bring to class a print, photograph, or a copy of a piece of art that appeals to you. Complete the items below, describing your piece of art. Then share your art and comments with the class.

1. Medium (material used to create the art piece—wooden sculpture, oil painting, photograph, etc.): _____

2. Subject (what it is about, what are the main figures or topics. Include the title if there is one): _____
_____

3. Style (How it is presented, colors, shapes, realistic or abstract, etc.):
_____
_____
_____

4. Theme or message: _____
_____
_____

5. What I like about it: _____
_____
_____

7 **Making a Comparison** Do artists tend to have similar types of lives even though they are from different cultures and time periods? Search the Internet or go to the library and look up information on an artist from any country other than the United States. Compare the life of this artist and that of Georgia O'Keeffe. Put these points into a Venn diagram like the one below. Write *Georgia O'Keeffe* above one circle and the other artist's name on the line above the other circle. Write points about the individual artists inside the appropriate circle. Write points that both these artists share in the shaded place where the circles intersect. Share your work with a partner.

Georgia O'Keeffe   _____

If there is no similarity, try to explain why:

_____

_____

Part 2	Reading Skills and Strategies

Chicano Poetry: The Voice of a Culture

Before You Read

1 **Previewing** Look at the map of the United States and answer the following questions. Then read the article to find out whether you are correct and to learn more about the largest minority group in the United States.

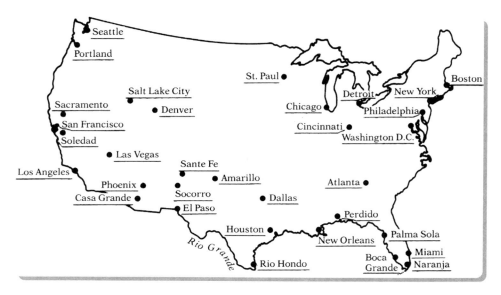

1. What cities on the map sound to you as though their names might be of Spanish origin?

_____

_____

2. What areas of the country seem to have the most Spanish names?

_____

_____

3. Do you know or can you guess why these areas have Spanish names?

_____

_____

2 **Matching Words to their Meanings** Match the adjectives and nouns from the column on the left to the correct synonyms or definitions on the right. Use clues from the word structure when possible.

1. _____ Anglo

2. _____ bilingual

3. _____ citizenship

4. _____ civil rights

5. _____ discrimination

6. _____ Hispanic

7. _____ inhabitants

8. _____ immigration

9. _____ mechanization

10. _____ migrant

11. _____ strike

a. speaking two languages

b. moving from place to place

c. unfair treatment against certain ethnic groups

d. change from working by hand to working by machines

e. a stopping of work by employees to gain benefits

f. English-speaking

g. entitlements to certain freedoms as citizens

h. Spanish-speaking

i. people who live in (inhabit) a place

j. condition or quality of being a citizen

k. arriving into a new country in order to live there

Read

Introduction

The following article gives some background on Mexican-Americans, who are often called Chicanos, and presents a few examples of their poetry. You might wonder why this group is singled out when there are so many ethnic groups, with their particular languages and cultures, living in North America, including millions of Spanish-speaking people from other countries. There are historical reasons, which you will read about, that explain why this group is different from most others.

- What do you know about (or imagine would be) the history of people of Mexican origin in the land that now constitutes the United States?

Chicano Poetry: The Voice of a Culture

The Hispanic Presence in the United States

A   According to 2000 census figures, 32.8 million Hispanics live in the United States. More than 80 percent of Hispanics live in urban areas. Most are concentrated in the five southwestern states of Arizona, California, Colorado, New Mexico, and Texas. There are also sizable Hispanic populations in New York, Florida, and Illinois.   5

▲ A Mexican mariachi band in San Antonio, Texas

B   There are countless Spanish geographical names in the United States, such as the state of Colorado (which means *red*), the city of Las Vegas (*fertile lowlands*), and the Rio Grande (*big river*). Many Spanish and Latin   10 American words have been incorporated into English. A large number of these words are related to geographical features: *mesa* (plateau) and *canyon*; to music: *tango, rumba*; to ranch life: *rodeo, corral*; to architecture: 15 *patio, plaza*; and to food: *chocolate, tomato*. Many colorful English slang terms are corruptions of Spanish words, such as *calaboose* (jail) and *macho* (big, tough male).

Mexican-American History

C   Where did all this Spanish influence come from? Didn't the United States start out as a colony of the British? In fact, the southwestern United States was settled by the Spanish and Mexicans centuries before the arrival of the first Anglos. Many people are unaware of this fact because until recently, all the history books were written from the point of view of the British. Let's examine the "true history" of the American Southwest.

D   The region was part of Mexico until it was lost in a war with the United States. Under the terms of the Treaty of Guadalupe Hidalgo, which ended the war in 1848, Mexico ceded to the United States the territory that is now New Mexico, Utah, Nevada, California, and parts of Colorado and Wyoming. On paper, the 75,000 Mexican inhabitants were guaranteed their property rights and granted U.S. citizenship. The reality, however, was different. They suffered racial and cultural discrimination at the hands of a flood of Anglo settlers, and many were dispossessed of their lands. Most worked for Anglo bosses as farm, railroad, and mine workers. Constant immigration from Mexico kept wages low.

E   World War II brought about fundamental changes. Many Mexican-Americans began to consider themselves U.S. citizens for the first time after serving in the war. Armed with new skills and faced with the rapid mechanization of agriculture, many moved to the cities in search of work.

The Chicano Movement

F   Inspired by the black struggle for civil rights, Mexican-Americans organized in the 1960s to gain reforms and restore ethnic pride. Members of this movement called themselves *Chicanos*, and the name has become popular, although some still prefer the term Mexican-Americans. The achievements of the Chicano movement are many. In 1962, César Chávez founded the strong and successful National Farm Workers Association in Delano, California, which has managed to raise wages and improve working conditions for migrant workers. In 1970, José Angel Gutiérrez established the *Raza Unida* political party in Crystal City, Texas, which has been successful in electing Mexican-American candidates to local office. Bilingual, cross-cultural education, and Chicano-studies programs have been established in schools and universities.

▲ Chicano arts are often expressed in outdoor wall paintings called murals.

Chicano Arts

G   The Chicano movement inspired a flowering of Chicano theater, art, and literature. Luis Valdés created the *Teatro Campesino* in the fields of Delano

in 1965 to strengthen the union's organizing efforts. This unique form of
theater draws on a variety of Latin-American and European traditions and   60
makes use of allegorical characters, masks, song, and dance. Originally
performed by farm workers for farm workers, it later broadened its focus to
include issues other than the strike, such as American foreign policy and
discrimination against Hispanics in schools. The *Teatro Campesino* has
gained international prominence and inspired the creation of many similar   65
companies across the country.

H   Colorful murals painted on the walls of public buildings in Mexican-
American neighborhoods are a collective expression of reborn hope and
ethnic pride. They depict the Mexican-Americans' Indian and Spanish
heritage, the history of Mexico and of Mexican-Americans in the United   70
States, and the problems of migrant workers.

I   The genre most cultivated by Chicano writers is poetry. Often written in
free verse, Chicano poetry creates an impression of spontaneity, freshness,
and honesty. It may be written in Spanish, English, or a combination of the
two languages.   75

Source: "The Hispanic Presence in the United States" (Deana Fernández)

After You Read

3 Recalling Information Based on the reading, tell whether each of the following
statements is true or false by writing *T* or *F* in the blanks. Correct the false statements to
make them true.

1. _____ There are more than 25 million Hispanics living in the U.S.

2. _____ Most Hispanics live in rural areas.

3. _____ Spanish and Mexican architecture and geographical names are
characteristics of the northeastern part of the country.

4. _____ The first Spanish and Mexican settlers in the United States arrived
after the first British settlers.

5. _____ After the war of 1848, Mexicans in the U.S. territory that used to
belong to Mexico suffered racial and cultural discrimination.

6. _____ After World War II, many Mexican-Americans moved from the
countryside to the cities.

7. _____ César Chávez is a Chicano who founded a powerful and effective
labor union for farm workers.

8. _____ José Angel Gutiérrez began a Chicano political party, but it has not yet managed to get Mexican-Americans elected to office.

9. _____ Chicano theater, begun by Luis Valdés, started out in the fields and was performed for and by farm workers.

10. _____ The literary genre most popular among Chicano writers is the novel.

4 **Summarizing Information About Specific Points** Write a brief summary of what you remember about each of the following people or things. If necessary, scan the article to refresh your memory.

1. Spanish words used in English

_____

_____

2. *Raza Unida*

_____

_____

3. Treaty of Guadalupe Hidalgo

_____

_____

4. César Chávez

_____

_____

5. *Teatro Campesino*

_____

_____

5 **Focusing on Words from the Academic Word List** Read the paragraphs on page 240 taken from Part 2. Fill in the blanks with the most appropriate word from the box. Do not look back at the reading right away; instead, see if you can remember the vocabulary. One of the words will be used twice.

achievements	established	issues	traditions
civil	ethnic	migrant	unique
discrimination	focus	policy	

Inspired by the black struggle for _____ rights,
Mexican-Americans organized in the 1960s to gain reforms and
restore _____ pride. Members of this movement called
themselves *Chicanos*, and the name has become popular, although
some still prefer the term Mexican-Americans. The _____ 5
of the Chicano movement are many. In 1962, César Chávez founded
the strong and successful National Farm Workers Association in
Delano, California, which has managed to raise wages and improve
working conditions for _____ workers. In 1970, José
Angel Gutiérrez _____ the *Raza Unida* political party 10
in Crystal City, Texas, which has been successful in electing
Mexican-American candidates to local office. Bilingual, cross-cultural
education, and Chicano-studies programs have been
_____ in schools and universities.

The Chicano movement inspired a flowering of Chicano theater, art, 15
and literature. Luis Valdés created the *Teatro Campesino* in the
fields of Delano in 1965 to strengthen the union's organizing efforts.
This _____ form of theater draws on a variety of
Latin-American and European _____ and makes use
of allegorical characters, masks, song, and dance. Originally performed 20
by farm workers for farm workers, it later broadened its
_____ to include _____ other than
the strike, such as American foreign _____ and
_____ against Hispanics in schools.

6 Guided Academic Discussion: History Discuss the following questions with a partner. Then compare your ideas with those of the rest of the class.

1. Why are there so many places with Spanish names in the United States? Why has English become the dominant language?

2. What does the author mean when she talks about the "true history" of the American Southwest? Do you think that the stories told in most history books are not exactly true? What difference would there be in the story of the war that ended in 1848 between an American history book and a Mexican history book? Why?

3. Are there any differences in the history books of your country between the official story of some events and different stories told by other groups?

4. What other events have you heard about that have two different versions? Explain.

5. The Greeks have an old saying: *In time of war, the first casualty is truth.* How would you explain what this means in your own words? If you think of wars that have occured, what different points of view are there about what happened?

Strategy

Reading Poetry

Just as any scene can serve as the subject of a painting, so any part of daily life can provide material for a poem. Of course, the choice that the artist or poet makes relates to his or her purpose. Poetry is usually short and compact, so it should be read several times, preferably aloud, to appreciate its meaning. Try to understand the main points that the poet wants to convey and the emotions the poet wants the reader to feel.

7 Reading Poetry Read the examples of Chicano poetry below. What are the main points the poet is trying to convey? Read it again. What emotions does the poet want the reader to feel?

To People Who Pick Food

I am the man
   who picks your food
   immigrant,
   tablecloths
   ignore my stare

I have children

a fake green card

a warm kiss

a cross to ward off rangers

a picture of St. Peter so

I will not drown in a river

   I pick apples

      cotton

      grapes

eyes follow me

   utter under their breaths,

I do not understand

   the lettuce canned

with my hands

   citrus pores

   inflame my eyes

my wife is   proud

   soft   gentle

   my   children

are brown   tender deer

   what eyes,

the sun cracks my skin

I am old and dark as the dirt

I drop on my knees before the sky

they can hate me, point me out in a crowd

but do not pity me the sun is there

every morning God follows my children

and I walk to the field to grow bread

   with my friends.

                   —Wilfredo Q. Castaño

Grandma's Primo

Grandma had a cousin

who lived in the big city

and looked like a gringo

He smoked a big cigar

and spoke English as well

as he spoke Spanish

He loved to tell jokes

would always tell them twice—

the first time in Spanish

to make us laugh

and the second time in English

to impress us.

—Leroy V. Quintana

8 **Understanding Poetry** To see if you understood the gist (the basic idea) of the two poems, write *True* or *False* before each of the following statements. If a statement is false, explain why.

1. _____ "To People Who Pick Food" is told from the point of view of a poor but contented Mexican farm laborer who works in the United States illegally.

2. _____ In the poem "Grandma's Primo," the cousin always told jokes twice because he wasn't sure that his relatives understood them the first time.

9 **Reading Poetry for Meaning** Read the following questions. Then reread the poems on pages 241–243 and answer the questions.

> **"To People Who Pick Food"**
> This poem is spoken from the point of view of a poor Mexican migrant who is working illegally in the United States, with "a fake green card."

1. What parts of the poem suggest that the man feels prejudice and discrimination from the people around him?

_____

_____

2. What work does the man do? How does he feel about it?

_____

_____

3. When so many rich people seem dissatisfied with their lives (as evidenced by alcoholism, use of drugs, nervous breakdowns, and so on), why is this man content? What things does he have that give him strength and pride?

_____

_____

4. What emotive words (ones based on strong feelings or emotions) are used? What emotions do you think the poet wants us to feel toward the man?

_____

_____

> **"Grandma's Primo"**
> Just as a painter might use only a few lines or brushstrokes to suggest a whole person, this poem is also the portrait of a person, shown in just a few words.

5. From whose point of view do we see this character?

_____

_____

6. What special qualities does he have?

_____

_____

7. Why do you think the poet found him memorable?

_____

_____

Strategy

Reading for Speed and Fluency: Previewing the Questions and Predicting

If you have time, it helps to preview the questions that follow a reading BEFORE you do the reading. By previewing the questions, you can get an idea about the content in the reading and it will help you determine what information you want to get from the reading.

10 **Timed Reading: Reading for Speed and Fluency** After reading the introduction in the box below, try to finish the reading and comprehension exercises in six minutes.

> **Introduction**
> Jackie Chan has long been one of the best-known figures in Asian popular culture and is now popular in mainstream Hollywood as well. Read the following biography to learn more about his background and road to success.

The Life of Jackie Chan

A   One of the most popular film personalities in the world, Jackie Chan came from a poverty-stricken Hong Kong family—so poor, claims Chan, that he was almost sold in infancy to a wealthy British couple. As it turned out, Chan became his family's sole support. Enrolled in the Chinese Opera Research Institute at the age of seven, he spent the next decade in rigorous training for a career with the Peking Opera, excelling in martial arts and acrobatics.

B   Billed as Cheng Lung, Chan entered films in his mid-teens, appearing in 25 productions before his 20th birthday. Starting out as a stunt man, Chan was promoted to stardom as the potential successor to the late *Bruce Lee*. In his earliest starring films, he was cast as a stone-cold serious type, determined to avenge *Lee*'s death. Only when he began playing for laughs did Chan truly attain full celebrity status. Frequently referred to as the *Buster Keaton*[1] of kung-fu, Chan's outlook on life is a lot more optimistic than Keaton's, but in his tireless devotion to the most elaborate of sight gags and the most awe-inspiring of stunts (many of which have nearly cost him his life), Chan is Keaton incarnate.

▲ Jackie Chan in action

C   From 1978's *The Young Master* onward, Chan has usually been his own director and screenwriter. His best Hong Kong-produced films include the nonstop action-fests *Project A* (1983), *Police Story* (1985), *Armour of God* (1986), and the Golden Horse Award-winning *Crime Story* (1993)—not to mention the multiple sequels of each of the aforementioned titles. Despite his popularity in Europe and Asia, Chan was for many years unable to make a dent in the America market. He tried hard in such films as *The Big Brawl* (1980) and the first two *Cannonball Run* flicks, but American filmgoers just weren't buying.

D   At long last, Chan mined U.S. box-office gold[2] with 1996's *Rumble in the Bronx*, a film so exhilarating that audiences never noticed those distinctly Canadian mountain ranges looming behind the "Bronx" skyline. Chan remained the most popular Asian actor with the greatest potential to cross over into the profitable English-speaking markets, something he again demonstrated when he co-starred with Chris Tucker in the 1998 box-office hit *Rush Hour*. Chan had another success on his hands with *Shanghai Noon*, a comedy Western in which he starred as an Imperial Guard dispatched to the American West to rescue the kidnapped daughter (Lucy Liu) of the Chinese Emperor.

Source: www.starpulse.com

---

[1] A classic American comedy actor and movie writer.
[2] They made a lot of money at the box office, the place where movie tickets are sold.

Comprehension Quiz: True or False Read each statement below about the Jackie Chan reading. Based on the reading, check *True* or *False* for each statement.

	True	False
1. Jackie Chan was the son of wealthy parents.	❏	❏
2. He trained for a career in the opera where he learned martial arts and acrobatics.	❏	❏
3. Jackie Chan started as a comedy actor and then moved into serious roles.	❏	❏
4. Chan started out as a stunt man.	❏	❏
5. In most films, Chan is not only an actor, but also his own director and screenwriter.	❏	❏
6. Chan was very popular in the United States right away with his first movie.	❏	❏
7. The last three movies mentioned, *Rumble in the Bronx*, *Rush Hour*, and *Shanghai Noon* were very successful.	❏	❏

Word count in reading: <u>469</u>

Your time for completing the reading and exercise: _____

 11 **What's Your Opinion?** Discuss the following questions about the Jackie Chan article.

1. Have you seen any Jackie Chan movies? Which ones? Describe them. Did you like them? Why or why not?

2. Do you think that only men like Jackie Chan movies and women don't? Explain.

3. What do you think of him as a person?

4. If he did not do all of his own stunts, do you think that Jackie Chan would still be popular and famous? Why or why not?

 12 **What Do You Think?** Read the paragraph below and discuss the questions that follow.

MUSIC

Of all the creative arts, music is probably the most popular. For some people, nothing is more beautiful than opera, or a symphony by Beethoven or Mozart. Classical music is indeed the choice of millions. Yet others shun classical music and prefer to listen to jazz, rock, world, folk, country, or hip-hop. Music taste is in the ear of the listener.

1. Do you enjoy many types of music? What are they? What is your favorite type of music? Why?

2. Are there any types of music that seem universal, that most people around the world seem to enjoy? What are they?

3. Ethnic music, like Mexican music, seems to have worldwide appeal. Can you think of some other ethnic music that's popular nowadays?

4. Sometimes when you travel around the world, you hear the same songs and singers anywhere you go. An example of this would be Frank Sinatra singing "My Way" or "Strangers in the Night." Can you think of any other songs you hear over and over, year after year, worldwide?

▲ Rock music has worldwide appeal.

Part 3   Tying It All Together

 1 **Making Connections** Do some research on the Internet and take notes on one of the following topics. Share your results with the class or in a small group.

Georgia O'Keeffe Find some more art works by Georgia O'Keeffe or more detailed descriptions of her style or biography. Describe what you find.

Chicanos Find more information on the Chicano movement, Chicano history, Chicano art, Chicano programs, or other information related to Chicanos that interests you.

Names of Places Besides the place names given on the map or in the article on Chicanos, there are many other places that have Spanish names in the United States. Look at a map and make a list of Spanish place names, such as the city of Los Angeles or the state of Nevada. Find the meaning of the names and write it down. What strange or unusual names are there where you live that may have an interesting history?

Jackie Chan What is Jackie Chan doing nowadays? Does he have a more recent movie than the one mentioned in the timed reading? Is he involved in other projects? Or find out more information about his personal life and early childhood.

Responding in Writing

WRITING TIP: USING A VENN DIAGRAM TO COMPARE AND CONTRAST

When writing a comparison and contrast essay, be careful to choose two people or items that have clear similarities and differences between them and structure your composition to best suit the comparison or contrast made. As you learned in Exercise 7 on page 234, a Venn diagram can help you better visualize similarities and differences.

---

2 Writing Practice Compare any two well-known figures in the world of art or entertainment. For example, compare Jackie Chan to Bruce Lee.

Step 1 Choose two well-known figures who are movie stars, musicians, dancers, or in some other area of art or entertainment. Choose carefully. Think of people who have very clear similarities and differences, so it is easy for you to write about them. Maybe both are similar in age, gender, and popularity, but they have different styles or talents. Or maybe one provides a good moral example, and one does not.

Step 2 Write down as many points for comparison as you can think of. Use a Venn diagram to help you see the points where the two figures differ and where they are the same.

Step 3 Looking at your points, choose which one of the following compositions best suits your topic. The structure you use will depend on what you want to say.

1. Describe the similarities between the two, then describe their differences. (Example: If the two figures seem similar, but you want to stress that there is an important difference between them, then you would use the first structure.)

2. Describe the differences between the two, then describe their similarities. (Example: If the two figures seem different, but there are some interesting similarities you want to point out, then you would use the second structure.)

3. Describe one artist or entertainer fully, then describe the other. (Example: If you are focusing more on just describing the two artists, and hoping to point out some similarities and differences between them in passing, then you would use the third structure.)

Step 4 Write the composition, using the examples you wrote down in Step 2.

Step 5 Add a title, revise your composition, and exchange with a partner to give each other suggestions for revision.

- Did your partner choose two figures that have a good basis for comparison and contrast?

- Does the structure that your partner chose make sense for the comparison they make?

TOEFL® iBT

Focus on Testing

Inference Questions

For each TOEFL® iBT reading passage, some questions focus on implied meanings. These are meanings that are clear to a skillful reader but are not specifically expressed in words. The reader understands these meanings by *inferring* them— by making reasonable conclusions from what is specifically stated.

Some inference questions focus on implied relationships among pieces of information. Other inference questions focus on your understanding of an author's stance or purpose. Does the author have a positive or negative attitude? How certain is the author about a piece of information? Why does the author mention a particular idea?

Practice Read the passage about public art. Then answer the inference questions that follow.

Ethnic Influences on Public Art

A   Most works of art are kept indoors, in a gallery, private home, office building, or museum. One category of artwork, fashioned to be on display outdoors, defies such cloistering. It is known as public art, and it is meant to be viewed easily by any passer-by. By definition, public art shapes the environment of a community. In recent decades, most supporters of public art have advocated a two-way relationship, in which the people of a community should shape public art as well.

B   North America provides excellent examples of the ways in which ethnicity shapes the impulse to create public art. Multiple and overlapping waves of immigration into the United States and Canada have ensured that any truly local art movement will draw subjects and styles from many traditions. The best of such art expresses what a given ethnic group has experienced in North America, not merely what their ancestors experienced in "the old country."

C   California's Chicanos—descendants of immigrants from Mexico—have led the way in making public art that depicts an ethnic community's interests. A critical aspect of this was the struggle by a predominantly Chicano labor union, the United Farm Workers (UFW), for better working conditions in California during the 1960s. To support the UFW's efforts, highly accomplished Chicano artists in Los Angeles, in Sacramento, and elsewhere, placed posters, murals, and other politically charged works in public spaces. They drew attention as much for their beauty as for their message. After the UFW issue faded, the demand persisted for public art in the styles pioneered during the campaign. The complex murals that adorn sides of buildings throughout central and southern California, featuring elements of indigenous Mexican cultures mixed with scenes and symbols from Mexican-American life, carry the expression forward.

D   The Mural Arts Program (MAP) in Philadelphia has supported some of the most ambitious community-based public art in North America. In 1984, the MAP was launched as part of a campaign to fight a plague of graffiti in the city. In a novel approach to the problem, young people caught spraying graffiti on structures in Philadelphia were directed to MAP to work under professional muralists and produce murals that beautified neighborhoods rather than graffiti that defaced them. The MAP has since left its graffiti-busting past behind and has become an outlet for community expression. Philadelphia's African-American community has been particularly active in helping design and paint murals that depict family life, express aspirations, and honor achievements. For example, a three-story mural titled *Holding Grandmother's Quilt* covers one end wall of a block of rowhouses in eastern Philadelphia. It shows three African-American children intently studying the complexities of a geometric quilt, all against a quilt-like background of pastel pink, blue, and lavender. Designed by professional muralists Donald Gensler and Jane Golden, it was actually painted by a group of student amateurs.

E   Public sculptures in many North American cities express traditional and modern aspects of American-Indian life. For example, Marvin Oliver, whose ancestors include members of the Quinault Indian Nation in the Pacific Northwest, has fashioned several large public works. His *Eagle Bearing Wealth* is an eight-foot tall column of Douglas fir carved and painted to resemble a totem pole traditional among Indians of the Northwest Coast. It stands on the campus of North Seattle Community College in Seattle, Washington. In a public park in Seattle, Remington Court Park, Oliver's *Spirit of Our Youth* depicts the dorsal fin of an orca whale in a massive bronze form 26 feet tall. More controversial are the works of Hachivi Edward Heap of Birds. His work *Wheel* outside the Denver Art Museum in Colorado incorporates 12 Y-shaped columns of red porcelain arranged in a circle near a curved wall carved with the names of 97 Indian families killed in a massacre in the 1860s. The public display of names is a hallmark of Heap of Birds' work. On the banks of the Mississippi River in downtown Minneapolis, his *Building Minnesota* is an array of 40 simple white aluminum signs, each of which bears, in red lettering, the English and Dakota-language name of an Indian hung in Minnesota during the 1860s by order of the president of the United States.

F Countless other ethnic groups have left, and are leaving, their marks on North American public art. The stonemason Torkjel Landsverk erected beautifully textured ornamental walls and monuments in Iowa and Minnesota during the late 19th century and early 20th. While a modern eye might skip over them as just more examples of stodgy, old fixtures expressing little, they are anything but boring. Their rough-hewn character skillfully reflects an aesthetic appreciation for hard-to-tame nature among Norwegian-Americans in the Upper Midwest. Along Toronto's Light Rail Transport (LRT) system, as it follows Spadina Avenue, several commissioned works of public art are expected to enliven the ride. One of these commissions, awarded to Millie Chen, is for an ornamental gateway to Toronto's Chinatown. Preliminary designs show its basic shape as the Chinese character for "gate," a character that also appears in several other Asian languages. Toronto has been a magnet for Asian immigration into North America, and Chen's work is meant to represent a strong, growing, cross-national segment of the Canadian public.

1. Which of the following best expresses the author's attitude toward indoor art, according to Paragraph A?

- (A) It is not as beautiful as public art.
- (B) It is only one type of public art.
- (C) It is not as easy to encounter as public art.
- (D) It is not shaped by the community.

2. Which of the following is most strongly implied by the last sentence of Paragraph B?

- (A) The best public art brings ancestral traditions to the attention of modern audiences.
- (B) The best public art expresses aspects of an ethnic community's life after immigration.
- (C) The best public art in the world is found in the United States and Canada.
- (D) The best public art is produced by artists with a lot of experience.

3. Why does the author mention the UFW struggle in Paragraph C?

- (A) to show support for better working conditions
- (B) to demonstrate that Chicano artists were originally farm workers
- (C) to show why Los Angeles and Sacramento are well-known for Chicano art
- (D) to explain the origins of much of California's Chicano public art

4. Which of the following is most strongly implied about graffiti in Paragraph D?

- (A) It is not beautiful.
- (B) It is a kind of public art.
- (C) It is dangerous.
- (D) It is best done by professionals.

5. What can most strongly be inferred about orca whales from Paragraph E?

- (A) They are very large.
- (B) They have cultural significance to some American Indians.
- (C) They are controversial.
- (D) They have bronze-colored fins on their backs.

6. Why does the author call the work of Hachivi Edward Heap of Birds "controversial"?

- (A) because it often includes names
- (B) because it uses the colors red and white
- (C) because it takes up a lot of public space
- (D) because it criticizes certain events of the past

7. What can be most strongly inferred from Paragraph F about Millie Chen's "gateway" work in Toronto?

- (A) It is not likely to be completed.
- (B) It has been delayed because of complaints from Asian groups.
- (C) It will probably be completed.
- (D) It is being promoted by Asian groups despite government opposition.

Self-Assessment Log

Read the lists below. Check (✓) the strategies and vocabulary that you learned in this chapter. Look through the chapter or ask your instructor about the strategies and words that you do not understand.

Reading and Vocabulary-Building Strategies
- ❑ Previewing
- ❑ Getting meaning through word structure and context: verbs
- ❑ Paraphrasing
- ❑ Expressing ideas
- ❑ Making a comparison
- ❑ Matching words to their meanings
- ❑ Recalling information
- ❑ Summarizing information about specific points
- ❑ Reading poetry
- ❑ Understanding poetry
- ❑ Reading poetry for meaning
- ❑ Reading for speed and fluency: previewing the questions and predicting
- ❑ Previewing the questions and predicting

Target Vocabulary

Nouns
- ❑ achievements*
- ❑ Chicanos
- ❑ citizenship
- ❑ civil rights
- ❑ discrimination
- ❑ focus*
- ❑ immigration*
- ❑ inhabitants
- ❑ issues*
- ❑ mechanization
- ❑ policy*
- ❑ strike
- ❑ traditions*

Verbs
- ❑ clarify*
- ❑ criticized
- ❑ embodied
- ❑ established*
- ❑ exhibited*
- ❑ faltered
- ❑ fascinated
- ❑ ignored*
- ❑ immortalized
- ❑ perceived*
- ❑ reject*
- ❑ stunned

- ❑ tilling
- ❑ translated

Adjectives
- ❑ Anglo
- ❑ bilingual
- ❑ civil*
- ❑ disappointed
- ❑ ethnic*
- ❑ Hispanic
- ❑ migrant*
- ❑ unique*

* These words are from the Academic Word List. For more information on this list, see www.vuw.ac.nz/lals/research/awl.

Conflict and Reconciliation

In This Chapter

The chapter opens with several instances of the surprising power of the apology and what it can achieve in terms of reconciliation. The second part is a poem by one of the world's great poets who reveals the human face of hatred, war, and compassion. In the timed reading, we then look at an unusual method of resolving conflict.

> **❝** What kind of victory is it when someone is left defeated? **❞**

—Mahatma Gandhi
Indian religious leader who championed
the concept of nonviolence (1869–1948)

Connecting to the Topic

1. What do you know about the life and work of Mahatma Gandhi, pictured below?

2. Read the quotation by Gandhi. What do you think it means?

3. What is meant by the word *reconciliation*? In what ways can people or warring countries be reconciled to each other?

Contrite Makes Right

Before You Read

Culture Note

To apologize or to make an apology means to admit that you have done wrong and to say you are sorry. An apology can be made in many different contexts.

1 **Previewing a Reading for its Organization** The article that follows is about the power of apologies. All of the contexts in the following list are mentioned in the article. Scan the article to see what order they are given in and number them from 1 (the first one mentioned) to 5 (the last one mentioned). Can you guess why they are organized in this sequence?

1. _____ during legal disputes

2. _____ from a government to a group that has been wronged

3. _____ from one nation to another

4. _____ in the home

5. _____ in the workplace

2 **Getting Meaning from Word Structure and Context** Using the word structure or context, figure out the best synonym or definition for each word in italics taken from the reading. Scan the word in the reading if you need more context.

1. Apologies . . . repair *schisms* between nations . . .
   - (A) books
   - (B) divisions
   - (C) families
   - (D) weapons

2. Apologies . . . restore *equilibrium* to personal relationships.
   - (A) anger
   - (B) balance
   - (C) conflict
   - (D) energy

3. Apologies . . . are one of a *bevy* of . . . speech acts . . .
   - (A) center
   - (B) front
   - (C) group
   - (D) question

4. In the American context . . . women are more inclined to offer an expression of *contrition* than men.

- (A) anger for the wrong that has been done to them
- (B) criticism and insults against wrongdoers
- (C) interest in meeting more people
- (D) sorrow for what they have done wrong

5. Showing that you *empathize* provides the contrition . . . central to apologies . . .

- (A) dislike the ideas of another
- (B) see what is wrong in the situation
- (C) think in a different way
- (D) understand the feelings of another

6. When he admitted . . . that he had made a mistake and then expressed *remorse* . . .

- (A) confusion for the problems caused
- (B) sorrow for having done wrong
- (C) happiness for having succeeded
- (D) tolerance for the faults of others

7. . . . it is distressing when the *litigious* nature of our society prevents us from [making apologies].

- (A) beneficial
- (B) lawsuit-loving
- (C) money-saving
- (D) peaceful

8. Germany responded by setting up a *philanthropic* fund for the benefit of the Czechs.

- (A) charitable
- (B) costly
- (C) false
- (D) popular

9. It is absurd—even *grotesque*—for members of the Khmer Rouge to offer the people of Cambodia brief regrets . . .

- (A) amusing
- (B) generous
- (C) difficult and good
- (D) strange and horrible

10. The statement is . . . inadequate in light of the massive *slaughter* and suffering . . .

- (A) benefit
- (B) killing
- (C) misunderstanding
- (D) payment

> **Introduction**
>
> The following magazine article was written by the popular American author and linguist Deborah Tannen. The first word of the title, *contrite* (meaning "sorry") gives us a clue about the theme. This is confirmed in the *lead* (the short explanatory statement that often comes before an article); it refers to the "mighty sorry" that has "proved effective." The article goes on to show examples of how powerful this simple word has been in various difficult situations in American society and also on the international scene. Read to see if you agree with the examples given and how you feel that apologies can be used to obtain useful results.
>
> - From your experience, what benefits can you get from apologizing?
> - Are you a person who apologizes easily or almost never? Do you know people who never want to apologize?

Contrite Makes Right

A   *Whether used to repair old, strained relationships or to lay the groundwork for new, productive ones, the mighty "sorry" has proved effective.*

B   Apologies are powerful. They resolve conflicts without violence, repair schisms between nations, allow governments to acknowledge the suffering of their citizens, and restore equilibrium to personal relationships. They are an effective way to restore trust and gain respect. They can be a sign of strength: proof that the apologizer has the self-confidence to admit a mistake.

C   Apologies, like so many other communication strategies, begin at home. They are one of a bevy of what some linguists call speech acts and are used to keep relationships on track. Each cultural group has its own customs with regard to conversational formalities, including conventionalized means of repairing disruptions.

D   In the American context, there is ample evidence that women are more inclined to offer an expression of contrition than men. One woman, for example, told me that her husband's resistance to apologizing makes their disputes go on and on. Once, after he forgot to give her a particularly important telephone message, she couldn't get over her anger, not because he had forgotten (she realized anyone can make a mistake) but because he didn't apologize. "Had I done something like that," she said, "I would have fallen all over myself saying how sorry I was . . . I felt as though he didn't care." When I asked her husband for his side of the story, he said apologizing would not have repaired the damage. "So what good does it do?" he wondered.

E   The good it does is cement the relationship. By saying he was sorry—and saying it as if he meant it—he would have conveyed that he felt bad about letting her down. Not saying anything sent the opposite message: It implied he didn't care. Showing that you empathize provides the element of contrition, remorse, or repentance that is central to apologies—as does the promise to make amends and not repeat the offense. In the absence of these, why should the wife trust her husband not to do it again?

F   Apologies can be equally powerful in day-to-day situations at home and at work. One company manager told me that they were magic bullets. When he admitted to subordinates that he had made a mistake and then expressed remorse, they not only forgave him, but became even more loyal. Conversely, when I asked people what most frustrated them in their work lives, co-workers refusing to admit fault was a frequent answer.

G   Given the importance of taking responsibility for the results of our actions, it is distressing when the litigious nature of our society prevents us from doing so. We are, for example, instructed by lawyers and auto insurance companies never to admit fault—or say we're sorry—following automobile accidents, since this may put us in a precarious legal position. The stance makes sense but takes a toll spiritually.

H   The power of apologies as a display of caring lies at the heart of the veritable avalanche of them that we are now seeing in the public sphere. Government, for instance, can demonstrate that they care about a group that was wronged, such as when the United States apologized in 1997 to African-American men who were denied treatment for syphilis as part of a 40-year medical experiment that began in the 1930s.

I   Offering an apology to another country is an effective way to lay the groundwork for future cooperation. In the late 1990s, the Czech Republic remained the only European nation with which Germany had not reached a settlement providing restitution for Nazi persecution during World War II. Germany refused to pay Czech victims until the Czechs formally apologized for their postwar expulsion of ethnic Germans from the Sudetenland. In the interest of receiving both reparations and Germany's support for inclusion in NATO, the Czech government offered the apology in 1997 (despite the opposition of many of its citizens). The gamble paid off, as Germany responded by setting up a philanthropic fund for the benefit of the Czechs,

and both NATO and the European Union have invited the Czech Republic to join their ranks.

₁ Sometimes it may seem 65 that a nation or group tries to purchase forgiveness with a facile apology. It is absurd—even grotesque—for the leaders of the Khmer Rouge to 70 offer the people of Cambodia brief regrets and immediately suggest that they let bygones be bygones. The statement is woefully inadequate in light of 75 the massive slaughter and suffering the Khmer Rouge caused while it was in power. Furthermore, by taking the initiative in suggesting the past 80 be laid to rest, they seem to be forgiving themselves—something that is not the offender's place to do.

▲ Apologies can help heal the wounds of war.

Source: "Contrite Makes Right" *Civilization Magazine* (Deborah Tannen)

After You Read

Strategy

Analyzing Cause and Effect
In a selection that describes a cause and effect relationship, such as *Contrite Makes Right,* analyzing which cause leads to which effect helps you understand the logic of the argument. You can use a cause and effect graphic organizer to organize information about cause and effect.

3 **Analyzing Cause and Effect** Describe the effects that occurred (according to the article) as a result of the following actions.

Cause	Effect
1. One woman's husband did not apologize to her for forgetting to give her an important telephone message.	→ As a result, the woman got very angry and couldn't get over her bad feeling toward her husband. She felt as though he didn't care.
2. A company manager admitted to his subordinates that he had made a mistake and felt remorse about it.	→
3. Lawyers and auto insurance companies tell us never to admit fault or say we are sorry after an automobile accident.	→
4. The U.S. government in 1997 apologized to African-American men who were denied medical treatment as part of an experiment.	→
5. The Czech government apologized to Germany for the expulsion of ethnic Germans from the Sudetenland.	→
6. The Khmer Rouge offered an apology to the people of Cambodia for the suffering that had taken place under their rule and suggested that they should let bygones be bygones (forget about wrong actions of the past).	→

4 **Inferring the Meaning of Idioms and Expressions** Look at the common phrases and idioms taken from the article and written in italics in the sentences below. Choose the correct meaning.

1. Apologies can *lay the groundwork* for new productive relationships.
- (A) prevent the growth of
- (B) contribute to the development of

2. If the woman had made such a mistake, she felt that she would have *fallen all over herself* saying how sorry she was.
- (A) tried hard to show her remorse by
- (B) made more mistakes by

3. When the husband was asked for *his side of the story* . . .
- (A) the words he had said
- (B) his point of view

4. Sometimes an apology can *cement the relationship*.
- (A) make a relationship weaker
- (B) make a relationship stronger

5. By expressing contrition, he would have shown that he felt bad about *letting her down*.
- (A) not giving her what she needed
- (B) not winning the argument with her

6. The promise to *make amends* is central to an apology.
- (A) do something to correct the wrong
- (B) think of a new explanation for what was done

7. Admitting that you have made a mistake can also be important in *day-to-day situations*.
- (A) situations that occur in the day
- (B) situations that are common

8. One company manager said that apologies are *magic bullets*.
- (A) effective ways to quickly make things better
- (B) hurtful ways of destroying some people

9. The instruction from lawyers to never admit fault *takes a toll* spiritually.
- (A) helps us to feel better about ourselves
- (B) makes us feel bad about ourselves

10. The power of apologies *lies at the heart of* the recent tendency to use them in public.
- (A) is the main reason for
- (B) is not an important part of

11. Both NATO and the European Union invited the Czech Republic to *join their ranks*.
- (A) leave their organizations
- (B) become members with them

12. Suggesting that the people of Cambodia *let bygones be bygones* seems absurd or even grotesque.

(A) just forget the whole thing as something in the past

(B) accept compensation and allow forgiveness to occur

5 **Focusing on Words from the Academic Word List** Read the paragraphs below taken from the reading in Part 1. Fill in the blanks with the most appropriate word from the box. Do not look back at the reading right away; instead, see if you can remember the vocabulary. One of the words appears twice.

acknowledge	cultural	resolve
conflicts	evidence	restore
context	inclined	strategies

Apologies are powerful. They _____ 1 _____ 2 without violence, repair schisms between nations, allow governments to _____ 3 the suffering of their citizens, and _____ 4 equilibrium to personal relationships. They are an effective way to _____ 5 trust and gain respect. They can be a sign of strength: proof that the apologizer has the self-confidence to admit a mistake.

Apologies, like so many other communication _____ 6, begin at home. They are one of a bevy of what some linguists call speech acts and are used to keep relationships on track. Each _____ 7 group has its own customs with regard to conversational formalities, including conventionalized means of repairing disruptions.

In the American _____ 8, there is ample _____ 9 that women are more _____ 10 to offer an expression of contrition than men.

6 **Guided Academic Conversation: Report from the Psychologists**

Working with a small group, complete a report on one of the following topics. Play the role of a team of psychologists who have been hired to make a serious list and give suggestions relevant to each topic. When your teacher calls time, one person from each group will be asked to read the list and another will be asked to give the suggestions.

1. **Conflicts at Home** "Apologies begin at home," according to the article. Your group has been asked to give advice to a clinic of marriage counselors. Make a list of at least five home situations in which an apology would be helpful. Then give suggestions to the following people on how to apologize: wives, husbands, children, parents. Or do you feel that certain groups should never apologize, such as parents to children? Do you agree with the author that women apologize more than men? Is that a difference that belongs only to North American culture? Explain.

2. **Conflicts at Work** You have to give a workshop for the directors of human resources of large companies. Make a list of five common conflicts that can occur in the workplace. Indicate for which ones an apology would be in order. Then give specific rules on this subject to be given to employees as well as to the managers and bosses. Who would apologize to whom? And for what? Would apologies be given by subordinates to managers and bosses or only the other way around? Or should they only be used among equals? Explain.

3. **Dealing with Errors at Schools or Universities** Is an apology a show of strength or is it really an admission of weakness? Think of three errors that the president or administration of a school or university could make? After each one, list the bad consequence or effect that would come from that error. What would you think of a teacher who apologized for a mistake in teaching or the president of a university who apologized for supporting a bad policy? Choose one of the errors, and give advice to those involved.

4. **Public Apologies** The government has made a serious mistake and asked you to advise it on how to apologize for it. First, invent the situation. Describe a serious mistake that you can imagine your government or some other government making. Then give five suggestions about how the politicians and officials can handle this. Should they admit that they made a mistake or not? When should they announce the apology and how? How would they state it— directly or indirectly?

5. **The Cultural Dimension** Your group has been asked to report on the cultural dimension in the article you just read. What does the title, *Contrite Makes Right*, mean? Why is this a particularly effective title? Even though the title is a good one, is the article really universal? Does it apply equally well to societies other than the United States? Why or why not? Do you know of different customs relating to admitting fault or saying that you are sorry?

7 **What Do You Think?** Read the paragraphs below and then discuss the questions.

Dealing with the Past

"The experience of others has taught us that nations that do not deal with the past are haunted by it for generations," said Nelson Mandela, leader of the movement against apartheid. Apartheid was the policy of racial segregation in South Africa, based on the belief in the superiority of

▲ Nelson Mandela with an official of the former apartheid regime

white people. For almost half a century, it denied basic rights to Black Africans and all people of color, such as the right to freedom of movement, good education, housing, work, and employment. Mandela was imprisoned for 27 years for his opposition to this system. He was finally released, and four years later in 1994, he was elected president of a new South Africa.

During his presidency, a Truth and Reconciliation Commission was established to uncover crimes committed during the apartheid era. The Commission could choose to give amnesty to those who confessed.

1. Some of the crimes included robbery, murder, and torture. Do you think it was correct to have the people who committed such crimes confess, tell the truth, and then be forgiven? Why or why not? In your opinion, can this model be used in other places in the world? Explain your opinion.

2. What do you think Mandela means when he says: "Nations that do not deal with the past are haunted by it for generations"? Explain. Can you think of any nations where this is true?

When One Person Reaches Out with Love

Before You Read

Strategy

Reading a Poem
Poetry is usually shorter than a selection of prose (non-poetic writing) and denser—more packed with detail, meaning, and emotion. So it is good to mentally prepare yourself before starting to read it, to shift gears from the normal everyday world and enter into the inner emotional world of another person. See Chapter 9, page 241 for more about reading poetry.

1 Previewing a Poem Look at the introduction and the poem on pages 267–268 and answer the following questions.

1. Think for a moment about the title. Then skim the poem for its main idea. What do you think is the dominant emotion of the poem?

2. Where and when did the events described in the poem occur? What was the world like in the year mentioned in the note?

3. The poem is a childhood memory of the poet, and the note says that it describes a transforming moment. What do you think is meant by a transforming moment? Do you think these moments happen mostly in our childhood, or are they possible throughout life? Can you give an example?

2 Identifying Synonyms Below are sentences from the poem with words in parentheses. Choose a more effective synonym from the box to fill in each of the blanks. Notice that the words used in the poem (those in the box) usually give a more vivid or complete idea of what is being seen or felt.

clenching	hobbling	roughened
dead	hunched	shuffling
demeanor	massive	tottering
disdainfully	plebeian	

1. The pavements (were filled) __*swarmed*__ with onlookers . . .

2. Russian women with hands (worn) _____ by hard work . . . and with thin, (bent) _____ shoulders . . .

3. The generals marched at the head, (large) _____ chins stuck out, lips folded (arrogantly) _____ . . .

4. . . . their whole (attitude) _____ meant to show superiority over their (low-class) _____ victors . . .

5. They smell of eau-de-cologne (*perfume*), the bastards (*a vulgar insult not used in polite company*) . . . The women were (tightening) _____ their fists.

6. They saw German soldiers . . . (walking weakly) _____ on crutches . . .

7. The street became (completely) _____ silent . . .

8. —the only sound was the (moving back and forth) _____ of boots and . . .

9. . . . a soldier, so exhausted that he was (leaning from side to side as if about to fall down) _____ on his feet.

Read

Introduction

Yevgeny Yevtushenko, one of the most loved Russian poets, transmitted a notable description of a transforming moment. In 1944, toward the end of World War II, Yevtushenko's mother took him from Siberia to Moscow. They were among those who witnessed a procession of 20,000 German war prisoners marching through the streets of Moscow.

▲ Yevgeny Yevtushenko

- What images come to your mind when you think of World War II?
- Do you have any childhood memories that are very powerful?

Read this short selection at least two times to get its full flavor and meaning. Try to imagine in your mind the pictures that Yevtushenko paints with words of the three different groups of people who are present at the scene and the contrasts between them.

When One Person Reaches Out with Love

The pavements swarmed with onlookers, cordoned off by soldiers and police.

The crowd was mostly women—Russian women with hands roughened by hard work, lips untouched by lipstick and with thin, hunched shoulders which had borne half of the burden of the war. Every one of them must have had a father or a husband, a brother or a son killed by the Germans.

They gazed with hatred in the direction from which the column was to appear.

At last we saw it.

The generals marched at the head, massive chins stuck out, lips folded disdainfully, their whole demeanor meant to show superiority over their plebeian victors.

"They smell of eau-de-cologne, the bastards," someone in the crowd said with hatred.

The women were clenching their fists. The soldiers and policemen had all they could do to hold them back.

All at once, something happened to them.

They saw German soldiers, thin, unshaven, wearing dirty, bloodstained bandages, hobbling on crutches or leaning on the shoulders of their comrades; the soldiers walked with their heads down.

The street became dead silent—the only sound was the shuffling of boots and the thumping of crutches.

Then I saw an elderly woman in broken-down boots push herself forward and touch a policeman's shoulder, saying: "Let me through." There must have been something about her that made him step aside.

She went up to the column, took from inside her coat something wrapped in a coloured handkerchief and unfolded it. It was a crust of black bread. She pushed it awkwardly into the pocket of a soldier, so exhausted that he was tottering on his feet. And now suddenly from every side women were running towards the soldiers, pushing into their hands bread, cigarettes, whatever they had.

The soldiers were no longer enemies.

They were people.

Source: "When One Person Reaches Out with Love" *A Precocious Autobiography* (Yevgeny Yevtushenko)

After You Read

3 **Using a Chart for Comparison** With a partner, make a chart similar to the one that follows and fill it in with as many details as possible to show the contrasts between the three groups from the scene described in the poem. Then answer these questions: How do these different groups react to each other at first? What emotional transformation takes place afterwards? Why?

Groups Present	Physical Appearance	Attitude and Emotions	What Happened in Their Past
Crowd of onlookers			
The German prisoners who were generals and officers			
The German prisoners who were common soldiers			

4 **Guided Academic Conversation: War and Peace** In small groups, discuss the following questions. Afterwards, compare your answers with those of another group.

1. What is your opinion of war? When is it justified? Are there good wars and bad wars, or are all wars bad?

2. What monuments do you know about to wartime victories? Do you like them? Do you think it is important to remember the soldiers who have died in different wars? How should this be done? Should ceremonies be held only for the winning armies or for both sides? Explain.

3. How do you feel about the idea of nationalism? Do you think every person should love his or her country? Do you believe in the idea: "My country, right or wrong!" Why or why not?

4. Some people think that nationalism is an old idea that should be left in the past. Today people should think of themselves as citizens of the world and feel loyalty to all of humanity. What is your opinion about this idea?

5. What would you be willing to fight and die for?

5 **Around the Globe** Read the introduction below. Then in a small group, read the following excerpt aloud, each person in turn reading two sentences. Then answer the questions at the end.

Introduction

Louise Diamond, a conflict negotiator, in her book *The Courage for Peace*, tells of a moment of enlightenment for someone who had been deeply hurt, longed to seek revenge, and then changed his mind and chose to let go of hatred in favor of forgiveness.

The Toy Rifle

In a conflict resolution workshop with Turkish Cypriots on the troubled island of Cyprus, I began by asking the usual question, "Why are you here?" One young man shared that his father had been killed by Greek Cypriots in the communal violence when he was a child, and that he had grown up full of hatred and bitterness toward his "enemy."

A few evenings before this meeting, the man had gone in to kiss his young son good-night. As he leaned over to hug the child, he noticed a wooden toy rifle tucked under the sheets beside the boy. "Why do you have that rifle in bed with you?" asked the father. "To kill the Greek Cypriots when they come for me in the night," replied his son matter-of-factly.

In that moment, something shifted in the father's heart. Seeing the need to break the cycle of violence, the man released his own bitterness and made a commitment to work for a future in which his son would not have to live in fear or repeat the hatreds of yesterday.

1. What do you know about the island of Cyprus and its history of conflict?

2. Do you think there are many places with conflicts that are somewhat similar? Explain.

3. What effect does the sight of the toy rifle have on the father? Why?

4. What did the father learn from his son? How did it change him?

Strategy

Reading for Speed and Fluency: Not Vocalizing Words as You Read
Our speaking speed is much slower than our reading speed. Vocalizing or saying words in our head as we read slows down our reading speed. If we want to improve our reading speed, one tip is to not vocalize the words as we read them.

Reading Tip

If you can complete the reading and the exercise in 5.5 minutes, you are reading at about 122 words per minute (wpm) with 1.5 minutes for the exercise; 6.5 minutes = 97 wpm with 1.5 minutes for the exercise; 8 minutes = 81 wpm with 2 minutes for the exercise.

6 **Timed Reading: Reading for Speed and Fluency** The following selection is very short, but even so, first quickly preview the comprehension activity on page 272 before beginning the reading. Then read the introduction. Once you begin the reading, try to finish the reading and comprehension exercise in six minutes.

Introduction

The timed reading is about a group of people in Vietnam during a war who tried to help find resolution to the conflict. It is an excerpt from Vietnamese author Thich Nhat Hanh's book *Being Peace*, which consists of teachings, lectures, and essays that include stories from his own experiences. Nhat Hanh is recognized throughout the world for his work towards peace. He was nominated for the Nobel Peace Prize by Dr. Martin Luther King Jr. He lives in exile in a meditation community that he founded in the South of France where he continues his teachings and assistance to Vietnamese refugees.

▲ Thich Nhat Hahn helps lead the search for peace.

Your beginning time: _____

Being Peace

During the war in Vietnam we young Buddhists organized ourselves to help victims of the war rebuild villages that had been destroyed by the bombs. Many of us died during service, not only because of the bombs and the bullets, but because of the people who suspected us of being on the other side. We were able to understand the suffering of both sides, the Communists and the anti-Communists. We tried to be open to both, to understand this side and to understand that side, to be one with them. That is why we did not take a side, even though the whole world took sides. We tried to tell people our perception of the situation: that we wanted to stop the fighting, but the bombs were so loud. Sometimes we had to burn ourselves alive to get the message across, but even then the world could not hear us. They thought we were supporting a kind of political act. They didn't know that it was a purely human action to be heard, to be understood. We wanted reconciliation; we did not want a victory. Working to help people in a circumstance like that is very dangerous, and many of us got killed. The communists killed us because they suspected that we were working with the Americans, and the anti-Communists killed us because they thought that we were with the Communists. But we did not want to give up and take one side.

The situation of the world is still like this. People completely identify with one side, one ideology. To understand the suffering and the fear of a citizen of the Soviet Union* we have to become one with him or her. To do so is dangerous—we will be suspected by both sides. But if we don't do it, if we align ourselves with one side or the other, we will lose our chance to work for peace. Reconciliation is to understand both sides, to go to the one side and describe the suffering being endured by the other side, and then to go to the other side and describe the suffering being endured by the first side. Doing only that will be a great help for peace.

▲ How would you express yourself as a river?

During a retreat at the Providence Zen Centre, I asked someone to express himself as a swimmer in a river, and then after 15 minutes of breathing, to express himself as the river. He had to become the river to be able to express himself in the language and feelings of the river. After that, a woman who had been in the Soviet Union was asked to express herself as an American, and after some breathing and meditation, as a Soviet citizen, with all her fears and her hope for peace. She did it wonderfully. These are exercises of meditation related to non-duality.

The young Buddhist workers in Vietnam tried to do this kind of meditation.

Source: *Being Peace* (Thich Nhat Hanh)

---

*The huge former Communist nation which included Russia and 14 other republics and was, for many years, the largest country in the world. It was established in 1922 and was officially ended in 1991.

Comprehension Questions Read the sentences below about the reading and choose the correct answers.

1. The young people seeking resolution for the conflict in Vietnam are _____.

   a. Muslims

   b. Buddhists

   c. Christians

2. The anti-Communists killed these young people because they thought they were working with the Communists, and the Communists killed them because they thought they were working with the _____.
   a. Americans
   b. Vietnamese
   c. Russians

3. These young workers feel you can only find reconciliation by _____.
   a. finding out who is right and helping them to win the war
   b. forming your own government and dominating both sides
   c. not taking sides, but instead helping each side to understand the other

4. Sometimes this group trying to resolve conflict in Vietnam would take the extreme action of _____ to get their message across.
   a. burning themselves alive
   b. leaving the country
   c. killing people

5. During a retreat, the author asked a man to "express himself" (to act as though he were) a swimmer, and then after meditation, to express himself as _____.
   a. the person rescuing him
   b. a sky diver
   c. the river

Word count: 486

Your time for completing the reading and exercise: _____.

 7 **Your Opinion** After you are have finished the timed reading, discuss the following questions with a partner.

1. Is it possible to be in a war zone and not take sides? How do you imagine Nhat Hanh would try to communicate to each side what the other was feeling?

2. Why do you think both sides were mistrustful of Nhat Hanh?

3. What is the point of the exercises of expressing oneself, for instance, as an American and then as a Soviet citizen?

4. Think of a conflict that is present in your culture or in today's world. What two opposite people or things could you express yourself as? Try to do this, by pretending first to be the one, and saying out loud what opinions this one might express. Then pretend to be the opposite and say out loud what this other might express.

5. Do you think this type of conflict resolution could work in the conflict between the two groups you mentioned in the last question?

1 Making Connections Do some research on the Internet and take notes on one of the following topics. Share your results with the class or in a small group.

Deborah Tannen Find a review of another one of Deborah Tannen's books. Summarize what the reviewer had to say about it. Did the reviewer like it or not? Why? Does it sound interesting to you?

Apologies Find an article about apologies or reconciliation by another writer and compare it to the article by Tannen.

Yevgeny Yevtushenko's Poetry Find another poem by Yevgeny Yevtushenko, read it, and explain what it is about. Make sure you look through a number of poems before choosing one, as some of Yevtushenko's poems are much easier and shorter than others. Some titles of shorter poems you might want to choose are "People," "Waiting," "Lies," or "Wounds."

Poetry about War or Peace Find a poem that deals with war or peace. It can be from your own culture if you like. Compare it to the poem by Yevtushenko.

Mindfulness See what you can learn about Thich Nhat Hanh and his writings. Report on what you learned.

TOEFL® IBT

Focus on Testing

Negative Questions and Sentence-Insertion Questions

Two types of TOEFL® iBT reading questions we have not yet discussed are negative questions and sentence-insertion questions. Negative questions ask you to identify the one option that does NOT relate to a certain idea. A sentence-insertion question asks you to identify the best possible place to add a new sentence to the reading passage.

Not every set of questions contains a negative question. In sets that do contain one, there is probably not more than one. The word *except* is almost always part of a negative question, as you can see from the questions in the practice section below.

There is one sentence-insertion question for each reading passage, and it is commonly the second-to-last question in the set. The question gives you a new sentence and asks you to look at four positions in the reading passage, each marked with a dark square. You answer the question by choosing the number of the square where the sentence would best fit.

Practice Read the following passage about peer mediation. Then answer the negative questions and the sentence-insertion question.

Peer Mediation on Campus

A   Things have not gone well lately between Anna and Carly, two roommates in a dormitory at a Midwestern public university. Anna likes to stay up late, and Carly is not happy about being kept awake night after night. Carly spends hours each day talking on her cell phone, driving Anna "crazy" with all the chatter. Mutually annoyed, they have become distrustful, suspecting each other of stealing small personal items and reading private correspondence.

B   This sort of conflict is so commonplace as to seem silly or trivial, but it could have serious consequences—bad grades, loss of personal confidence, and even perhaps physical violence. Colleges and universities have to take them seriously and try to resolve them. The old-school solution is simply to threaten the disputants with some disciplinary action if they don't stop fighting. This approach wrongheadedly treats a personal conflict as a violation of the university rules. It may drive the dispute underground but is unlikely to resolve it. Another "solution" that seems obvious is to separate the roommates by re-shuffling room assignments. If only one such conflict erupted each semester, this might defuse the conflict (again without actually resolving it), but a room-shuffling policy is doomed by its own impracticality. Any university following such a policy would be so overwhelmed that its residential-life staff would do little else all semester but process room-change requests. In search of a sustainable, pragmatic policy, many universities have turned to a highly successful conflict-resolution strategy called peer mediation.

C   In any kind of mediation, a third party—the mediator—helps both sides in a conflict come up with possible solutions and a plan for implementing them. The mediator arranges meetings between the parties, directs the conversation, and helps clarify the issues. Beyond that, conflict resolution is up to the disputants themselves.

D   Mediation differs from another conflict-resolution strategy, arbitration, in that a mediator does not propose or impose solutions. An arbitrator listens to both sides, asks questions, and then issues a judgment about the best way to resolve things. Any plan for moving forward is constructed by the arbitrator, not by the disputants, who may or may not think the arbitrator's decisions are fair and practical. The parties in the conflict comply because they have to, not necessarily because they want to. Especially with independent-minded young people, such coercive methods rarely work. In mediation, by contrast, there is no plan for resolving the conflict unless the disputants come up with one.

E   Peer mediation is a unique version of the process in that the mediator is someone close in age or status to the people involved in the conflict. [1] Up to a point, the closer the better. To resolve dorm-room disputes, for example, the mediator should not only be a student but, if possible, a dorm resident as well. [2] If racial or ethnic tensions are part of the conflict, it would be best to bring in two mediators, each of which has one of the relevant backgrounds but is committed to an unbiased examination of the problem. [3] If this is not possible, a lone mediator should be prepared to demonstrate fairness and an understanding of both sides. Disputes between undergraduates should be mediated by other undergraduates, not by graduate students whose concerns are quite far removed from those of younger students. [4]

F To ensure impartiality, however, the mediator should not be someone too close to the problem. The mediator should absolutely not be a friend or even an acquaintance of either party. Nor should the mediator have any prior experience of the problem. A mediator from the same dorm floor as the disputants, someone who has been kept awake by Anna or subjected to Carly's cell phone chatter, will probably not approach their dispute with focus and clarity.

G Peer-mediation programs at public universities in the United States all follow similar outlines. A group of student volunteers is assembled under the direction of one or more faculty mentors. The mentors and the volunteers discuss ways in which to customize standard mediation programs so they suit local circumstance. Whatever the resulting structure, it must operate on a very limited budget because peer mediation is offered free of charge to all students. With the rules and a practical funding structure in place, the volunteers go through training sessions in effective conflict resolution. On many campuses, such as the University of Texas at Austin or the University of Maryland, the training comes in the form of a credit-bearing conflict-resolution course. Students fulfill course requirements by working in the peer mediation program, and their grade depends on how well they apply principles they've learned in the course.

H The greatest potential drawback of a peer mediation system derives from the youth and inexperience of the mediators. Even with training, college-student mediators may lack a broad view of interpersonal relations. For this reason, faculty mentors must carefully monitor the progress of all mediation cases and step in if something seems to be going amiss. The benefits of peer mediation are numerous. Students are likely to trust that their peers understand their problems better than adults do. The parties in the conflict must cooperate in finding solutions to their problems, and this shared experience can help break down barriers of personal distrust.

Because any plan for resolving the conflict is developed by the parties themselves, they are not likely to feel that some unworkable scheme has been imposed from the outside. In other words, the disputants have "buy-in," a personal stake in making the solution work. Finally, peer mediation addresses the underlying causes of a problem, not merely its obvious symptoms. This increases the chance that a resolution will be effective over the long term.

1. Paragraph A mentions all of the following as part of the problem between Anna and Carly EXCEPT that
   - (A) they annoy each other
   - (B) they distrust each other
   - (C) they are suspicious of each other
   - (D) they do not talk to each other

2. Paragraphs B–D mention all of the following as being ineffective ways to solve college-student disputes EXCEPT
   - (A) mediation
   - (B) arbitration
   - (C) disciplinary action
   - (D) roommate separation

3. In Paragraph G, all of the following are mentioned as steps in establishing peer-mediation programs at public universities in the United States EXCEPT
   - (A) getting volunteers
   - (B) getting course credit for volunteering
   - (C) setting rules
   - (D) identifying sources of funding

4. In Paragraph H, all of the following are mentioned as reasons for the success of peer-mediation programs EXCEPT
   - (A) "buy-in" by the disputing parties
   - (B) a sense that the mediators understand the disputants
   - (C) the willingness of faculty mentors to step in as needed
   - (D) cooperation between the parties who are in conflict

5. Look at the four numbered squares in Paragraph E. Which square indicates the best possible place to insert (add) the following sentence?

   A student who lives off-campus is likely to be perceived as less attuned to the problem.
   - (A) 1
   - (B) 2
   - (C) 3
   - (D) 4

Responding in Writing

WRITING TIP: WRITE A STRONG FIRST SENTENCE

When you write a story to illustrate a particular point, start out with a strong beginning sentence. This makes the point clear and it draws in the reader. See for example the way Deborah Tannen begins her essay with narrative examples on page 258. Her first sentence is, "Apologies are powerful." Her lead also provides an example of a good first sentence, "Whether used to repair old, strained relationships or to lay the groundwork for new, productive ones, the mighty 'sorry' has proved effective."

2 Writing Practice Write a narrative essay on one of these topics. Remember that a narrative tells a story. Follow the steps listed below the box.

Topic 1
Write about a childhood memory, explaining how it was a transforming moment in your life.

Topic 2
Write about an apology that had a significant effect on you or another person, explaining the effect.

Step 1 Choose one of the two topics above and brainstorm, writing a list or using a cluster diagram to develop all your ideas on the topic.

Step 2 Determine what you want to prove with your story. Write it out as a sentence; for example, "I want to prove that. . ." Note: You will not use this sentence in your essay; it is only meant for you to clearly identify your main point for your own reference.

Step 3 Now revise the sentence you just wrote into a first sentence for your composition that will say something direct about the cause and effect relationship between your memory and its impact on your life (for Topic 1) or on the apology and its effect (for Topic 2). Even if you are doing Topic 2, make sure your point is not exactly the same as Tannen's.

Step 4 Write the rest of your narrative. Include clear examples and details that help prove the point you described in your first sentence.

Step 5 Read and revise your composition. Make sure that your main idea is clear and that there are details to support the main idea. In addition, check the spelling and punctuation. Add a good title that will make someone want to read it.

 Step 6 Exchange your paper with another student. Read each others' compositions and make suggestions for improvements. Does your partner's composition prove the first sentence? Do you have any suggestions for making the first sentence stronger or more precise? Then hand in your paper.

Self-Assessment Log

Read the lists below. Check (✓) the strategies and vocabulary that you learned in this chapter. Look through the chapter or ask your instructor about the strategies and words that you do not understand.

Reading and Vocabulary-Building Strategies

- ❏ Previewing a reading for its organization
- ❏ Getting meaning from word structure and context
- ❏ Analyzing cause and effect
- ❏ Inferring the meaning of idioms and expressions
- ❏ Reading a poem
- ❏ Identifying synonyms
- ❏ Using a chart for comparison
- ❏ Reading for speed and fluency: not vocalizing words as you read

Target Vocabulary

Nouns

- ❏ bevy
- ❏ conflicts*
- ❏ context*
- ❏ contrition
- ❏ demeanor
- ❏ equilibrium
- ❏ evidence*
- ❏ remorse
- ❏ schisms
- ❏ slaughter
- ❏ strategies*

Verbs

- ❏ acknowledge*

- ❏ clenching
- ❏ empathize
- ❏ hobbling
- ❏ resolve*
- ❏ restore*
- ❏ shuffling
- ❏ tottering

Adjectives

- ❏ cultural*
- ❏ grotesque
- ❏ hunched
- ❏ inclined*
- ❏ litigious

- ❏ massive
- ❏ philanthropic
- ❏ plebeian
- ❏ roughened
- ❏ swarmed

Adverbs

- ❏ dead (as in dead silent)
- ❏ disdainfully

Idioms and Expressions

- ❏ cement the relationship
- ❏ day-to-day situations
- ❏ his/her side of the story

- ❏ join their ranks
- ❏ lay the groundwork
- ❏ let bygones be bygones
- ❏ letting her down
- ❏ lies at the heart
- ❏ magic bullets
- ❏ make amends
- ❏ takes a toll
- ❏ would have fallen all over herself

---

* These words are from the Academic Word List. For more information on this list, see www.vuw.ac.nz/lals/research/awl.

Vocabulary Index

---

*These words are from the Academic Word List. For more information on this list, see www.vuw.nz/lals/research/awl.

incandescent
inconsolable
mausoleum
media*
minarets
mixed blessing
Mogul design
mosque
nose jobs
notable
oblong
octagonal
prominent
redefining (style)
region*
retract
sacred
serene
shimmering
standard
surgical makeover
symmetric
temporal
tranquil
trend*
tuned in
worthy

Chapter 5

achievements*
commitments*
computer*
concreteness
excessiveness
exhausted
exorbitant
exquisite
finally*
financial*
found (find)*
framework*
Herculean
indefatigable
inebriated
inspecting*
marshy
materialistic
mundane

nasty
next of kin
polluted
pollution
prosaic
rejuvenated
restrictions*
roam
significance*
waste

Chapter 6

adequately*
at length
bade (bid)
bosom
ceased*
convinced*
cooperate*
detected
distinct*
effortlessly
exceptional
exclusive*
extraordinary
fancy
fashionable
found*
hypothesis*
impressed
insure
intellectual skills
in vain
labors*
memorized
novice
rare (describing
    meat)
removed*
secure*
subordinate*
vex

Chapter 7

achievement*
art nouveau
aspects*
Belgian

broad human beings
chiseled
concluded*
crane
cultural
curly
cut corners
European
exposure*
finally*
goals
hard knocks
industrial
integrity
in the short run
(a) labor of love
landmarks
liberal*
mantel
memorable
monumental
mythological
occupied*
options*
pilgrimage
raw brain power
sense of integrity
Sicilian
traditional*
urns
Victorian*
warehouse

Chapter 8

advocacy*
analyze*
benefit*
be routine
conservation
degradation
desertification
detection*
deterioration
erosion*
go that route
half dead
(a) handful
harassment

(a) normal life span
not (a procedure) to
    be taken lightly
nutritious
predict*
primarily*
rainfall
researchers*
respond*
sequence*
sequenced*
spot
started making sense
take (her concerns)
    more seriously
topsoil
trigger a flood
unsuitable
vision*
worldwide

Chapter 9

achievements*
Anglo
bilingual
Chicanos
citizenship
civil*
civil rights
clarify*
criticized
disappointed
discrimination
embodied
established*
ethnic*
exhibited*
faltered
fascinated
focus*
Hispanic
ignored*
immigration*
immortalized
inhabitants
issues*
mechanization
migrant*

---

*These words are from the Academic Word List. For more information on this list, see www.vuw.nz/lals/research/awl.

perceived*
policy*
reject*
strike
stunned
tilling
traditions*
translated
unique*

Chapter 10

acknowledge*
bevy
cement the
   relationship

clenching
conflicts*
context*
contrition
cultural*
day-to-day
   situations
dead (as in dead
   silent)
demeanor
disdainfully
empathize
equilibrium
evidence*
grotesque

his/her side of the
   story
hobbling
hunched
inclined*
join their ranks
lay the groundwork
let bygones be
   bygones
letting her down
lies at the heart
litigious
magic bullets
make amends
massive

philanthropic
plebeian
remorse
resolve*
restore*
roughened
schisms
shuffling
slaughter
strategies*
swarmed
takes a toll
tottering
would have fallen all
   over herself

---

*These words are from the Academic Word List. For more information on this list, see www.vuw.nz/lals/research/awl.

Skills Index

PHOTO CREDITS

LITERARY CREDITS

Page 6 "English as a Universal Language" From *Megatrends 2000* by John Naisbitt and Patricia Aburdene. Copyright © 1990 by Megatrends Ltd. Reprinted by permission of HarperCollins Publishers, John Naisbitt and Patricia Aburdene. **Page 16** "Mongolians Learn to say 'Progress' in English" by James Brooke, *International Herald Tribune*, February 15, 2005. Copyright © 2005 by The New York Times Co. Reprinted by permission. **Page 31** From *Into Thin Air* by Jon Krakauer, copyright © 1997 by Jon Krakauer. Used by permission of Villard Books, a division of Random House, Inc. **Page 40** "The World We Lost" from *Never Cry Wolf* by Farley Mowat. Copyright © 1963 by Farley Mowat Limited; Copyright © 1991 by Farley Mowat Limited. By permission of Little, Brown and Co., Inc. and Farley Mowat Limited. **Page 58** "Finding Real Love" by Cary Barbor, as appeared in *Psychology Today*, January–February, 2001. Reprinted with permission of Cary Barbor. **Page 61** "Oh When I Was in Love with You" by A.E. Housman, from *A Shropshire Lad*. Reprinted with permission of The Society of Authors as the Literary Representative of the Estate of A.E. Housman. **Page 65** "'Bare Branches' Might Snap in Asia" by Valerie Hudson and Andrea Den Boer. Copyright © 2004, *Edmonton Journal*. Reprinted with permission. **Page 83** "Taj Mahal, India" from *The Grand Tour Individual Creations* by Flavio Conti, translated by Patrick Creagh, 1978, pp. 69–72. **Page 88** Adapted from *The Story of Architecture* by Jonathan Glancey. New York: Dorling Kindersley Publishing, Inc.: 2000, pp. 106, 49. **Page 93** "Korea's Makeover from Dull to Hip Changes the Face of Asia" by Gordon Fiarclough, *The Wall Street Journal*, October 20, 2005, p. A1. Midwest Edition by Gordon Fairclough. Copyright © 2005 by Dow Jones & Co., Inc. Reproduced with permission of Dow Jones & Co., Inc. in the format Textbook via Copyright Clearance Center. **Page 112** "Conversations in Malaysia" from *Among the Believers: An Islamic Journey* by V.S. Naipaul. Copyright © 1981 by V.S. Naipaul. Used by permission of Alfred A. Knopf, a division of Random House, Inc. and Gillon Aitken Associates. **Page 121** "Grisha Has Arrived" by Tanya Filanovsky, *Newest Review*, August/September 1990, translated from Russian by Ruth Schacter. Reprinted by permission of Tanya Filanovsky. **Page 138** "A Memory for All Seasonings" by Stephen Singular. Reprinted with permission from *Psychology Today* magazine. Copyright © 1982 (PT Partners). **Page 161** "Mays Boy" by Maija Penikis. Reprinted by permission of *The Post-Crescent*, Appleton, WI, 1993. **Page 169** "The San Francisco Sculptor Who Created Nicholas Cage's 'Dreadful Dragon'" by Kristine M. Carber, *San Francisco Examiner*, November 17, 1993. Reprinted by permission. **Page 178** "A Lifetime of Learning to Manage Effectively" by Ralph Sorenson, *Wall Street Journal*, February 28, 1983. Wall Street Journal. Eastern Edition by Ralph Sorenson. Copyright © 1983 by Dow Jones & Co., Inc. Reproduced with permission of Down Jones & Co., Inc. in the format Textbook via Copyright Clearance Center. **Page 184** "Izumi Kobayashi" by Andrew Morse, *Wall Street Journal*, October 31, 2005. Wall Street Journal. Midwest Edition by Andrew Morse. Copyright © by Dow Jones & Co., Inc. Reproduced with permission of Dow Jones & Co., Inc. in the format Textbook via Copyright Clearance Center. **Page 185** "Kim Sung Joo" by Seah Park, *Wall Street Journal*, November 8, 2004. Wall Street Journal. Midwest Edition by Seah Park. Copyright © 2004 by Dow Jones & Co., Inc. Reproduced with permission of Dow Jones & Co., Inc. in the format Textbook via Copyright Clearance Center. **Page 186** "Maria Asuncion Aramburuzabala" by David Luhnow, *Wall Street Journal* November 8, 2004. Wall Street Journal. Midwest Edition by David Luhnow. Copyright © 2004 by Dow Jones & Co., Inc. Reproduced with permission of Dow Jones & Co. in the format Textbook via Copyright Clearance Center. **Page 188** "The Worst Recruiters Have Seen," *Wall Street Journal*, March 12, 1995. Wall Street Journal. Eastern Edition by Staff. Copyright © 1995 by Dow Jones & Co., Inc. Reproduced with permission of Dow Jones & Co. Inc. in the format Textbook via Copyright Clearance Center. **Page 201** "Trees for Democracy" by Wangari Maathai, *The New York Times*, December 10, 2004. © 2004, The New York Times. Reprinted by permission. **Page 208** "A Revolution in Medicine" by Geoffrey Cowley and Anne Underwood. From *Newsweek*, April 10, © 2000 Newsweek, Inc. All rights reserved. Reprinted by permission. **Page 217** From *Are Computers Alive?* By Geoff Simons. Reprinted with permission of The Harvester Press/Simon & Schuster Ltd., International Group. **Page 229** "To Paint is to Live: Georgia O'Keefe, 1897-1986" by Miki Prijic Knezevic. Reprinted by permission of the author. **Page 236** From "The Hispanic Presence in the United States, by Deana Fernandez. **Page 245** "The Life of Jackie Chan," www.starpulse.com. Reprinted by permission of Hal Erickson, All Movie Guide. **Page 258** "Contrite Makes Right" by Deborah Tannen, *Civilization* magazine, April/May 1999, copyright Deborah Tannen. Reprinted by permission. **Page 268** "When One Person Reaches Out with Love" from *A Precocious Autobiography* by Yevgeny Yevtushenko, translated by Andrew P. MacAndrew, copyright © 1963 by E. P. Dutton, renewed © 1991 by Penguin USA. Copyright © 1963, renewed © 1991 by Yevgeny Yevtushenko. Used by permission of Dutton, a division of Penguin Group (USA) Inc. **Page 271** *Being Peace* by Tich Nhat Hanh. Berkeley: Parallax Press, 1987, pp. 69–70.